JOAN WULFF'S

Fly Casting Techniques

Illustrated by
Francis W. Davis

THE LYONS PRESS

Printed in the United States of America

10 9 8 7 6 5 4

Library of Congress Cataloging-in-Publication Data

Wulff, Joan.
      Joan Wulff's fly-casting techniques.

      Includes index.
      1. Fly casting. I. Title. II. Title: Fly-casting techniques.
SH454.2.W85 1987   799.1'2   87-3587
ISBN 0-941130-38-X (cloth)
ISBN 1-55821-354-6 (paperback)

Lee and Joan on the Godbout River.   *Photo by Stan Bogdan.*

JOAN WULFF'S

Fly Casting Techniques

CONTENTS

Special thanks to Mary and Frank Visconti
and to Connie and Neil Marvin

JOAN SALVATO WULFF'S TOURNAMENT CAREER
1937–1960

First National title in 1943 after state and regional titles
  as Sub-Junior and Junior.
17 National casting titles
1 International title
Fishermen's Distance Fly title against all-male competition (1951)
Longest cast in registered tournament—161 feet (1960)

> **Use the drawings in this book as a guide rather than as absolutes. They are of a 5′5″ tall person using an eight-foot rod. The moves may be smaller or larger for you.**

JOAN WULFF'S

Fly Casting Techniques

INTRODUCTION

My first conscious thought about fishing developed at the end of a summer's evening on Greenwood Lake in New Jersey in the early 1930s. Dad was the fisherman and Mom was rowing the boat.

Jimmy Salvato loved to fish with a fly rod, especially for bass. He was a whiz at casting big hair bugs on his nine-foot bamboo rod and of these, mouse imitations were his favorites. I watched as he cast the deer-hair lure into a pocket in the lily pads and let it sit, perfectly still, until all the disturbance rings had disappeared. Then he let the hair bug sit some more. The minute or two he did nothing was an eternity to me, a child of six or seven. Finally he would twitch and hop the bug back toward the boat, and then he'd cast again—unless Mom had allowed the boat to drift too close or too far from bass cover. Mom wasn't a fisherman (or an expert at rowing) and did not quite understand how important it is to accommodate the fisherman by being at the perfect casting distance from every likely looking bass hangout. The magical sounds of fly fishing were heavily punctuated with Dad's critical comments about the boat's position; I had never heard him speak to Mom like that before.

When a fish took Dad's mouse I was startled by the ferocity of the strike and thrilled by the acrobatic jumps of the large-mouth bass. Then, when he'd brought the fish close to the boat, Dad suddenly handed the rod to me. A bass was strange to me—and so was the process of playing a fish. I stared at the great head with the hair mouse in its mouth—and as I stared, the bug suddenly floated free. For a second or two, the bass stayed still—then it slowly submerged. Dad promised this tearful kid that we'd get another—but we didn't.

Still, something had happened to me. I could not wait to go fishing again for the exciting creature that lived in dark water under lily pads. Even more important, I reacted to Mom's dilemma as a boatman with the strong thought forming in my young mind, "It's better to be the fisherman than the rower." And so I am.

In the late 1930s, Dad started to teach my younger brothers Louie and Jimmy to cast; I was bypassed because I was a girl. But I did not want to end up rowing the boat, so I asked Mom if I could try fly casting by myself, borrowing Dad's fly rod. A couple of waves of the rod, back and forth, and the tip section shot out of the ferrule and went down into the deep, dark water of the pond. I was so afraid of Dad's anger that I cried all the way home—but a neighbor came to the rescue by going back with me and retrieving the rod in the tines of his garden rake. When I told Dad what had happened, he surprised me by asking if I'd like to join him and the boys at the next casting-club practice session.

That was the beginning. Fly casting in the thirties was still traditional, taught by putting a book or handkerchief between the elbow and the body of the student, to promote the use of the wrist. I tried to cast that way, but as a skinny ten-year-old with a weak wrist, I was only able to reach the close targets. Finally, as kids often do, I stopped listening to my elders, dropped the handkerchief and lifted my elbow to use more of my whole arm's strength and accompanying leverage. It worked; I could reach the far targets. I went on to win the Junior All-Around title for New Jersey the next year, regional titles in subsequent years, the Women's Dry Fly Accuracy event in my first National in 1943 and, eventually, six national titles in one year (1951) including the Fisherman's Distance Fly title against all-male competition.

Tournament casting was great fun—a sport in itself—but was sterile when compared to fishing. I left tournament casting in 1960. Since then I've had the best of both worlds, with the skills learned as a tournament caster shortening the time it has taken to grasp the intricacies of fishing for everything from trout, bass, and bluegills to bonefish, tarpon, and Atlantic salmon. The fly fisherman's world is exciting, providing never-ending challenges that will interest me for the rest of my life.

There is an axiom among fisherman that, as beginners, they want to catch fish by the numbers; most is best. The second stage, naturally, is to want to catch the biggest fish; and the final challenge is to catch the most difficult. Fly casting can be viewed in similar fashion. The beginner is happy just to have his line and leader land on the water without tangling. The second stage is to cast great distances. Finally, a fly fisher wants to execute each cast, short or long, with grace and precision.

There is a lot more casting than catching in fly fishing. My husband, Lee, and I counted casts one afternoon on an Atlantic salmon river. Casting sixty-three feet of line, plus the leader, in the wet-fly technique of casting down-and-across the stream, to let the current swim the fly back to the close edge, fifteen casts were made and fished in eleven minutes. A different area of stream with shorter line requirements produced twelve casts in six minutes; another length line, twelve casts in eight minutes. For a short dry-fly drift, over a fish we knew was there, thirty casts were made in seven minues. Multiply these numbers by the hours in your fishing day and you'll realize that if fly casting doesn't give you pleasure and satisfaction, it is just hard work.

Fly casting is not difficult. The motions are quite simple with one length of fly line. It becomes complex because of changing lengths of line (changing *weight*) and the changing conditions under which you must cast, such as wind, less than enough backcast room, how deeply you must wade, and the weight of your flies. If you can master the casting of one length of line to start with, you'll be able to master the rest, taking it step by step. In addition to words and principles you'll need mental images, and the drawings by Francis Davis will reinforce these for you.

Practice is absolutely necessary to develop your skills. In a world that is computer conscious, you might wishfully think that you can pass a learning sequence through your muscles just once and have them perform perfectly from then on. Muscle skills are developed by repetition only and that takes time. There is no real short cut except that certain thoughts, in the form of "cue words," can make your muscles and reflexes respond to your mind's direction and may actually shorten learning time. Look for such words in this book—words or phrases you can repeat to yourself as you practice, which make everything go just right.

If the book is used well, you will be able to look at a target area, aim your hand, and watch the line unroll to it. You'll cast under tree limbs, into wind—fore and aft—double haul for effortless long casts, and make fewer false casts between presentations to keep your fly on the water more of the time. You'll solve casting problems with both straight-line and circular form casting and be able to cast in any plane between horizontal on the right and horizontal on the left as the needs arise. You'll know where to use power and where to rest, on each stroke, for less casting fatigue.

My ideas break with tradition, with the clock face so familiar in casting instruction articles, and with the restrictive arm movements I myself was started on. I'll present a basic system, a set of what I call the "mechanics," though they are simply the parts of the cast, that can explain any cast that anyone can do, even if the style is different from my own. With this system, you can reach your full potential as a caster and solve any problem that is solvable within your personal physical limitations. The necessary skills will be laid out in a suggested learning order.

This book is also a pioneering effort in the development of a fly-casting language. Because I have analyzed the moves of the cast to a greater depth than I can find in the available books, I have had to develop explanations and terms for moves that have existed but have not been understood. It is ironic that fishing is one of America's top participant sports, and fly fishermen are

Top: **With other youngsters on the Paterson Casting Club dock at Oldham Pond, North Haledon, New Jersey—about 1939. Jim Tracey is in the foreground.**

Above: **A fishing contest at Haledon Reservoir, North Haledon, New Jersey, about 1939.**

Right: **At the Dry Fly Accuracy competition in 1941, Eastern Tournament—age 14.**

Preparing to cast at Little River event, French National Tournament, Bois de Boulogne, Paris, 1948.

Photo by A. J. McClane.

Same tournament. Caught in the trees!　*Photo by A. J. McClane.*

at the top of the heap, intellectually, yet our language and understanding of what makes fly casting work are at first-grade level. We are long overdue in articulating the mechanics of our sport so that the average fly fisherman can derive maximum benefit from a casting language, written or spoken.

Lee Wulff came into my life thirty years after I started to use a fly rod. What he did for me (and I think I've done for him) was to broaden the scope and my understanding of fly casting. In order to be able to encompass the completely different style of casting he practices, I had to analyze the mechanics more deeply than ever in order to know what made his style work. Lee challenged me all the way. I had to "get to the guts of it" on any difference of opinion. He is an instinctive caster and his style developed naturally to suit stream fishing conditions. I have incorporated his methods as part of the whole picture I wish to present to you. If you can use the straight-line casting of the basic discipline and the circular-line casting that broadens its scope, you'll have at your command techniques that will make you comfortable in any fishing situation.

Here is one final thought on the importance of being good at fly casting. There are two areas of expertise that are deemed most important to fishing success, and fly fishermen, especially those who pursue trout, often argue about which is more important. The first is *knowing where the fish lie* (reading water) and the second is *being able to present the fly* (presentation/casting). My thought is this: if you don't know where the fish lie but can cast well enough to cover all of the water with finesse, you are likely to solve the mystery and catch fish. If you know where they lie but can neither reach them nor present the fly naturally, you are not even in the game. Hence this book.

one

GETTING STARTED

You Start With The Line

The basic difference between fly casting and all other casting lies in the weight of the lure. You can throw a bait-casting or spinning lure by hand, almost as far as you can cast it because it is a contained weight, like a rock, that carries an almost weightless line behind it.

As a fly fisherman, you'll use imitations of insects that are, essentially, weightless—flies made with fur, feathers, tinsel, and yarn. Have you ever tried to throw a soft feather for any distance? It is impossible. It has no weight and it has air resistance. In fly casting, the weight you'll cast is not in the lure, it is in the *fly line*, spread throughout its length or concentrated in the forward thirty or forty feet. The fly goes along as a passenger, at the end of a monofilament *leader* which, in turn, is attached to the fly line. The leader is a nearly invisible, tapering connection between the fly line and the fly and it too is essentially without weight.

So it is the line we cast and, because it is long and flexible, compared to a lure, its weight cannot flex the rod with just the short, snapping motion used in bait casting or spinning. The fly-casting stroke is a straight-line movement of the whole rod by the rod hand, in an *acceleration to a stop*. During the acceleration, the weight of the fly line flexes the rod from the tip downward. When the acceleration is ended and the butt section of the rod is stopped, the limber rod tip flips over and the long flexible line continues on its path, passing over the tip, to form an open-ended unrolling loop.

7

This action happens on each casting stroke. It must be done backward (the backcast) and forward (the forward cast) to give you a complete cast. *Two strokes*. The length of the strokes may vary from being as short as a few inches to as long as a few feet, depending on the length of the rod, the length of the line, and your physical height and arm length.

Two strokes to every cast. There is no other sport in which this is true. In other sports, which are mostly ball sports, you'll set up slowly on the back-swing and whack the heck out of something to drive it forward. Not so in fly casting; here you'll need just as much force on the backcast as on the forward cast. This is crucial to your understanding. The line must unroll behind you just as it unrolls ahead of you in order for you to control it. If you set up slowly on the backcast and whack the heck out of the forward cast, you'll hear your leader and fly crack like a whip and you may lose the fly in the process. The speed and power must be equal backward and forward for a constant length of line.

Unfortunately we all arrive at adulthood without having developed muscles for throwing backward. This is why so many fly fishermen have trouble learning to cast well without professional help. There is no short cut; you'll have to develop and train your muscles, telling them what to do on each backcast until they respond automatically. Throwing backward is your first challenge.

The fly line is the focal point of your tackle. You should choose the weight and design of the line to suit the fishing you enjoy and then find a rod that will cast it perfectly. In the range of available line weights, designated by numbers from 1 to 12 (relative to the ascending grain weight of the first thirty feet)*, the ideal weight for you to use in this casting instruction is a #6 floating fly line. It is heavy enough to give you a good feeling of weight (as compared to #5 on down), and the rod balanced to cast it will be light enough to keep you from tiring too quickly in practice. You cannot put a #6 line on any rod—only on a rod designed specifically to cast a #6. Such information is found on the shaft of the rod between the hand grip and the first guide on contemporary rods.

Line Design

The illustration shows the basic line designs and the common names used to designate their different sections.

1. The **level line** has only one diameter. It has limitations as a casting line if you use tapered leaders and featherweight flies and does not lend itself to "shooting," the technique in which more line than the primary line you

*See chart, page 183.

FLY LINE NOMENCLATURE

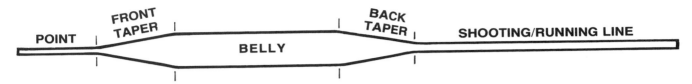

BASIC DESIGNS

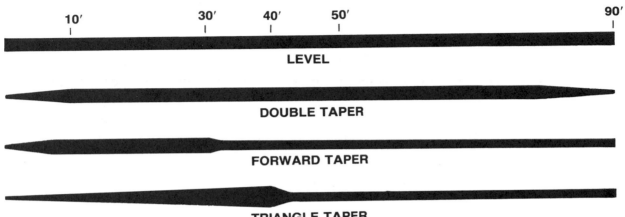

handle is extended on the cast. As a fishing line it is better for bass than for general trout fishing.

2. The **double taper** line has roughly eight to ten feet of taper at its front end, for delicate presentation. (A leader will extend this taper to handle nearly weightless flies.) The *belly* of this line is seventy feet long. The *back taper* is non-functional but allows you to reverse the line if the front end has worn out. The limitation of this line is that the constant diameter of the belly section makes it difficult to shoot line more than ten or twelve feet at a time. You must make more casts, after the thirty-foot mark, to cast a longer line than with the forward taper designs, and you may never reach your full distance-casting potential with it. However, the double taper is America's traditional trout fishing line, lacking only that one capability.

3. The **forward taper** line answers the need to make long casts with a minimum number of casting strokes. The *front taper* is short and the belly is short too, making a total weight package of approximately thirty feet. It has a quick back taper, followed by smaller diametered *running line* for the rest of its thirty-yard length. When the belly of this line is out of the rod tip, a cast can carry many feet of the running line behind it to reach longer distances with ease. In theory it is a bit like a spinning lure that carries weightless line behind it, the difference being that a spinning lure's weight may be contained in only two or three inches, while the concentrated fly line weight is spread

over thirty feet. Until the belly is out of the rod tip, the forward taper line casts like a double taper.

There are many variations within the forward taper family: long belly, rocket, torpedo, bass, saltwater; each is suited to particular fishing conditions and fly weight or bulkiness, for every species of gamefish from trout to tarpon.

4. The **triangle taper** line, so named for the form of the taper when drawn on paper, is a single, continuous taper for its first forty feet. A quick back taper follows, and running line makes up the rest of its ninety-foot length. This line has no real belly section but "thickens" slowly from the *point* backward. This aspect of the design makes it an excellent roll-casting line. When the forty-foot taper is out of the rod tip, the triangle taper performs like the conventional forward taper, carrying light running line behind it for easy shooting and maximum distance potential. It is an all-purpose line, depending on the weight, for everything from trout to tarpon.

Setting up your Tackle

This basic trout-fishing outfit will be good for a lifetime.

Rod:	8 to 8½ feet, weighing 3 ounces or less
Line:	#6 weight, light-colored, floating, of weight forward, triangle taper, or double taper design
Leader:	9-foot, knotless, tapering from .021 at the butt section to .008 or .007 (3X or 4X) at the tip
Fly:	For practice, brightly colored yarn or a conventional dry fly with the hook cut at the bend
Knots:	If you are unfamiliar with knots use the simple knots shown in the illustrations

The Rod: If the rod's *ferrules* are made of metal (external) put the sections together with the guides lined up and use a straight pull to take the sections apart. If the ferrules are internal, of the rod's own material (glass or graphite), line up the sections with the ferrules offset 90°, then turn them as you seat them to line up perfectly. When you take the sections apart, twist 90° in reverse.

The Reel: Illustrations in this book will always show the reel being wound left-handed. The rod hand is superior to the line hand for playing fish because it is stronger and is cued to your master eye to react quickly to changing situations. The line hand can learn to "go around" on the reel's track quite easily if given the opportunity (spinning fishermen do it). Most reels come from the factory set up to be wound right-handed and must be altered internally before they can be wound left-handed.

FLY TACKLE NOMENCLATURE

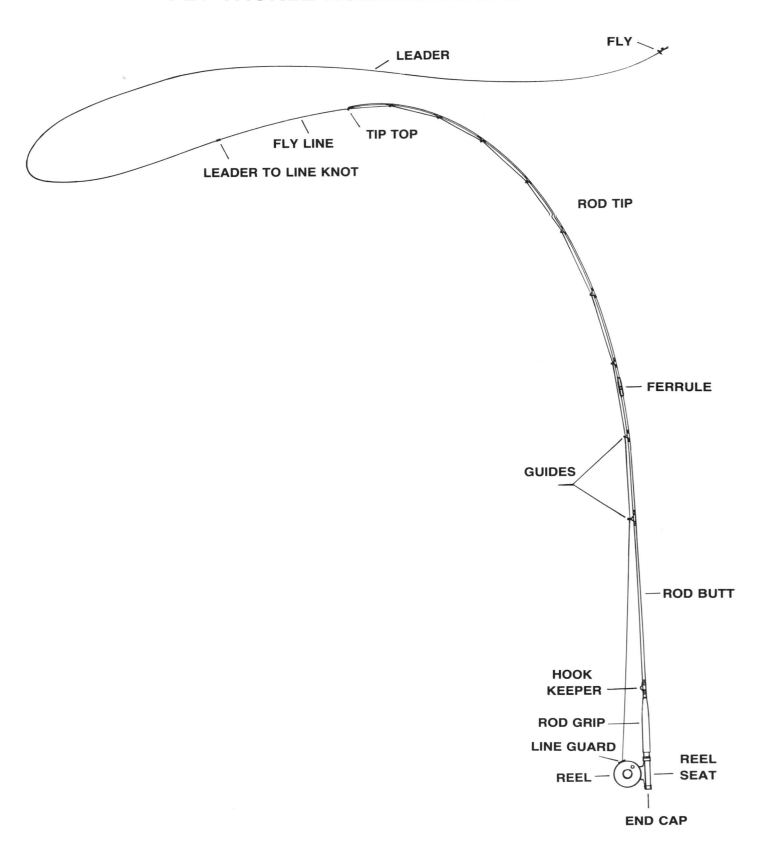

LEADER

FLY

FLY LINE

TIP TOP

LEADER TO LINE KNOT

ROD TIP

FERRULE

GUIDES

ROD BUTT

HOOK KEEPER

ROD GRIP

LINE GUARD

REEL

REEL SEAT

END CAP

SIMPLE KNOTS

OVERHAND KNOT

LEADER TO LINE KNOT

1

2

LEADER TO YARN—SLIP KNOT

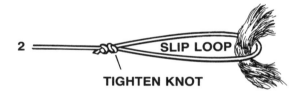

SLIP LOOP

1 OVERHAND KNOT AROUND LEADER

OVERHAND KNOT AT END

2 SLIP LOOP

TIGHTEN KNOT

3 TIGHTEN THE LOOP AROUND THE YARN

JOAN'S CLINCH
LEADER TO FLY KNOT

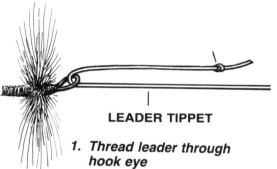

LEADER TIPPET

1. Thread leader through hook eye and make overhand knot near end.

2. Five turns with end around leader. Bring overhand knot through loop at eye.

3. Hold knot against hook eye.
Pull leader away from hook, jamming turns against eye and knot. Trim end. Careful! Not so close as to lose the overhand knot.
Trim end beyond knot.

TRIM

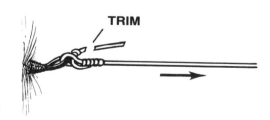

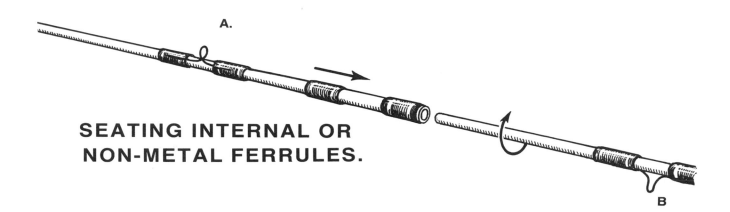

SEATING INTERNAL OR NON-METAL FERRULES.

OFF SET GUIDES 90° TO START. TWIST TO LINE THEM UP AS YOU SEAT THEM.

Always rewind the fly line under a little tension and with some guidance from a lower finger of the rod hand, to keep peaks and valleys from forming on the spool.

After fishing, whether or not you remove the fly, wind the leader a bit loosely on top of the line and allow a few final inches to hang from the reel. Fine-diametered tippets are hard to pull from between layers of fly line. Find out, from the instructions that come with the reel, how to remove the spool in case it is necessary to untangle either the line or the leader.

Stringing Up

Make sure the line is coming from inside or above the *line guard* (*inside* a round one, *above* a bar) on the reel as you string up the rod. Pull the leader and enough fly line from the reel to equal double the length of your rod.

Set the butt of the rod on the ground in a clean, dry place. Double the leader over on itself, about halfway, and thread it through the guides of the slanted rod. When the loop is through the *tip top*, pull all of the leader and line on through and then check to see that you have not missed any guides.

General Tips

Always start to cast with a few feet of fly line out of the rod tip, because the leader has almost no weight. Once the line is out of the rod tip, hold tension on the leader or keep the rod tip below a horizontal level until you are ready to begin casting. This is to keep the line and leader from sliding back down the rod to undo the stringing up.

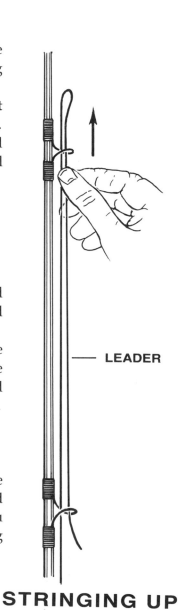

LEADER

STRINGING UP

Length of the Cast

The length of a cast is measured from where you stand, to the inch of water on which the fly lands. If you intend to make a thirty-foot cast with a nine-foot rod and a nine-foot leader, you will have to cast only twelve feet of line. I categorize the lengths of casts as follows:

Short: up to 30 feet
Medium: 30 to 50 feet
Long: 50 to 80 feet
Very Long: over 80 feet

You can quickly become familiar with line lengths if you will measure your line, inward from the "point," to thirty feet, and put a one-inch black mark there, before you begin the instruction. Use a quick-drying paint or an indelible laundry marker.

Warming Up

Become familiar with the feeling of the tackle by doing the following in a clear space with no obstructions:

Pull six to ten feet of line out of the rod tip in addition to the leader and fly. Hold the rod as shown in "The Grip" chapter, and, with a bent arm, make patterns in the air that you can see in their entirety: circles, ovals, figures-of-eight. Make them large and make them small. Make them quickly, make

A general guide for carrying your rod, after it is set up, is as follows:
1. Passing through a doorway
   Rod tip first is the safest way.
2. Walking alone in open areas
   Rod tip forward
3. Walking alone in wooded areas
   Rod tip backward
4. Walking with other people in single file
   a. First person carries rod with tip forward
   b. In-between people carry rod with tip forward
   c. Last person carries rod either way

them slowly, but don't let the line or leader tangle. Even though you have only a short line, with very little weight, try to recognize that subtle feeling of weight on the rod tip. Notice that *wherever the rod tip leads the line will follow*. This is absolutely fundamental. Let your eyes confirm this for you.

Focus your attention on your arm. Do the patterns you have just tried, in these ways:

1. Move the rod with just hand motion, *hinging at the wrist*.

2. Keep your wrist straight and move your forearm and hand as a unit, *hinging at the elbow*.

3. Use the whole arm in its bent position, moving only *from the shoulder* to form the different patterns.

The feeling of better control should be apparent with full-arm movement as compared to using isolated parts of the arm. I'll cover this aspect more deeply in "The Area of Focus."

To become operational as a caster you'll start with the roll cast and then progress through the basic discipline to more complex techniques.

The Grip

The way in which a fly rod is held during the cast is extremely important. A good grip can enhance the cast; a poor grip can kill it. Your hand is the connecting link in the power sequence that starts in your muscles, is magnified by the rod's action and is transferred, in the form of energy, to the fly line. The link must be secure.

The illustrations show some of the many grips from which fishermen may choose. #1 extends the thumb on top of the grip and #2, the forefinger. Grip #3 has neither finger extended and the V, between thumb and forefinger, lines up with the shaft of the rod. #4 has both thumb and forefinger extended in another version of #3.

I have always used my thumb on top of the grip except for rods less than six feet long (there aren't many) and for Fly-O, the indoor practice rod that is only three feet long. I use my forefinger on these rods, feeling that my thumb adds more punch than these short, really light-action rods can take for a smooth cast. Therein lies the heart of the matter. The thumb does add punch to the cast, forcefully pushing the rod shaft through a short arc at the end of the forward casting stroke. This push of the thumb maximizes the

Grip #1: Flexed thumb on top is the recommended grip.

A. Flattened thumb is less effective.

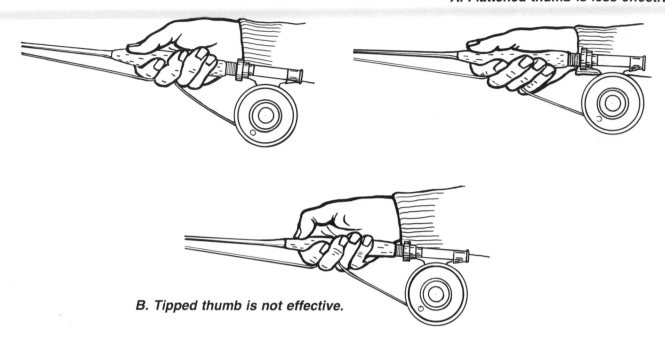

B. Tipped thumb is not effective.

Grip #2: Forefinger on top.

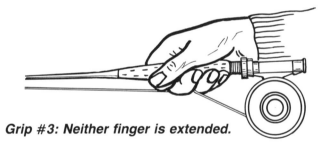

Grip #3: Neither finger is extended.

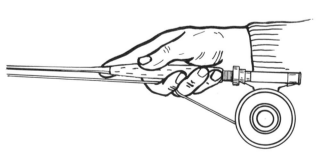

Grip #4: Thumb and forefinger extended.

No grip. Totally ineffective.

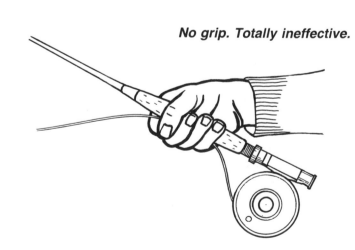

SCREEN DOOR HANDLE ANALOGY.

wrist's action, adding speed and direction to the forward cast and helping to unroll the line and leader perfectly along the way.

Orthopedic surgeon G. Pierce Jones II has this to say: "Positioning the thumb on top of the rod handle puts the strongest muscles of the hand in the correct position to aid in moving the fly rod forward. The combined action of the muscles (flexor pollicus longus and adductor pollicus) brings the thumb toward the index finger when the hand is in the hand-shaking position or in a plane perpendicular to the ground, as at the start of the forward cast."

The hand action on the forward cast is the same kind of action we use on common screen door handles: push with the thumb, and pull back (the end of the rod grip) with the lower fingers.

Pierce says of the forefinger-on-top grip, "The muscles mentioned are in an unfavorable position to assist in moving the fly rod forward. The muscles that flex the index finger (flexor digitorum profundus and sublimus) are not nearly as strong as the intrinsic muscles of the thumb that occupy the meaty portion of the hand."

The forefinger is a good pointing mechanism and many new students use it in the early learning stages in place of the thumb, feeling that they can direct the rod shaft with more control by pointing rather than pushing. Lee uses his forefinger on top all of the time with light rods but, with heavy tackle, uses grip #4 which takes some advantage of the pollicus muscles.

The sometimes long road to becoming proficient with tackle of all weights can be shortened by using the thumb on top as your permanent rod grip.

Grip #1 shows the way to position the thumb to use the pushing muscles. It should be flexed, with the first section pressed against the grip and a little space under the lower section.

Figure A shows a flattened thumb, which cannot take full advantage of the thumb muscle for pushing forward. Figure B shows a tipped thumb. There is not enough thumb surface on the grip to really push the rod. This latter position usually cramps the thumb.

Grip #3, a "free wrist" grip, does not take advantage of pushing muscles. It relies on the speed of the arm's motion alone, with no help in the form of a direct push from the thumb on the forward cast. It seems more suitable for throwing a contained weight, like a ball, than for directing a rod shaft with

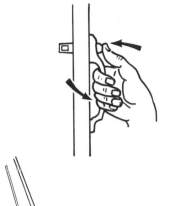

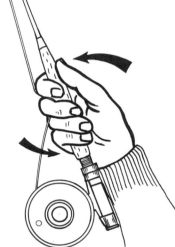

On the forward cast, pushing forward with the thumb as you pull back with the lower fingers is remarkably similar to the action required with a screen-door handle.

The length of the ideal rod grip is slightly longer than your hand in its gripped position. The thumb should then be close to the forward end of the rod shaft. If the grip is much longer, position your hand back farther, closer to the reel, to keep the reel from "swinging out" too far in the stroke.

the flexible weight of a fly line behind it. This "free wrist" grip may have been useful when casting-arm motion was limited by keeping the elbow against the body and the wrist could be bent back farther on the backcast than if the thumb were on top, to improve leverage for the forward cast.

If you have any doubt about which grip to use, check them out and see which one straightens out your leader and helps best to deliver your fly to the target. No matter which grip you choose, never allow your hand to shift its position during the cast. Shifting is a common fault. Be consistent in the basic grip position and be sure to hold it steadfastly throughout the cast.

NOTE: Throughout this book, the thumb will be used on top of the rod grip in all descriptions and illustrations. I will write as a right-handed caster. Left-handers, fortunately or unfortunately, have much more experience than anyone else in translating right-hand directions for their own use. So it must be.

The Roll Cast

The roll cast is not only the beginning caster's security blanket but remains an extremely valuable technique throughout every fly fisherman's career. It is best known as the cast to use if you have no room above or behind you for a conventional aerial cast. With it, you can present a fly even if you are backed up against a bush or an abutment.

The roll cast is taught as a first technique because, in addition to its value, it's easy to learn. You'll be operational in short order. There is no backcast—just a forward stroke (an exception to the rule) and, consequently, no hurrying with the roll cast. To put it simply, the rod is moved into a nearly vertical position, with part of the line bellied behind you. The front end of the line, plus leader and fly, remains on the water in front of you. A forward and downward movement of the arm and rod unrolls the line ahead of you *on the water.*

It is essential, in learning to roll cast, that you do it *on water.* Water's surface tension is needed to activate the rod's action and grass is a poor substitute. The line will slide across grass without friction or drag.

To begin the roll cast, you'll need to extend line outside of the rod tip.

1. Be sure that two or three feet of fly line are pulled out of the rod tip, in addition to the leader and yarn fly. Just throw the fly into the water.

2. Keeping the rod tip low to the water, strip fifteen to twenty feet of line from the reel and let it lie, just as it falls, on the ground at your side.

3. Holding the line in your line hand and keeping the rod slanted downward toward the water, *stroke* the rod back and forth (six inches of hand motion—about three feet of rod-tip motion) releasing line to work its way out through the rod. You will be transferring the coiled line from the ground, through the rod guides, to form loose coils on the water.

4. When it is all out of the rod tip except for what is in the guides, put the line under your rod hand and put your line hand in your pocket. You are ready for the roll cast.

Face the target area squarely, but drop your right foot back a little. Start with the rod tip low to the water and your elbow bent.

1. Moving slowly, raise the rod and your whole bent arm until your hand is slightly above your eye level. Your wrist should be straight, your forearm should be in line with your upper arm; your elbow should be in front of, and in line with, your shoulder. The rod tip will be pointing straight up. The line will have followed the tip in and be hanging down limply in front of the rod.

2. Cock your hand to the right (bend at the wrist, about 45°) to tilt the rod so that the tip is outside the edge of your body. As you tilt, move your elbow toward the center of your body just a little, so that the hand is "outside" the elbow. This will move the fly line to the side, separating its path from that of the rod, so they won't collide when you start the forward stroke.

3. Shift your weight to your back foot and let the line swing behind your shoulder without changing the position of the rod. If you can't see the line with an easy turn of your head, it is too far behind you. Check your rod position.

4. Let the bellying line come to rest behind your shoulder, dead-stopped.

5. Look forward now to choose a target area. It must be a little to the left of whatever fly line remains on the water. Shift your weight to the forward foot and follow this shift immediately with a forward and downward stroke of the rod. Within this stroke, apply power with an accelerating snap of the forearm and hand, pushing forward with your thumb as far as your wrist will allow you to go. Follow through on the cast by lowering the rod so that the tip will be pointed where you expect the fly to land. The line should have rolled out straight on the surface of the water, carrying your leader and fly with it to straighten out ahead of it.

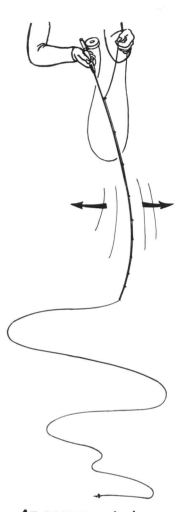

An easy way to increase the length of line out of the rod tip: stroke the rod from side to side, while releasing slack line. It will move through the rod to lie on the water.

THE ROLL CAST

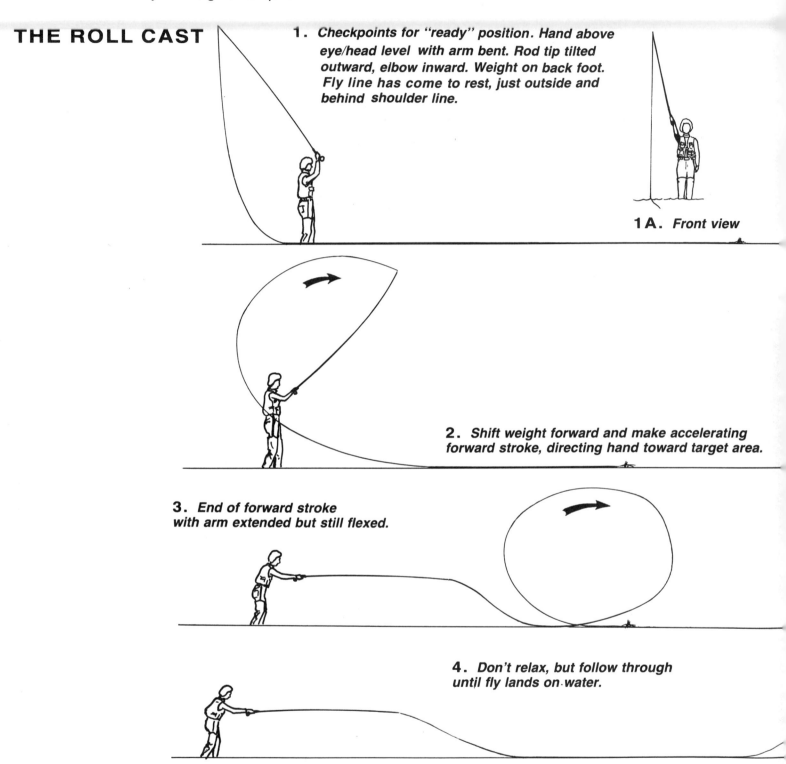

1. **Checkpoints for "ready" position. Hand above eye/head level with arm bent. Rod tip tilted outward, elbow inward. Weight on back foot. Fly line has come to rest, just outside and behind shoulder line.**

1A. *Front view*

2. **Shift weight forward and make accelerating forward stroke, directing hand toward target area.**

3. **End of forward stroke with arm extended but still flexed.**

4. **Don't relax, but follow through until fly lands on water.**

When you are familiar with the five moves given, you will find that you can blend everything together, tilting the rod as you draw it back, and shifting your weight at the same time. Then you need only wait for the line to come to rest behind you. Shift your weight forward and make the stroke in one smooth motion.

Troubleshooting:

1. If the line did not come out of the water where you piled it originally, it may have sunk due to elapsed time. If it has sunk, it may take two or three roll casts to get it up to the surface. Don't despair; getting out of this kind of trouble is one of the valuable uses of the roll cast.

2. If all went well except that the leader and fly didn't straighten, be sure to drive forward with your thumb during the "power snap" and continue to push until the leader and fly have landed.

3. If the line hits the water too heavily and doesn't straighten, you may have lowered your arm too quickly or too far. Concentrate on the *forward* motion of the stroke, the forearm and hand action of thrusting forward.

4. If the line unrolls *above* the water, lower your arm more quickly as you begin the forward stroke. It is perfectly all right to unroll line above the water on a roll cast if that is, in fact, what you set out to do. As a first discipline, work on unrolling it *on* the water so that every inch of line and leader straighten out.

Wind blowing from your left may force you to aim a little left of the target area. Wind from behind will help the cast. Headwinds could be countered with extra force forward and a fast lowering of your arm.

Backhand Roll Casting

If your target area must be to the right of the fly line as it lies on the water, or if the wind is blowing from your casting side, you must tilt the rod to position the line behind your left shoulder in what is a *backhand* position. Change the position of your feet so that the foot that was back is now forward and vice versa. Start the cast by positioning the rod hand centered on your body, then tilt your hand and forearm to the left (lift the elbow outward slightly) to move the rod tip, and connected fly line, behind your left shoulder. It takes an inch or two of movement of the forearm and hand, no more, to move the rod tip and line a few feet. Keep your thumb and the open edge of the reel pointed toward the target area. Look at the target inch of water, and make the forward stroke.

As a beginner, you can roll cast a fly line twenty-five or thirty feet with a minumum of energy. However, your ultimate length of cast will be determined by the design of the fly line. To lengthen the line, just strip it from

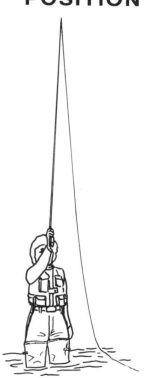

BACKHAND POSITION

Center arm on body, tilting the rod tip to carry line outside and behind left shoulder.

the reel and stroke it through the rod as you did earlier. Experiment to find out how far you can roll cast the line of your choice. These are the advantages and disadvantages of the various tapers:

1. A double-taper line can be roll cast the farthest, because of the seventy-foot belly that follows the front taper.

2. A triangle (single) taper can be roll cast most easily because a heavier part of the line is always turning over a lighter part ahead of it. There is no level "belly" section. The single taper is forty feet long and that length, plus your rod and leader's length, will be the limit of the roll cast.

3. Like the triangle taper, a forward taper line can be roll cast only until the rear end of the taper is out of the rod tip (about thirty feet of line in this case). The light running line, behind the heavy belly, cannot transfer casting energy from the rod to the heavy part of the line, once the line weight overhangs two or three feet out of the rod tip.

As a fishing technique, the roll cast, right *on* the water, is fine for wet-fly fishing, when you cast quartering downstream. For dry-fly fishing, the roll can be made a few feet above the water and the use of a long leader tippet will help the fly to land lightly. Because you will not have false casts to help dry the fly between presentations, you might have to dress your fly more heavily with floatant than you would when aerial casting.

You can shoot line with a roll cast. Aim the cast well above the water and release line from your line hand after the forward power snap is made.

As mentioned under "Troubleshooting," whenever your line has sunk, use roll casts to bring it to the surface, or use it to eliminate slack line before taking line off the water for aerial casts. There is a technique, called the *roll pick-up*, that combines a roll and an aerial cast, effective when there is slack in the line prior to pick-up. This will be covered later.

After you have read "Rod-Hand Mechanics," this additional information may be helpful.

The high starting position of the rod hand gives you time and space to build up speed, which in combination with the drag of the water's surface tension (static friction) will load the rod more efficiently than if you start from a lower position.

The forward cast is a combination of downward and forward motion. Lead with your elbow, and end with your hand. When you are ready to start, consciously start your elbow downward, an inch or so, as you would in an aerial loading move, to position the rod shaft 90° from the target area. Then power snap the rod forward, pushing with the thumb. The roll-casting stroke is an overall acceleration, in the same manner as an aerial cast.

The Area of Focus

I do not know what a fly rod is, in engineering terms. Is it a lever? A spring? A flexible lever? A fly rod is a long and progressively flexible shaft that will cast my fly line. The more limber upper section of the rod responds to my control of the relatively stiff butt section that is linked to me through my hand. Under the load of the line, the upper section of the rod can bend, from a few inches to a few feet, depending on the line's length. It is much too difficult to judge how far to move the rod by the position of the tip, because the tip is always lagging behind the butt. I focus on the *butt*—specifically, the first few inches of rod shaft above the *grip*—as an indicator of rod arc movement. It has never let me down.

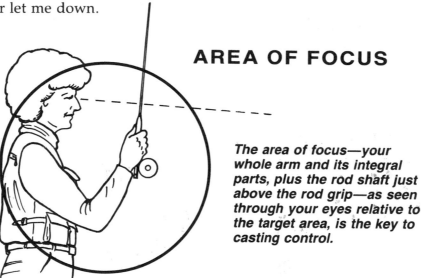

AREA OF FOCUS

The area of focus—your whole arm and its integral parts, plus the rod shaft just above the rod grip—as seen through your eyes relative to the target area, is the key to casting control.

Additionally, arm and body movement are an integral part of the cast and so the area of focus must include hand and arm motion, backed up by body motion, as it directs the lower part of the rod shaft.

Our arms have three movable joints: the wrist, the elbow, and the shoulder. Good fly casting includes movement of all three in varying amounts. The hand, forearm, and upper arm can move as one or be hinged at one or more of the joints so that one part of the arm may move within the move of another. We have at our disposal a full sphere of motion in which to use the casting arm but we will start with *straight-line* motions as our basic discipline in fly casting.

Before you put a rod in your hand, hold a pencil as you would a rod. Become familiar with the possible movement of the different parts of your arm and how this will determine rod movement in the stroke.

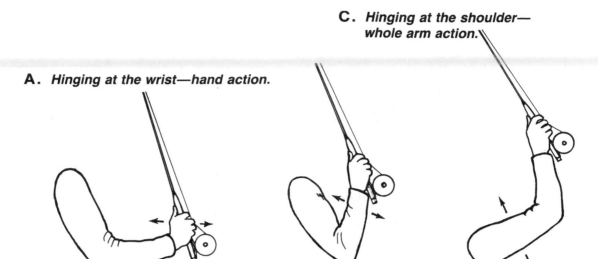

C. Hinging at the shoulder— whole arm action.

A. Hinging at the wrist—hand action.

B. Hinging at the elbow—forearm action.

1. With the elbow bent and the forearm parallel to the floor, position your forearm so that your thumb is on top of the pencil and your palm is facing left. Keep the rest of the arm still and swing the hand up and down, hinging at the wrist alone. This is *hand-wrist* action.

2. Keep your wrist straight as you hinge at the elbow, moving your forearm and hand, as a unit, up and down. (Touch your forearm to your upper arm.) This action also moves the pencil-rod back and forth through a simple arc. This is *forearm-elbow* action.

3. Keep the wrist and elbow joints motionless and move from the shoulder, lifting and lowering the whole bent arm as a unit. This is *upper arm-shoulder* action.

Fly casting is a backward and forward movement of the forearm and hand within the up-and-down range of movement of the whole arm. It is *compound movement*, moves within moves. What determines how much movement you will use at each joint or part of the arm is the guidance of making a *straight-line path with your hand* in the casting stroke. In vertical-plane casting, the path will be inclined upward on the backcast but may be inclined either downward or upward on the forward cast, depending on the distance to the target. Use the parts of your arm as you need them to make sure the path of your hand is straight.

Let's go back in time, for a moment. Traditionally, the caster's elbow was held tightly at his side and the casting stroke was a simple 90° arc, hinging on the elbow joint. The forearm and hand were like a radial arm. Wrist action was added to the forearm's movement on the backcast to gain a little more arc length and to have better leverage with which to start the forward cast and power application. In addition to the forearm motion forward, wrist action (and pushing forward with the thumb) could project the line to unroll above the water. Upper arm motion was left out entirely. The cast was made through a simple 90° arc that could be explained on a clockface.

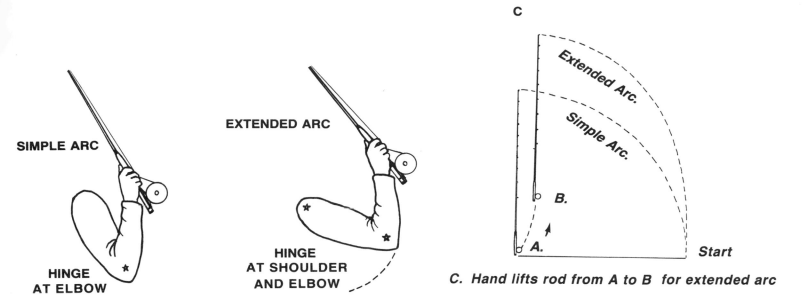

SIMPLE ARC

HINGE AT ELBOW

EXTENDED ARC

HINGE AT SHOULDER AND ELBOW

C

C. Hand lifts rod from A to B for extended arc

With this method it could take years for the caster to develop a smooth forward stroke for a relatively long line, having to get the rod and line moving and adding power, all in such a restricted length of movement. Can you imagine running with your knees tied together? Or not using the upper part of your legs to lengthen the stride and smooth out the jolts? That's what the stationary elbow is similar to. I untied my elbow, early on, and shortened the time it took to become proficient. You should do the same, lifting and lowering the whole arm, as you sense the need, to keep the casting stroke on a straight path.

Lifting and lowering the arm extends the 90° arc through which the rod will pass. On the backcast, the base of the radial arm (the elbow) will start low and end higher. Therefore the rod tip will end higher with this "extended arc" than it would with a simple arc. The line will follow the rod tip's path.

The backcast becomes a backward/upward move, instead of just a backward one and it will help to think of the word "up" as you do it. Because of the bending of the rod tip and the way in which your arm is attached to your shoulder, the line can't help but be thrown backward. The upward impetus must come from the lifting of your elbow (shoulder movement).

Arm motion is backed by body motion to further lengthen your stroke if needed. Shift your weight, back and forth, from one foot to the other (standing with one foot ahead) on backcast and forward cast to smooth out your strokes on long casts. Body motion will reduce the actual movement of your arm, for easier casting and less fatigue.

Use the Butt of your Fly Rod

Having used a pencil to familiarize yourself with the joints of your arm and how they might be used, try the same thing with the butt of your fly rod (with a reel mounted).

Notice that:

1. Hinging at the wrist alone makes the rod move like a metronome, in a simple arc, with the reel swinging in and out.

2. Hinging at the elbow, with forearm movement and the wrist straight (but not stiff), moves the rod through a 90° arc, with a little movement but *no swinging* of the reel.

3. Moving the bent arm as a unit, from the shoulder, makes the rod move up and down, on an inclined straight-line path, through an extended arc. Focus on the elbow's change of position. Again, as with the elbow hinge, there should be no swinging of the reel.

Now go back to #2, hinging at the elbow, and combine it with lifting and lowering of the whole arm, from the shoulder, accelerating to a stop on each stroke. On the backcast, *squeeze* the cork grip to end the acceleration of the stroke (the wrist should "crack" slightly) and, on the forward stroke, push with the thumb and squeeze the other fingers on the grip to end the acceleration. The thumb push creates noticeable wrist action. There will be movement of all three joints on each casting stroke with the wrist *restricted on the backcast* to just cracking. If you check on the position of the reel, relative to the underside of your forearm, it will help you gauge whether or not you are using too much wrist.

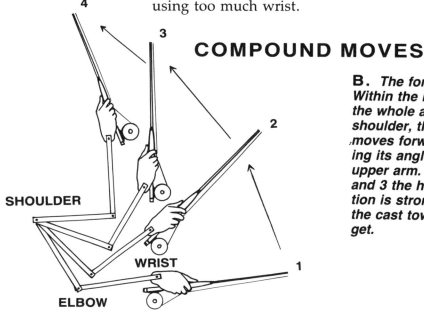

COMPOUND MOVES

A. The backcast.
Within the movement of the whole arm, from the shoulder, the forearm moves backward to lessen its angle with the upper arm. Wrist action is negligible.

B. The forward cast.
Within the movement of the whole arm, from the shoulder, the forearm moves forward, enlarging its angle with the upper arm. Between 2 and 3 the hand/wrist action is strong to project the cast toward the target.

SHOULDER

WRIST

ELBOW

Use a Mirror

To get the best look at this combination of movements, stand in front of a mirror with your rod butt and reel.

Line up the ferrule end of the rod butt with the inside edge of the mirror, with your bent arm at waist level. Move your hand in a casting stroke backward-upward, along the edge, in slow motion. Keep your arm in front of your shoulder, forearm lined up with the upper arm. Don't let the rod shaft go outside the mirror edge.

At the end of the backcast stroke, if you have lifted your elbow, your hand will be above eye level. If you didn't, it will be at chin level. Free your shoulder joint to lift your elbow.

Start the forward casting stroke with a movement from the shoulder that lowers the elbow an inch or two. Then extend the forearm, pushing forward with the thumb *at chest level*, toward your mirror image. "Follow through" by lowering the arm/rod to waist level. Do the same motions, smoothly accelerating to a stop, in a backcast and forward cast. On the backcast *lead with your forearm*; on the forward cast, *lead with your elbow*.

Turn sideward to the mirror, your casting arm visible, and make sure that, at the end of the backcast, your hand and the rod butt are not behind your head or shoulder. Your casting hand should never go behind your shoulder to end the stroke in this vertical plane casting. If it does, the line will be thrown downward by the tip of the rod.

AS SEEN IN THE MIRROR

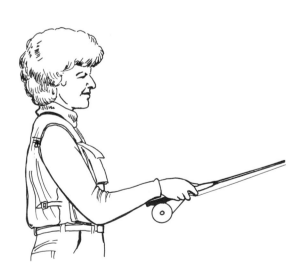

A. *Starting and ending position of full cast.*

B. *End of backcast and rod position, relative to shoulder and head.*

Body Motion

In this same position, shoulders perpendicular to the mirror, drop your right foot behind the other. As you make the backcast stroke, shift your weight to the back foot. Shift it *forward* as you make the forward stroke. This *body motion* can *extend* the *length* of the arc through which the rod passes, although the relative position of your rod hand to your shoulder will remain the same.

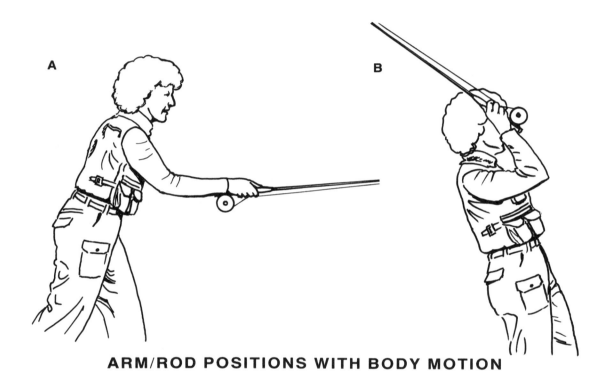

ARM/ROD POSITIONS WITH BODY MOTION

Common Faults

The most common fault is for the wrist to bend sharply on the backcast. Usually the forearm is angled slightly upward and the wrist takes it from there, bending backward to throw the backcast downward. If you recognize that you have this problem, put the very end of the rod grip inside the cuff of your shirt sleeve. This should make you bend your elbow and restrict the movement of your wrist. Unfortunately, the shirt sleeve will restrict wrist movement on the forward cast, where you really need it. If you are unable to solve the problem in a short time, there is a commercial product, "Wristlok," available from Simms/Life-Link in Jackson Hole, Wyoming, which is better than the shirt sleeve in that it allows *some* wrist motion.

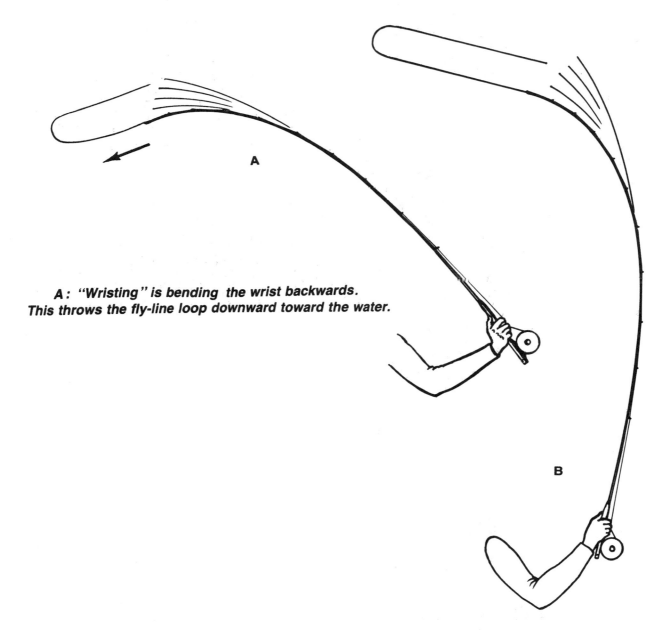

A: *"Wristing" is bending the wrist backwards.*
This throws the fly-line loop downward toward the water.

B: *Good form. With just a "cracked" wrist,*
the fly-line loop will unroll well above the water.

The second most common fault is to swing the whole arm outward from the shoulder. This moves the rod butt in a semicircular motion instead of in a straight line and the fly line will follow suit.

These faults seem to develop because the caster is afraid he is going to be hit by the hook of the fly. (I once had a student who not only swung his arm outward but turned his head to the far side, on every backcast.) The fly line follows the rod tip and, if the rod tip lifts upward, the line, leader, and fly will lift upward too, following its path. At its closest point, the fly will pass your head the length of the rod away.

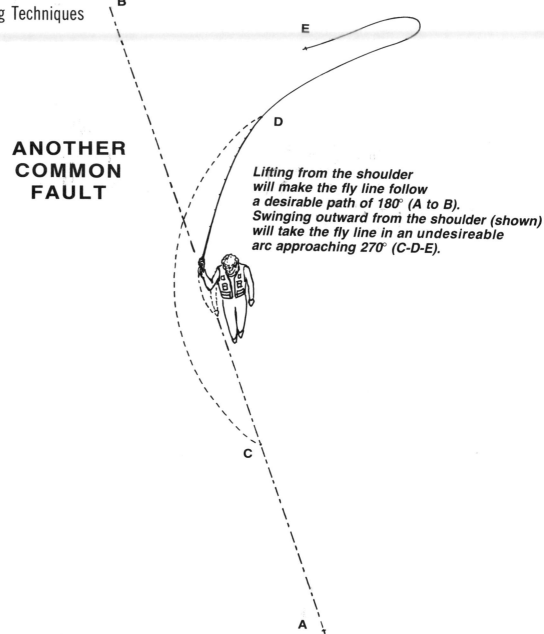

ANOTHER COMMON FAULT

Lifting from the shoulder will make the fly line follow a desirable path of 180° (A to B). Swinging outward from the shoulder (shown) will take the fly line in an undesireable arc approaching 270° (C-D-E).

In your "area of focus" you can see the motion of your casting arm, *directly* to start and finish the stroke, and *peripherally* during the stroke, as it directs the rod shaft. In addition, the effects of your actions can be seen at the end of every forward cast in your view of the whole rod and the unrolling line. Always watch the way, and the angle at which, the line unrolls forward, to get clues to your performance of the cast. Is the line unrolling smoothly, or did you use too much power? Is it angled toward the target too low, too high, or just right? Is every bit of the line going to unroll before it hits the water, or is the line speed too slow? All of these factors have as their source the movement of the rod shaft, backed by the movement of your casting arm and your body; this is your *area of focus*.

two

A BASIC DISCIPLINE

Knowing the Mechanics

Tournament casting gave me a basic discipline, developing the eye/hand/rod coordination that was necessary for both accuracy and distance. Casting was done in the vertical plane, with no obstructions behind, ahead, or on either side. Because I started as a ten-year-old, I didn't analyze the way I cast; I just did what felt good—and worked—to place the fly where I wanted it.

When I was sixteen and had won my first national title, casting stylist Bill Taylor became my mentor. He taught me to narrow my casting loop and to "hover" the fly for better accuracy. He taught by example. He never analyzed my casting in words; he just said, "Do this." It was like starting from scratch as I struggled to analyze both what he was doing and my own casting, to make the necessary changes in what had been my natural, comfortable style. It destroyed my casting confidence for about a year but, when I came up from that low point, I had started to understand what made casting work—and I was the better for it. Taylor had refined my style . . . or perhaps *we* had refined it. He taught me to cast distance fly in the same manner. I ghillied for him (tended his line) and he would ask me to tell him what was wrong with his imperfect casts. Examining his motions and the form the line took as it unrolled, I came to know what perfectly beautiful casting looked like and what he did to produce such casts. Duplicating them is a lifetime project.

When I gave up tournament casting and moved seriously into the world of fly fishing, I was in for some shocks. The wind was not always behind me and, in places like the flats of the Florida Keys, could be formidable. I had a caster's tendency to hit the fish on the head instead of leading them—and I made too many false casts. For a while I thought my fishing companions were right when they told me that tournament casting was a handicap and that I was stuck with it. But of course that wasn't true. I had to adapt and I did. The basic discipline of overhead casting still stands as one of my strengths as a fisherman. Another is being able to adapt that discipline to fishing situations, because I understand the casting mechanics.

I want you, too, to understand the mechanics and have a basic discipline so that you can solve your own problems as they arise. Start by practicing in the best of circumstances, with no obstructions, and the wind at your back, until you understand the parts of the cast in a vertical plane and the time and space they use. You'll have a set of rules you can use as is, or break as you then adapt them to fishing conditions. You'll have a standard cast that unrolls the back and forward casts exactly opposite each other, along a 180° line, and unrolls the forward cast completely, above the water, before it lands. You will be able to produce a loop that is wide or narrow at your command and enjoy expertise in line control through the precise use of the line hand. You'll have the strength of the basic discipline no matter how tough the conditions under which you must fish.

The Casting Stroke

It has been traditional to think of the casting stroke as one move, backward or forward. In recent years it has come to be recognized as an (overall) acceleration to a stop. Is the acceleration an even one? We hear the term **"power stroke"**. That sounds as if power should be applied all through the stroke. Should it? If power were isolated to be used in one part of the stroke, where, exactly would that be?

How do some anglers take their lines off the water without a whisper, while others *rripp* them off? And why do some anglers never tire while others have become fatigued in an hour? And doesn't the old clockface answer all of these questions?

Let's start with power stroke . . . a misnomer. The whole arm and rod movement is a stroke, just as in sports like tennis or golf. If you use equal power through the whole stroke, your line will rip off the water and the casting loop will be anything but smooth. Full power is used in only part of the stroke. You may read instructions that say to lift the line *first* and *then* power stroke. Lifting the line must be considered part of the overall stroke.

The backcast stroke begins when the line moves under tension. It ends when the fly comes out of the water. Who can tell you how many inches or feet long your stroke will have to be? On a clockface a short line might lift off by 10:30, a medium length by 12:45. Being told to move from 11:00 to 1:00 doesn't make sense. You can't begin to lift line at 11:00 o'clock effectively unless there are only three or four feet out of the rod tip. If you were lifting thirty feet of line you'd end up with the rod at 2:00 or 3:00 o'clock by the time the fly came out of the water. You might "false cast" line within the parameters of 11:00 to 1:00, but that length stroke will be good only for one length of line, not all lengths.

Clockface instruction tells you only that the rod moves through an arc, but the hands of a clock move from one central position, with a stationary base, to produce a simple arc. As stated earlier, that is not good enough; the base should move to extend the arc . . . and that base is your forearm and hand, *as an extension of the rod*, moving back and forth from the elbow, which itself lifts on the backcast and lowers on the forward cast from the shoulder, to extend the arc farther. There's another problem with this traditional method of determining rod movement. Because the rod tip is always lagging behind the butt, you can only know where it is, relative to the clock face, after the rod has unloaded and has stopped vibrating. That's late. The rod shaft, just above the grip, is a much better reference.

I have analyzed the casting stroke as having two parts within the overall *acceleration to a stop*. The first part of the stroke must overcome the static friction of the water's surface and the inertia of the line (or, in false casting, the change of direction against air resistance) to start the rod and line moving as a unit along the desired path. It begins the *loading* of the rod, the bending from the tip downward, by the weight of the line; so I call this the "**loading move**." It is done with a firm grip and little force to begin the acceleration.

The second part of the stroke *continues* and *maximizes* the loading action, as the rod and line are accelerated with force to a sudden stop, completing it. As a result of this powerful ending, the rod tip then springs to the opposite side, unloading the rod and forming a new loop. I call the second part of the stroke the "**power snap**" because it encompasses the one instant of real force in the cast and because the rod, through the action of the forearm and hand, snaps from one position to another.

While the new loop is unrolling, you have the option of keeping your casting arm exactly where it ended the stroke or following through. **Follow-through** helps to smooth the shock of the power snap and gives you a feeling of staying connected to the fly line's weight as it unrolls. On the backcast, follow-through is called "**drift**" and the time and space it provides will have an additional use for you, to reposition the arm and rod, when you must change planes between back and forward casts. The follow-through on the forward cast extends the distance slightly and softens the landing of line and leader for delicate presentations.

The power snap is the heart of the cast, moving the fly line loop from one side of the rod to the other. It is executed on every casting stroke, backward and forward. The loading move may not be necessary if you are fishing with just a few feet of line between rod tip and leader, because there is negligible weight to be moved. The quick acceleration of the power snap may be enough. As the line is lengthened, however, the initial resistance to its movement increases. The loading move, then, becomes absolutely necessary both to take the line off the water smoothly and to give sufficient length to the stroke to keep the cast smooth.

There is an outside factor to be aware of; this is **slack line**. Slack is line with no rod tension on it; it is the opposite of *tight*. It works against you and can spoil the cast. The first place to look for it is between the rod tip and the water, before you begin the cast. Slack in other parts of the line may or may not be critical, depending upon where it is in the line and how much there is proportionate to the line's length.

The cast cannot effectively begin, the rod will not load, until the slack line between the rod tip and the water is eliminated. A good roll cast will get rid of it if you then lower your rod tip on the follow-through to keep slack from forming again before you can begin your pick-up. You'll learn a roll pick-up technique to help solve this problem. For a first technique, use a roll cast or, if it will not shorten the line too much, strip the slack back in with the line hand, through a finger of the rod hand. Look for slack before you begin every cast so that it will become second nature to eliminate this.

Casting mechanics are the responsibility of the rod hand alone. It is really important that you do not use your line hand as you are working to understand, and recognize in your own cast, particular parts of the mechanics. Careless use of the line hand, haphazardly adding or subtracting line weight during the casting stroke, will keep you from feeling the rod and line as a unit. A constant length of line, secured under the rod hand, is your best bet for learning. After you are comfortable with one length, and its constant weight, add more and work with it until you master the new length too.

I'll separate the back and forward casts and their parts. I suggest that, as you read through these instructions, you use a pencil, or better still, the butt section of your favorite rod (with reel attached) to get used to the moves. Then set up the whole outfit and use it on water, except where noted that grass might be better.

Work with thirty-five feet of combined rod length, line length, and leader (with practice fly attached) so that you can utilize both parts of the stroke and drift. If you are a beginner, start with the roll cast to become operational.

Rod Hand Mechanics: The Backcast

Begin the cast believing that your hand and forearm are an extension of the rod butt, *all the way to your elbow*. Concentrate on these essentials:

No slack. Lowered rod tip. Firm but relaxed grip with rod butt against underside of wrist. Attention focused on the line where it first touches the water near the rod tip.

1. Raise your arm, hand, and rod, as a unit (with some speed) on an upwardly inclined path and in line with your shoulder. Watch the lifting fly line *where* and *as* it leaves the water, inch by inch. When you have lifted all of the line, right up to the line/leader connection, the *loading move* is finished and you will

2. Accelerate the stroke in a straight line, on the same, inclined path, lifting your whole arm and, within that motion, adding a forearm and hand thrust, to take the leader and fly out of the water. This is the *power snap*. End the move, dead-stopped, as the fly comes out of the water. The backcast stroke is finished.

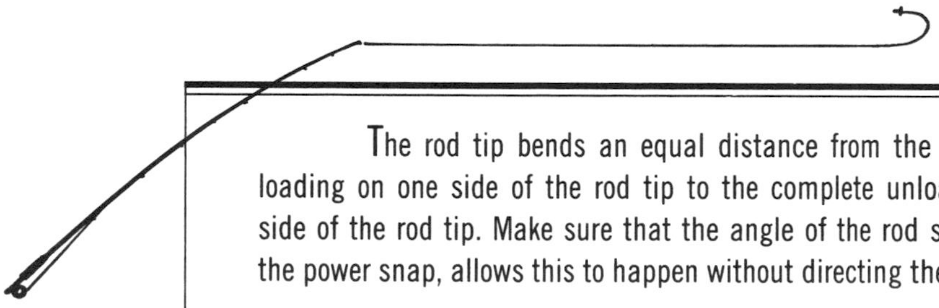

The rod tip bends an equal distance from the point of maximum loading on one side of the rod tip to the complete unloading on the other side of the rod tip. Make sure that the angle of the rod shaft, at the end of the power snap, allows this to happen without directing the fly line downward.

Rod Butt/Underside of Wrist

The end of the rod butt stays against the underside of the wrist through the loading move. On the power snap, when the forearm and hand thrust backward, within the lifting movement of the whole arm, the rod butt will move away from the wrist. *Squeeze-stop* the hand and rod butt before your wrist bends too far. The wrist should just "crack" and the rod butt's position should change just an inch or two. Use the fourth and fifth fingers of your hand to keep the butt close.

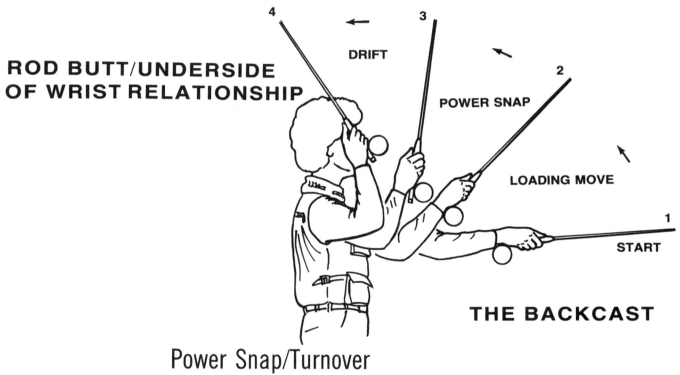

ROD BUTT/UNDERSIDE OF WRIST RELATIONSHIP

DRIFT

POWER SNAP

LOADING MOVE

START

THE BACKCAST

Power Snap/Turnover

The change in the rod-butt/wrist attitude indicates to you that the line has been transferred from one side of the rod tip to the other; I call that transfer the *turnover* as well as the power snap. Power snap tells what the move is and turnover tells what happened to the rod and line as a result. You'll powersnap the rod hand and forearm to turn the line over the rod tip, to form a new loop. Try to make the turnover smooth, with just the right amount of power.

> The arm moves in two ways on the backcast: the forearm and hand move as one within the movement of the whole arm from the shoulder socket.

A.

1 Starting position
1-2 Loading move
2-3 Power snap—end of stroke
3-4 Drift (follow-through backward)

B. *The line sags and slack is formed between the rod and the water when the loading move is done with too little speed.*

Loading Move/Power Snap Lengths

You have lifted the line and power-snapped the leader and fly in one smooth stroke. It's over in an instant! The loading move is a relatively long part of that instant, because of the line's length, and the power snap is proportionately short because of the lesser length of the leader and fly and their near weightlessness. The briefness of the power snap will test your reflexes. Don't let the rod hand recoil at the end of the power snap. Stop it dead!

Speed and Position of the Loading Move

The speed with which the loading move is made is important. If the move is too slow, the line will come toward you, below the rod tip, instead of lifting off the water. Slack will form and the rod will not load. It will kill the cast. A minimum speed must be maintained from the start, increasing gradually so that the line does not sag, but has tension on it as it lifts.

If, conversely, the line "rripps" off the water, disturbing it, you are using too much speed and/or too much force. The line cannot be lifted all at once;

The end of the power snap and the release of the fly from the water's surface film coincide exactly. Not another fraction of an inch of stroke length is necessary.

it is flexible and must be lifted inches at a time from where you started, close to the rod tip. This will give you a smooth-as-silk lift-off with minimal water disturbance. Your eyes and ears can tell you when it is just right. Notice now, in the illustration, that the angle of the line, as the fly lifts off the water, is the projected path of the backcast.

Speed and Position of the Power Snap

When you power-snap the leader and fly, you are accelerating the already moving fly line. That is why both speed and force are important, to complete the move in the time and space it takes to get just the leader and fly out of the water. This is the most difficult move of the cast because we lack training for throwing backward. Find a word that helps you do the move, such as *throw* or *snap* or *thrust* (I like that one) or *power*, and say it every time you make a backcast power snap until it is second nature.

The power snap is an instant, like the coming together of a bat, or golf club, and ball. Wherever in the stroke you power snap, wherever the face of the rod's bend is aimed, will determine exactly where the line will go. So the loading move becomes important in positioning the power snap. As with a bat and ball the power snap must be made at roughly 90° from where you want the line to unroll.

If, instead of starting the loading move with a lowered rod tip, you start with a high rod tip, at say, 11:00 o'clock, by the time the rod bends with the load of the line's weight, the face of that bend will be aimed downward behind you and that's where the line will unroll. This is a common fault. Start with the rod tip lowered and no slack in the line to position the parts of the stroke effectively.

The Path of the Line

At the end of the power snap, the rod tip will vibrate (oscillate) from the shocking action of the suddenly stopped butt, but the new loop will start to form when the tip first springs from its deepest bend on one side of the rod,

To avoid "hinging" at the wrist, think of lifting the forearm and the fly reel as if they were glued together.

to the other side. The illustration shows what occurs without all of the vibrations. Notice that the formed beginning of the loop is already directional. You can tell just where the fly line will unroll. The unrolling path should be a continuation of the angle of the line, between the rod tip and the fly, observed just as the fly left the water, at the end of the power snap. The line, leader, and fly will have traveled along a straight-line path, unrolling in a 180° change of direction. The rod will have moved through an arc of only about 90° for this length of line.

After the power snap, immediately relax the rod hand. As the line unrolls, rest your muscles until you need them again on the forward stroke. This is important. Knowing where to use power and where to relax can take the work out of fly casting.

Looking Back

In the old, traditional backcast stroke, the forearm did the loading move and the wrist did the power snap. The power snap could be only as long as the hand was large, no matter what the length of the line. If the wrist hinged backward as far as possible for long lines, the rod tip would move farther than 90° in its simple arc and throw the line downward in back. The caster had to end his wrist power snap at a precise angle.

Because the elbow was stationary, the move of the forearm and hand could be likened to the shape of the letter "V." Today's straight-line, straight-wrist power snap, because of the lifting from the shoulder to extend the arc without throwing the line downward, is shaped like an off-angle "U".

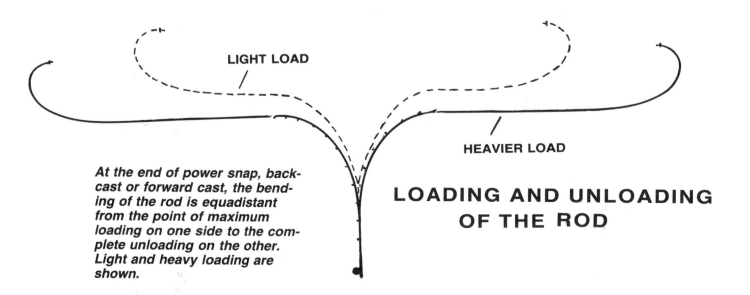

LIGHT LOAD

HEAVIER LOAD

At the end of power snap, back-cast or forward cast, the bending of the rod is equadistant from the point of maximum loading on one side to the complete unloading on the other. Light and heavy loading are shown.

LOADING AND UNLOADING OF THE ROD

Drift

Any stroke in any sport has a follow-through. You know all about it in one-stroke sports like tennis and golf. It is a natural extension of any forward stroke and, because we have two strokes in fly casting, you can make it a natural extension of the backcast stroke as well.

When I learned to cast there was no follow-through on the backcast. How far could you have gone with the elbow pinned to the body? You could only cock your wrist backward. True follow-through would have meant full movement of the arm and that was bad style.

When I freed my elbow I still didn't know about follow-through but used body motion to fill the time between back and forward casts. Some ten years later, when I became a distance caster, I learned to follow through backward with both arm and body motion, to give me the longer forward strokes and smooth power application so necessary for long lines. Distance casters called the move *drift*, and it became a conscious part of my casting mechanics, even in accuracy casting where I then substituted it for some of the body motion I had been using. It gave me a distinctive casting style.

The drift move can improve your casting in two ways.

1. It can give you perfect timing. Because you move the rod tip with the unrolling line, at the same speed as the lower level of the line loop and in the same direction, you will feel connected to the line and its weight, through its pressure on the sensitive rod tip. Drift is the *constant pressure* move, constant pressure being the key to perfect timing. By feeling the subtle weight of the line throughout its unrolling, you will know exactly where it is and when to start the forward cast. One move follows another in continuous motion.

2. The drift move can reposition your arm and rod for the forward stroke, giving you better leverage, through additional height or a farther-back starting position, even if you keep the cast in the same plane. It will allow

In addition to this first use of drift (following through on a backward/upward line) it can (later) be utilized to reposition the rod hand sideward or upward or downward, between the backcast and the forward cast.

you to reposition for a *change* of *planes*, slightly or dramatically, so often necessary for ease of presentation. If you can mentally separate the back and forward casting strokes as not having to be made along exactly the same path, then the drift move, between the strokes, can be the exciting key to new casting control our fly-fishing forefathers never dreamed of. In this first use, stay in the same plane.

The time during which you can drift is the time it takes for the fly line to unroll behind you. At the end of the power snap, the new loop has formed. Your forearm and the butt of the rod are in front of, or even with, your shoulder, your grip once more relaxed. As the line unrolls, keep the rod/hand/forearm position *static* while you raise your arm from the shoulder and extend the forearm to follow through backward. Follow through for just a few inches, maintaining your feeling of being connected to the line. That's all there is to it; you are ready to start the forward stroke.

Angle of the Drift Move

The drift move continues the rod hand along the path started by the backcast stroke, at the same time positioning it to begin the forward stroke. On short-line backcasts, the hand/rod position should drift almost directly upward because the angle of short backcasts is relatively steep. With longer lines, the angle of the cast is less steep. Continuing on that angled path, the drift move will be more backward than upward, because of the limitation of shoulder movement, and the rod angle will change to a lower one. This new rod position will give you more space ahead of your rod hand through which to make the longer forward stroke smoothly and it will allow you to raise the angle of the forward cast to provide for shooting line.

At the end of the drift move, the arm should still be flexed (never completely straight) so that you can start the forward cast smoothly. You are carrying weight, above your head, and the next move will begin with movement of the bent elbow, just as if you were splitting wood with an axe.

Drift is a move without power and you cannot expect to drift against a strong backwind.

Although the stroke should end with the rod hand above, or in line with, the shoulder, the drift move can then take the rod hand behind (but above) the shoulder without negative effect.

When you first add drift to your cast, you may feel that this move between backcast and forward cast is square-cornered, but, as you become familiar with it, it will *round*, with one move following another smoothly to give the feeling of constant pressure between rod tip and line. Drift could be the missing link in your casting style. I think of it as a magic movement linking the backcast and forward cast to make fly casting look and feel beautiful as well as enabling us to use a full range of angles and planes within a single cast, to solve the problems of presentation.

A Common Fault

It is fairly common among students to drift forward instead of backward, because we don't "follow through" backward in other sports.

If, at the end of the power snap, you move your rod hand forward at all while the line is unrolling, you will reduce the space you have available in which to make the forward cast. You will be restricting yourself, shortening the potential length of your forward stroke, which is just the opposite effect of the right use of drift. Be careful of this one. Use body motion to help solve the problem, keeping your weight on the back foot *through* the drift move.

Rod-Hand Mechanics: The Forward Cast

The forward cast is made on a straight line, from where the rod hand ends the backcast (or drift move) toward the target area. At the beginning of every forward presentation cast, look directly at the particular inch of water on which you want your fly to land and imagine a line between your hand and that inch. Start the cast along that "hand/target" line.

The drift move is *optional* and is "outside" the casting stroke.

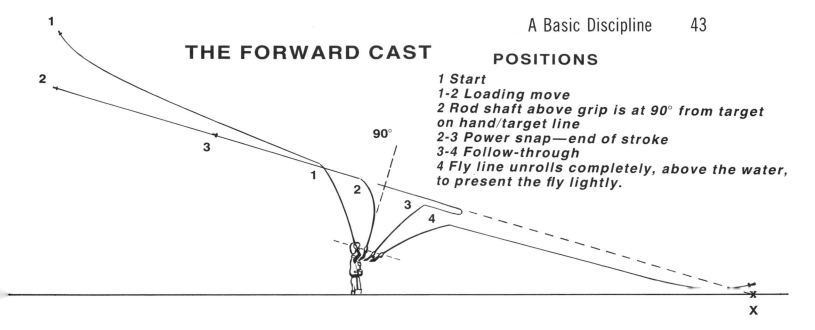

THE FORWARD CAST

POSITIONS

1 Start
1-2 Loading move
2 Rod shaft above grip is at 90° from target on hand/target line
2-3 Power snap—end of stroke
3-4 Follow-through
4 Fly line unrolls completely, above the water, to present the fly lightly.

The Forward Loading Move and Power Snap

When this instructional cast was started, your arm and rod were fully visible on the backcast loading move and you could see and feel the static friction of the water as it resisted the line's movement on the pick-up. On the forward cast, you can see only your arm and the rod grip as the loading move completes the "turning around" of the line and leader, still extended behind you, and starts it all (rod, line, leader, and fly) moving forward as a unit, beginning the acceleration that will end with the power snap. Form a good mental picture of the line as it straightens and starts forward, fully extended behind the rod tip.

The *forward loading move* and the *backcast drift move* occupy the same space and, in terms of arm movement, one is the reverse of the other. The backward drift move is a movement of the arm, from the shoulder, with a slight extension of the forearm, backward/*upward*. As seen in the illustration, the forward loading move is a movement of the arm, from the shoulder, with a slight retraction of the forearm, forward/*downward*. The whole, bent arm, led by the elbow, starts forward just before the line and leader are straightened out behind the rod tip.

1. The loading move positions the rod for the power snap. Focus on the rod shaft, just above the grip. See where it is at the end of the backcast (it is likely to be tilted backward) and then just move it forward, along the hand/target line, until it is 90° to, or perpendicular from, the target. Your elbow will have moved down/forward just an inch or two before the rod shaft is in position, and you should feel the subtle weight of the fully extended fly line on the rod tip.

2. Now that you are in position, *power snap* the rod through a 30 to 45° (maximum) **turnover arc** as you accelerate to a stop. Start the forearm forward and, at the same time, push the rod grip forward with your thumb, pulling the end of the rod grip back against the underside of your wrist. This thumb/wrist motion is the turnover arc, a move within a move (hand motion within the forearm motion) and they both are within the movement of the whole arm. What makes this easy to do is your focus on the rod shaft above the grip. You started with it positioned 90° from the target, and you'll move it through an arc of no more than 45° toward the target, on a straight line. (This will give you a narrow loop.) Check the rod shaft position at the end of the power snap. It should be no less than 45° from the target on the hand/target line. Follow-through will take it the rest of the way.

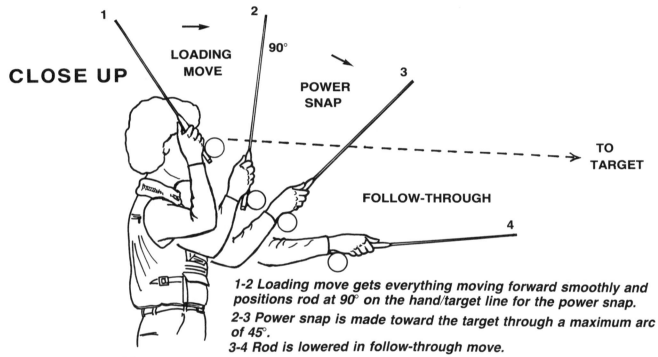

CLOSE UP

LOADING MOVE

POWER SNAP

FOLLOW-THROUGH

TO TARGET

1-2 Loading move gets everything moving forward smoothly and positions rod at 90° on the hand/target line for the power snap.
2-3 Power snap is made toward the target through a maximum arc of 45°.
3-4 Rod is lowered in follow-through move.

The power snap contains the one instant of real power in the forward cast, as it did in the backcast. Remember the screen door handle and, as you push with your thumb, pull the rod butt back up with your lower fingers.

The arm moves in three ways: the movement starts with the whole arm, from the shoulder, then the forearm projects forward, and, within that move, the hand, led by the thumb, moves forward independently.

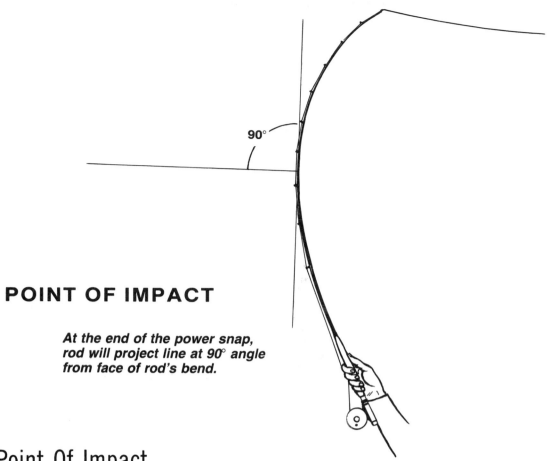

POINT OF IMPACT

At the end of the power snap, rod will project line at 90° angle from face of rod's bend.

90°

Point Of Impact

The position of the power snap in the casting stroke can be likened to the point of impact when a ball and bat come together (or golf club or racquet). When you hit the ball, you impact it with the bat, club, or racquet, perpendicular to where you want the ball to go. The power snap is the point of impact in the casting stroke, determining where the line will go. The loading move positions it to be at 90° to the target, analogous to the point of impact in these other sports.

Guidelines

The numbers of degrees, 90° for the start of the power snap and 30 to 45° for the turnover arc, are to be used as guidelines with your rod. They may not be the same with every rod action or length. For instance, if the rod is soft-actioned, the flexing will extend deeper toward the butt and the tip will lag farther behind. The power snap might need to start a little before 90° and the turnover arc, as measured with the rod shaft above the grip, would be on the short side, closer to 30° than to 45°. The overall movement of the rod tip, on this soft-actioned rod, would be through a very large arc, because of the deep bending, much more difficult to see and measure for constancy of the casting stroke than the movement of the shaft above the grip.

You may have to experiment with each different rod you use to find the perfect starting position for the power snap and the perfect size of the turnover arc to give you a narrow loop. Check the rod shaft at the beginning of the loading move, the beginning of the power snap, and the end of the power snap. Once you have it figured, it will simplify your forward stroke. You can expect to be able to cast beautiful, narrow loops, accurately, on every cast.

Forearm Extension

As you do the power snap, your forearm will extend. For short casts, it may need to move only a few inches. For longer casts you may need to extend it forward a foot or two. The length varies with the tackle and the caster. Extend the forearm only as much as you need to, to make a beautiful, smooth cast, and be sure it is still bent at the end of the power snap. You can injure your elbow joint if you power snap to an absolutely straight extension of the arm; this is the caster's version of tennis elbow. Any full extension of the arm is done on the follow-through, slowly and without force.

More on the Forward Loading Move

Let me go back to the need, or lack of it, for the forward loading move now that you know that it is a positioning move. If you were casting just the few feet of line and a leader (mentioned earlier as a situation in which you would not need a backcast loading move, because of lack of line weight) and you stopped the backcast when the fly came out of the water, chances are the rod shaft would be 90° from the target on the hand/target line (already in position for just a power snap forward). No forward loading move would be necessary.

If your line is long enough to need a loading move on the backcast, you most certainly will need one on the forward cast to get the rod shaft positioned before the turnover. Positioning the rod shaft at 90° from the target also tells you how long the loading move needs to be, so that you need not rely on the subtle feeling of weight alone. It's a real shortcut to a perfect forward cast.

The 90° positioning of the rod shaft, prior to the power snap, is not perpendicular to a line between the sky and the water. It is perpendicular to the hand/target line, which is usually inclined.

In my experience as an instructor, lack of a forward loading move, when it is needed, is the most common cause of tailing loops. A tailing loop is one in which the end of the fly line, leader, and fly, move forward below the rest of the unrolling loop, resulting in poor presentations and, perhaps, the formation of a "wind" knot in the leader.

Common Fault

A common fault on this forward casting stroke is to lower the rod hand too much on the power snap. The power snap is the instant of projection of the hand, directly toward the target. The overall stroke may be on a downward slant, but the rod hand, on the power snap/turnover, must continue to move on a straight line toward the target.

Forward Cast Follow-Through

The forward casting stroke is finished; the line is unrolling along the path determined by your power snap/turnover arc. If you have accelerated through the stroke, good line speed should unroll the fly line completely above the water before it drops lightly to the surface. The next move is to *follow through* by extending and lowering your arm and the rod as the fly line falls to the water. In this way, every inch of the line will be fully extended. Without follow-through, the line, between the rod tip and the point where it first touches the water, will become slack line, cheating you of a few feet of length and delaying your precise control of the line as you begin to fish it.

Follow-through softens the landing of the line and fly and can often save an over-powered cast from landing too heavily (if you follow through very quickly). It is a natural move and gives the feeling that the cast is completed.

One of the nice things about fly-casting, as opposed to bait casting or spinning, is that, after you have made the cast through the power snap, you can still move the line or a portion of it, before it hits the water, to alter the form in which it will, then, lie on the water. This is called **aerial mending**. Forward follow-through gives you the time and space in which to do it. You can alter the cast then, just as you can use drift time (in a different way) at the end of the backcast, to alter the path of the forward cast.

After the Mechanics

There will probably be a time lag between your ability to understand and execute the mechanics. The *backward power snap*, so short and sharp, is probably the most difficult move. It requires competence in those backward-throwing muscles. But once you feel a good backcast, you'll never again be satisfied with anything else. It's as sure a feeling as a friendly hug!

Drift may be a stumbling block until the backcast power snap is a natural move to you. Don't worry about drift; leave it out until you can recognize the time and space in which to use it, the time it takes for the line to unroll. Without drift, everything else in the cast has to be more precise (especially determining *when* to start the forward cast) because your arm's motion is more limited and the rod will be moving back and forth on exactly the same path. Include drift as soon as you can. Meanwhile, a little body motion can take its place to smooth your timing and power application.

The Heart of the Cast

You can do without a *loading move* if the line is very short and you can do without drift on short to medium casts, but you should always use a power snap. That's the heart of the cast. Without a power snap there is no real loop; the line will follow the rod tip, but your control as to where it will unroll and how it lands cannot be precise. The sharp turnover arc of the power snap forms the loop and gives it direction.

Choosing the term *power snap* to describe that portion of the cast was not a quick decision but I think it tells what happens. However, you might prefer *power turnover*, *power thrust*, *power move*, or *turnover arc*. You might think *power thrust* on the backcast and *turnover arc* on the forward cast. Use whichever term triggers muscle response, especially on the backcast.

Notice, in the illustrations, that the placement of the moves of the forward cast is the reverse of the backcast, with this constant length of line. The power snap is the heart, the backcast loading move and the forward cast follow-through are in the same space; the backcast drift move and the forward loading move are in the same space.

If your hand, forearm, and upper arm muscles tire, that is normal. If your shoulder, neck, or underarm muscles hurt, you are doing something wrong.

By understanding the rod hand's mechanics, you will recognize the time and space limitations within which additional coordinating actions must fit. This list will give you an idea of where coming line-hand techniques will coordinate with the basic rod hand moves.

While the rod hand does this:	The line hand can do this:
Backcast loading move	Move the line, independent of the rod's motion.
Backcast power snap	Coordinate a single haul; pull in the line on the double haul.
Drift move	Release line for shooting; give line back on the double haul.
Forward loading	Shoot additional line in "slide loading" technique.
Forward power snap	Coordinate a single haul; pull in line for double haul.
Forward follow-through	Release line for shooting; give back line on double haul.

Additionally, drift time can be used for the repositioning of the rod to change planes between back and forward casts. Follow-through, on the forward cast, can be used for aerial mending of the line on presentation.

Is That Dancin'?

As a dancing teacher for twelve years, I taught a lot of "steps" to would-be dancers. There's a world of difference between the two (steps and dancing), just as there is between mechanics and fly casting. "Mechanics" is a word at odds with the beautiful form and feeling of fly casting and, once you learn what the mechanics are, you can forget the word, but you mustn't forget the immutable laws of physics.

Good mechanics will bring to life the rod's individual action and the interaction between rod and line. You'll soon be making casting moves that flow one into another as you use speed and strength in just the right

Clutching the rod grip throughout the cast will tire you quickly. Hold the rod in a relaxed but firm grip to begin the stroke, gradually increasing the firmness as you accelerate. Use maximum force to complete the power snap, then instantly relax as the line unrolls.

proportions—dashed by precise touches of crispness and delicacy. Your arm and body can move with grace, the muscles contracting and relaxing in the lovely cadence of the casts. A little power here, the feeling of floating there . . . an unleashing of the rod's power; an inanimate tool coming to life, the sweet satisfaction of knowing you are in control. The nuances of beautiful fly casting enrich the soul as well as they enrich the art. Once you have felt them you'll be satisfied with nothing less and, "Yes, mon, *that's* dancin'!"

Variable Basics: Stroke Length, Power, and Timing

Variable basics are those elements of the cast that are not constant. They are the same elements you will find in other sports: the length of the stroke and variations in power and timing. They vary according to the tackle, the conditions, and the length of the line for each individual caster.

Stroke Length

The casting stroke has a specific length because it has a beginning and an end. Its length will change with the length of the line that is out of the rod tip. To move a length of fly line smoothly takes a particular amount of movement of the whole rod, from butt to tip. If I use thirty-five feet of line as a reference, it would take more movement of the rod to move that length than

STROKE LENGTH AND ANGLE OF CAST: SHORT

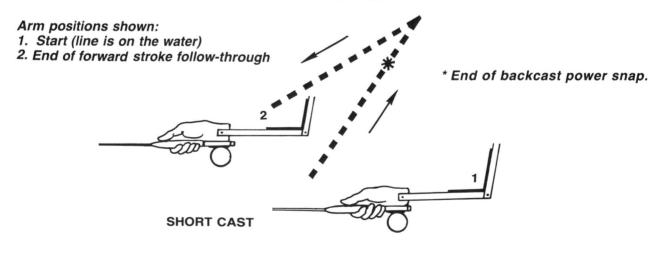

Arm positions shown:
1. Start (line is on the water)
2. End of forward stroke follow-through

* End of backcast power snap.

SHORT CAST

HORIZONTAL

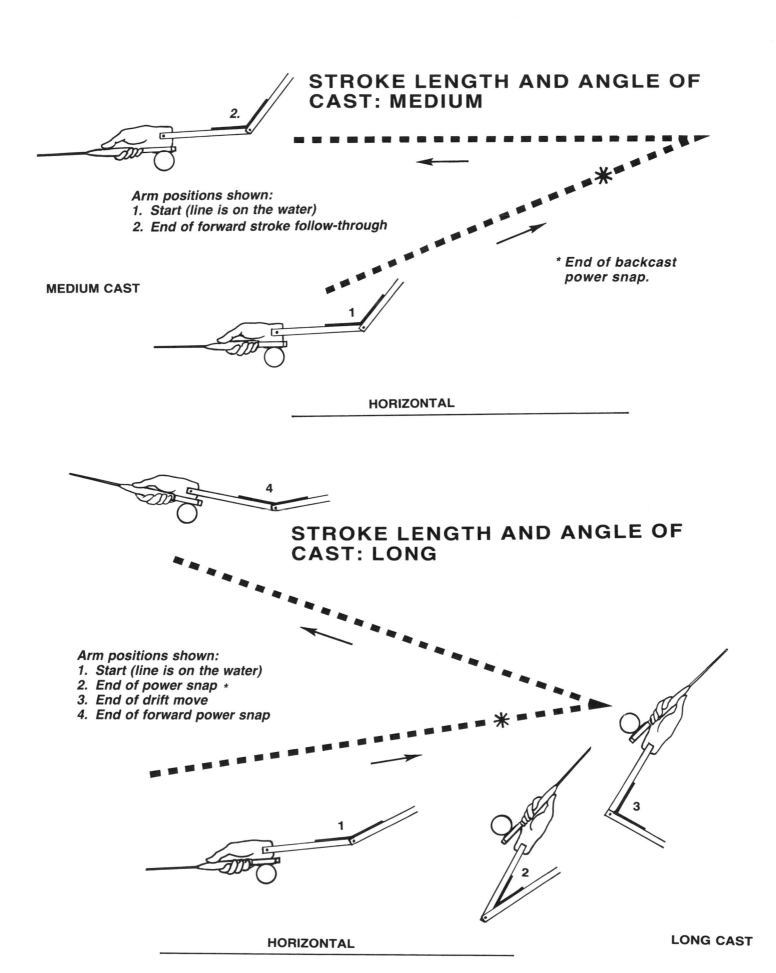

STROKE LENGTH AND ANGLE OF CAST: MEDIUM

Arm positions shown:
1. Start (line is on the water)
2. End of forward stroke follow-through

MEDIUM CAST

* End of backcast power snap.

HORIZONTAL

STROKE LENGTH AND ANGLE OF CAST: LONG

Arm positions shown:
1. Start (line is on the water)
2. End of power snap *
3. End of drift move
4. End of forward power snap

HORIZONTAL

LONG CAST

it would to move only twenty feet of line; forty-five feet would take more movement, proportionately. With control of the rod at the butt, the casting stroke (both loading move and power snap) lengthens by inches as the line lengthens by feet. Simply put, it is short line/short stroke, long line/long stroke.

The result of perfect stroke length (plus the right amount of acceleration) for a given length of line is for the line to unroll exactly opposite the preceding (or following) backward or forward cast. The backcast unrolls 180° from the forward cast and the reverse is true, as you have seen in the illustrations of the casting stroke.

Imperfect Lengths

If a stroke is too short, the front end of the line and leader may move under the rod tip instead of following it to turn over, as it should, above the rod tip. The fly may come at your head on a backcast or give you a tailing loop on the forward cast. There may not be enough momentum or line speed to unroll the whole length smoothly.

Strokes that are too long unroll the line at more than 180° and usually generate more energy than is necessary, causing the leader and fly to react violently, often sending the line downward on the backcast or causing the loop to open up on the forward cast.

Rod Length

The length of your rod helps to determine stroke length. It takes more arm movement to cast thirty-five feet of line with a seven-foot rod than it does to cast it with a nine-foot rod. Short rods require longer strokes. The length of the radial arm, in this case made up of the length of your forearm and hand and the rod's length, determines the circumference of a circle. The extended quarter-circle distance of the casting arc will be longer with a long rod and, at its base, you won't have to move your hand as far as you would with a short rod. The stroke length for a very short rod—six feet, for

The final "force" of the cast is in the hand. On the backcast, the hand squeezes the rod grip to bring it to a stop. On the forward cast, the push on the rod grip with the thumb is the final force.

example—may have to be nearly twice as long as with a nine-foot rod for a given length of line.

Arm Length

Your arm's length determines how long a straight line path you can make. Longer arms can make longer strokes. If a long arm is set high in the air, it will afford the caster better leverage than if it were closer to the ground. It follows that short fishermen should use longer rods, as a general rule, to lessen the work of casting, as should fishermen who must sit in a canoe, or boat, to fly fish.

Stroke length for really long casts must include particular stances and body motion. These will be covered in the long-line section.

Power

The controlled application of power changes a limp, flexible fly line into something that has a definite form and sufficient force to carry the fly to a predetermined spot, even against a wind. As you have learned, power is generated in the casting stroke in a precise way.

Power requirements vary with an outfit according to the weight and length of the line it must cast and the wind conditions. It is common sense to realize that you will need more power to cast forty feet of line than to cast twenty; that you will use more on a forward cast if you will shoot line, than on the backcast when you didn't; and that you will use more power against the wind and less with it. If you are aware of the problem, it's pretty easy to figure out the solution.

Rod actions can affect your power application. Soft-actioned rods cannot take as sudden a power snap as can fast-actioned rods. You can tell, by observing the fly line's unrolling, whether or not there is room for improvement. If the line unrolls with bumps in it, there is either too much power or its application is in the wrong place. If the line falls before it unrolls completely, or if the loop just collapses, perhaps there was not enough power applied (check also the speed and length of the stroke).

Analyzing the way your forward cast unrolls will help you develop the perfect power application for any length line on any rod. It may take five or ten minutes when you first use a new rod to determine this. Each one responds best to a power snap of particular intensity and length. Be patient and you'll find it in any rod, through constant use and what you know of the mechanics.

Strength

"The heavier the object, the more force required to set it into motion or bring it to a stop." —Newton's Law of Inertia

The literal weight of your tackle is a factor in power application. The power snap moves the rod through a *short turnover arc*. If your outfit is heavy (for a #9 or #10 line), it will require more strength on your part to accelerate that rod through the arc in its allotted time to a dead-stop ending than if the outfit was a #5 or #6 weight. Compare the weight of a trout outfit with that of a tarpon outfit.

Tackle	Trout	Tarpon
Rod	3 oz. or less	4½ to 6 oz.
Reel and line	5 oz.	8 to 14 oz.
Total:	8 oz. or less	12½ to 20 oz.

There's no need to spell out further that you had better develop your casting muscles and build your strength when you move from trout to tarpon, or even to bass, fishing.

Constant Pressure Timing

Timing is a thing of feeling. It transforms mere mechanics into beautiful fly casting, a thing of beauty to the caster himself and to the eyes of the beholder. Perfect timing takes the fatigue out of casting because you know when to use power and when to relax. Knowing the mechanics, particularly *starting* the cast perfectly—with rod tip lowered and no slack—will improve your timing automatically. The "pieces" will be in the right place. The big challenge will be in the unrolling of the backcast. How long should you wait? Should the backcast unroll completely, or not quite? What are the factors that affect timing?

To answer the last question first, the timing of your backcast's unrolling can be affected by factors such as whether or not you are shooting line, using heavy flies, have wind from the rear or, perhaps, the amount of backcast room available to you. Specific solutions to these problems will be covered in the appropriate sections.

In regard to a constant length of line I have two suggestions on timing that helped me as a beginner:

1. Be aware of the shock waves you can feel in the rod shaft at the end of the power snap. After they have dissipated, and the rod shaft is still, immediately start the forward cast.

2. You can *see* how long it takes for the fly line to unroll on the forward cast; it takes just as long to unroll on the backcast. Develop a cadence for back and forward strokes.

You could determine perfect timing *mentally*, with your brain going through this kind of monologue: "Let's see; I let out a little over 3 feet of line on that cast, making the total length of line and leader 37½ feet. It should take about 2½ milliseconds longer for the line to reach the turnaround point on this backcast than it did on the last one. That will be just about . . . *now!*"

What a chore, even if you could do it! No! Your sense of feeling has a much better chance of solving the problem. Rely on it.

The secret to perfect timing is *constant pressure*, a feeling of the line on the rod tip, through every inch of the cast, and instant recognition of its loss. Constant pressure was familiar to us as children when we waved pennants or banners, never allowing them to falter. The drift move, in the cast, is the constant pressure move, connecting the backcast and forward cast so that there is no faltering. If your power snaps are strong and the right length, yet you find yourself feeling disconnected on the backcast, you are ready for the *constant pressure drift move*: follow-through backward.

Too Late

If your backcast timing is less than perfect and you let the line unroll so long that, after it straightens, it "flops out," the feeling of the line's weight will be lost at the rod tip. When you start the forward cast, under these circumstances, there may be a lag and the line may start forward with a jerk, affecting the loading move and making it difficult to accelerate the line smoothly.

Too Early

If the line is only half or three-quarters unrolled when you start forward, there will be no pressure (no load) on the rod tip and you may be uncertain as to when to power snap. The line is likely to tangle on the forward cast.

The easiest way to understand backcast timing is to see it and feel it at the same time, in horizontal casting, as suggested in the next chapter. All of the mystery will be taken out of backcast timing as you look at the whole picture.

Visualize the force of the cast putting an *arc* in the rod as it is moved against air resistance.

Getting the Whole Picture

It is nearly impossible to cast in a vertical plane and watch your backcast. If you swing your head more than 90°, as you must in order to look back, your shoulders must swing too and you'll put the backcast out of line. Seeing the mechanics on paper is helpful because you get mental images, but "tipping them over" so that you can see them from a full-view position, has to be a thousand times better, and it is time to do that. I want you to cast in a horizontal plane to get the *whole* picture!

This exercise must be done on grass so that you can isolate the moves: loading, power snap, and drift, in what is almost slow motion, on both the backcast and the forward cast. You'll cast parallel to the ground; from left to right for the backcast and from right to left for the forward cast. You'll see line speed, backcast timing, and the effect of your stroke length, things you wouldn't normally be able to see when casting overhead. You can then transfer all this to your sense of feeling. You'll save months of time, knowing exactly what the casting motion is and within what parameters the line should unroll.

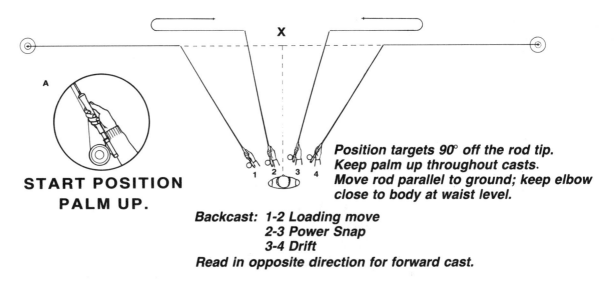

START POSITION PALM UP.

Position targets 90° off the rod tip.
Keep palm up throughout casts.
Move rod parallel to ground; keep elbow close to body at waist level.

Backcast: 1-2 Loading move
2-3 Power Snap
3-4 Drift
Read in opposite direction for forward cast.

Perfect stroke length and rod arc and unrolling the line 90° from the rod tip have been mentioned but not fully explained. This exercise should make things clear and may be the most important chapter in the book if it can make you independent—able to solve your basic casting problems.

You'll need two targets. They can be stones, sandbags, garbage-can lids, whatever. To place them, hold the rod at your waist, with the tip pointing straight ahead of you. Lay it down on the ground in that position. Pull line from the reel, through the rod, until fifteen or twenty feet are out of the rod tip. Lay out this line, and the leader, to make a 90° angle at the rod tip and put a target under the fly. Pick up the line and walk to the opposite side of the rod tip and put the second target under the fly. The targets should be 90° off your rod tip on either side. You'll stand where your rod butt lies, and your goal will be to unroll the line *to* the targets, both right and left, in a horizontal cast.

Body Position

The way you stand and your hand and arm positions are very important. Stand with your feet apart, sideward, so that you may look easily from side to side to see the full length of line, leader, and fly, as each backcast and each forward cast unrolls toward the target. You'll have to turn your head and focus your eyes rather quickly, but pretend you are watching a tennis match. Shifting your weight in the direction of the cast can make the casting easier and, perhaps, smoother.

Rod and Arm Position

Hold the rod as you normally would for overhead casting, with your thumb on top, and rotate the rod hand 90° to the right so that your palm will be facing upward. Notice that your forearm turns with your hand so that the inside of your wrist is facing skyward. The flat sides of the reel should be parallel to the ground and the sky. This rod and arm position will keep the flexing spine of the rod, and the guides, lined up with the cast as they were in the overhead casting plane.

The Horizontal Cast

First make any kind of a cast to put the fly on or near the target on the left. This will be your forward cast target.

Keep your elbow bent and close to your body, so that your casting stroke will move parallel to the ground. The rod tip should also move parallel to the ground (it will if your hand does), and if your stroke is not straight it will show up in the path of the line. Any dips or bumps included in your hand's path will be mirrored in the way the line unrolls.

Gripping the rod butt comfortably in this new position, and with your eyes on the stretched-out line, leader, and fly, move your arm and rod as one piece to start the loading move. When you see that everything, including the fly, has started to move, accelerate through the power snap to a dead stop. Follow through (drift) to the right by extending your arm as the line unrolls and falls to the grass. Try it in the other direction, moving as a unit to load, then power snapping to end the stroke and following through to soften the landing. Remember to push with your thumb on the forward power snap. (Is your palm still facing up?)

Just as your fly line unrolled completely before it landed on the forward cast in the instruction for vertical plane casting, make sure the backcast unrolls completely before it lands in this exercise. You can see line speed on the backcast in this plane, as well as the smoothness of your power application.

TROUBLESHOOTING

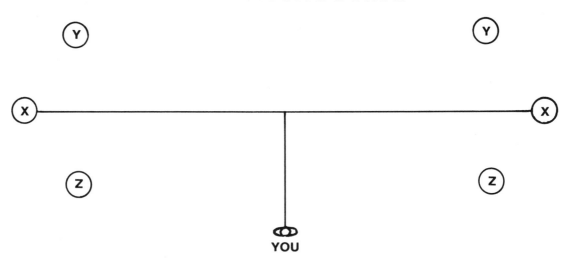

If the fly line, leader, and fly unroll to X positions, the stroke is perfect. If they unroll to Y positions, the stroke is too short; to Z positions, too long, or curved.

Stroke Length

Now is the time to be precise. Before you begin each stroke, determine a hand/target line. In order for the fly to land on the target, the length of the stroke, on the hand/target line, has to be perfect. As each cast falls to the grass, notice its relationship to the target. If it lands above the target, the stroke was too short. If it lands below the target, the stroke was too long. Adjust the length of your stroke until the line and leader straighten out *to* the target each time. This may take you a few minutes.

It will be helpful if you remember that stroke length translates to rod arc. Use those special few inches above the grip as your focal point and you can make the loading move position the rod for the power snap (90° to the target) in both directions. After the short turnover arc, drift/follow-through will take the rod another few degrees toward the target. When you can see this and the movement of the entire rod, you'll know exactly what happens in vertical-plane casting. Doing this exercise on grass should let you make the moves in close-to-slow motion.

Backcast Timing

After you have determined how long your stroke must be and can see the parts of the cast and how they fit in the overall arc of rod movement, keep the backcast, the one to the right, off the ground. "Aerialize" it as a real backcast is aerialized in vertical casting, and let the forward cast land on the target. The fly should pass over the target on the backcast and land *on* the target on the forward cast. Check your line speed (your overall acceleration) to make the backcast unroll straight off the rod tip, toward the target, without noticeably dropping. If you wait until the leader and fly are fully extended over the target before you begin the forward cast, gravity may score and they may touch the ground as they start forward. Use the forward loading move to begin the turning around of the leader and fly, before they straighten completely. This is *perfect timing* for a constant length of line with no plans to shoot additional line on the forward cast. (Yes, that timing would be different.) The fly line itself may be straightened but the leader and fly will straighten on the turnaround. You can see it when it is right.

When the backcast looks good several times in a row, make the same cast but keep your eyes on the left-hand target, transferring what you have seen a good backcast to be to something you can feel.

False Casting

The next step is to keep the forward cast off the ground too. When both backcast and forward cast are aerialized, it is called *false casting*. Now you should be able to really feel the line weight and, by not putting the line down between backcast and forward cast, you'll see the confines of your stroke length a little more clearly. The fly must pass over the target in both directions and not touch the ground as it turns around.

CHECK LIST:

1. Forearm and hand are moving as one. No hinging of the wrist on the backcast.

2. The elbow is close to the body during the power snap; and it moves away a little during the follow-through or drift move.

3. The reel and the palm of the hand remain faceup through all of the moves (this is the most difficult part of horizontal casting the first time you do it.)

4. The rod/wrist attitude is the same as in the vertical casting plane for you to check: Backcast—end of rod is against the wrist to start and away a bit at the finish. Forward cast—end of rod is away from the wrist to start and is against it at the finish.

5. The rod tip, although it is bent, moves in a straight line, parallel to the ground, just as your hand does.

6. You are accelerating to a stop through the power snap, then resting as the line unrolls.

You may be surprised at how short a false cast stroke can be, for fifteen to twenty feet of line. It should be in the range of six to eight inches, if your rod is eight feet or more in length. Try to relax mentally as you watch the cast in both directions (now you're at the tennis match), an instant of power and an instant of relaxation. The loading move is only an inch or so long, but if you use it to position the power snap you won't have to measure it. Do these false casts in sets of five or six at a time so that you don't tire and can give each set your full awareness.

When you are able to accomplish the goals in this horizontal plane, you can gradually transfer the action to the vertical plane. Move your arm upward, a few inches at a time, making two or three good casts in each of the planes you stop at, between horizontal and vertical. The palm of your hand will continue to be visible until, on reaching the vertical plane, you turn your feet and body toward the left-hand target and move your arm over in front of your body, your thumb on top and your palm facing left.

Acceleration is an important factor in the performance of the cast. The right stroke length with too little acceleration will produce a cast that falls before it is unrolled. As the length of the line and the stroke increases, so must the speed of the acceleration.

Because you have been casting parallel to the ground, the end of the line, the leader, and the fly are probably too high above the target for you to be accurate. Change the angle of your cast, now, to include some up-and-down motion from the shoulder, raising the backcast and lowering the forward cast. The angle will be close to the one you used when you took line off the water in the basic cast. Center your arm to move up and down in front of your face, to line up with the target most easily.

Try to unroll the line and leader on an angle that places the fly about two feet above the target at the end of each false cast. Your backcast should be angled 90° off the rod tip in the opposite direction from the forward cast. Keep the casting arc small and your arm bent. When you can see that the fly is centered on the target, as you unroll the cast above it, just follow through and lower everything at once. Yes, you might be tired by now, but this is the way you build casting muscles. Take it a little at a time.

This exercise will give you the whole picture in regard to various lengths of line. Change the length and, correspondingly, the target placement. Notice that the length of your stroke must change to accommodate the new line length. No matter how long or short the line, the parameters are the same: a total unrolling of the line of 180°. For longer lines, shifting your weight sideward, from foot to foot will help lengthen the stroke. Remember to increase the overall acceleration as the line lengthens.

This exercise does more for my students than any other in providing a way to analyze their own casting and solve their own problems. It should do the same for you. When you are ready for double hauls, we'll use the same pattern again.

Casting horizontally is an extremely valuable technique, on its own, in fishing situations when obstacles make overhead casting too risky. By turning your body 90° from the target area, you can see your backcast, if that will help, in tight situations. However, if you do take your eyes off the target to check your backcast, always look back at the target again before you start the forward casting stroke, to maintain your accuracy.

False Casting

In the basic cast, you take the line off the water, turn it over behind you, and put it back down on the water. If, on the forward cast the fly line were to be unrolled in the air, above the water, and not allowed to land before another backcast is made, it is called a **false cast**, and it was introduced in "Getting the Whole Picture."

False casting is a major part of your quiet approach to wary fish and lets you extend line without disturbing the water. More than that, a false cast, with extra power, can shake water from your dry fly; a few false casts, with a sideward rotation of the upper body, can help you change direction easily, and it is a technique that lets you accurately measure your cast before you deliver it.

When you know how to shoot line, you will start with the fly in your hand and false cast your way out to the target area, shooting a little line on each forward cast.

For now, work with a few constant lengths of line and check out the mechanics. You may have to expend some effort to be comfortable until you've built up the capacity of your muscles to hold the line in the air through several casts. You'll need more overall speed on the backcast stroke than if you were taking the line off the water (the air gives less resistance than the water). Do sets of five or six false casts at a time, to keep the mechanics sharp, as you practice.

The Forward Cast

The forward false cast must be made a little higher than a presentation cast, and the follow-through move will not be as pronounced but it *is* necessary, to lower the arm and rod's position, so that the following backcast stroke doesn't start too high. On short casts, the lowering will be an inch or two and the arm will remain sharply bent. On long casts, the lowering may be three or four inches and the arm will extend somewhat on the follow-through. Whether you are right or wrong in your movements will become clear as you do them.

The Backcast

The loading move reverses the direction of the line and leader and gets it all moving as a unit, just as it turns your out-of-sight backcast around to go forward. This is easier; it is *visible*! Watch the line as it unrolls forward and, when you see the leader and fly starting to unroll, begin the backward loading move, smoothly. Increase the speed and when you see that the fly has actually turned around and started back toward you, power snap to end the backcast. It's all very quick!

Body Motion

Shifting your weight back and forward can be the key to reducing the work of false casting in practice, especially if it is a new technique for you. Body motion can take the place of drift or can be used in addition to drift on longer casts. Try it to see if it doesn't make everything easier and your casts smoother. Body motion helps, too, to reduce the tension brought on in a learning situation.

The Rounding

When all of the false-casting mechanics, including drift, are in place, you can see by the illustration that the arm takes on a rotary motion, with one move following another smoothly. Focus on your elbow's movement to help make it happen. On short casts, the rounded movement is quite obvious; on longer casts the shape elongates and "elliptical" may better describe it.

FALSE CASTING:

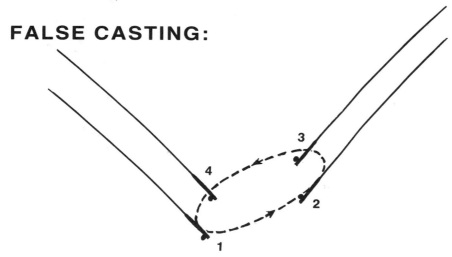

2-3 Drift; 4-1 Follow-through
One move follows another to "round" the whole cast.

The *literal speed* of your casting arm's movement must be greater on the backcast than is necessary on the forward cast. You don't have the independent thrust of the hand on the backcast power snap as you do on the forward power snap. Greater acceleration on the backcast makes up the difference.

Troubleshooting

If your fly comes at your head or hits the tip of the rod, check first to see that you are lifting from the shoulder on the backcast power snap. Another possible solution is to *cant* the rod a fraction of an inch to the right on the backcast.

If the loop has a sideward "pouch" in it on the forward cast, you are rolling your hand during the power snap. Think "direct drive" with your thumb as the pointer.

three

REFINEMENTS TO THE CAST

Line Speed

Line speed determines the rate at which the fly line will unroll and is controlled by the overall acceleration of the casting stroke, the sharpness of the power snap, and the inherent action of the rod.

(Fast) High Line Speed

Fast-actioned rods—rods that recover most quickly from the shock waves of the power snap—will automatically cast your line with more speed, for a given effort, than will soft-actioned rods, which bend more deeply and oscillate for a longer time.

High line speed is desirable for these reasons:

1. It will unroll the line 90° from the rod tip before it falls.

2. It will help you feel the weight of the line on the rod tip throughout the backcast for better timing.

3. It will make shooting line easier, both backward and forward.

4. It will help you drive a line into wind—backward or forward.

5. It is essential for really long casts, when, on the final backcast, you must shoot additional line to be unrolled in a limited amount of time.

6. It fights the effects of gravity.

Single and double hauls are techniques used to increase line speed.

Slow Line Speed

Slow line speed on a good forward cast will make your line land on the water at about the middle of its length, unrolling from there—and that can be desirable.

On a vertical plane backcast, slow line speed is generally undesirable, under open-space casting conditions, because it will unroll the line too low for a good start to the forward cast, asking of it that it travel more than 180° to the target. However, slow line speed on the backcast can be helpful if you have *limited backcast space* and want to control how far the line will unroll (to be covered later).

Once you are aware of line speed, a little experimenting with your acceleration, in the stroke, will let you exercise complete control.

LINE SPEED

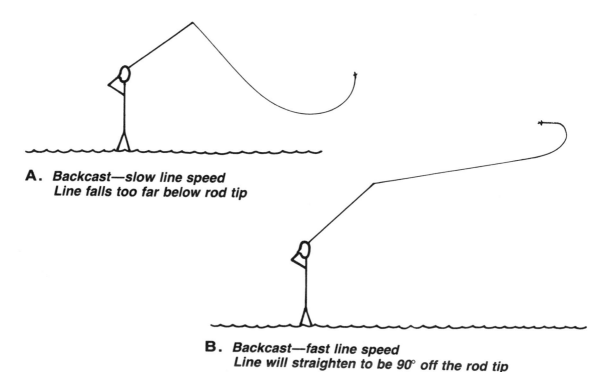

A. *Backcast—slow line speed*
Line falls too far below rod tip

B. *Backcast—fast line speed*
Line will straighten to be 90° off the rod tip

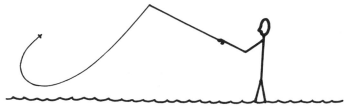

C. Forward cast—slow line speed.
   Line hits water before it is unrolled.

D. Forward cast—fast line speed.
   Line unrolls above the water.

Accuracy: Lining Up

Dorothy Vogel was a competitor of mine in my early tournament years. My mental picture of her includes the shaft of a rod held upright between her eyes. She put it there on every backcast. She was young, seven or eight years old, when she started to cast. Because she was small, and with no real strength, her dad, Archie, figured out a system for her. She used *two hands* on the rod. Using two hands centers the casting stroke and she would bring back the rod between her eyes, hesitate, and push it forward. She was deadly accurate and I thought of her as a little machine; she left so little to chance.

There is a great joy in being accurate—even in every-day activities; and I take every chance I can get to improve my eye/hand/target coordination by throwing towels into the hamper, crumpled paper into the wastebasket, or car keys to my husband—all from far enough away to make it a challenge. Good shots can make my day.

Although high line speed is generally desirable for use with weight-less flies, it can be one cause of "wind" knots with heavy flies. On the backcast, the fly can hit the end of the unrolling loop with a *jerk* that will cause it to be thrown in the opposite direction, overtaking or doubling back on the leader, to knot around it within the cast. Use slower line speed with heavy flies.

There are two imaginary straight lines at the heart of accuracy. The first is the line between your eyes and the target, the eye/target line. You must look at a target in order to hit it. The second is the line on which your hand moves in the casting stroke, the hand/target line. You already know the formula for being accurate: position the rod shaft at 90° to the target on the hand/target line, and make a *turnover arc* (power snap) that is 30 to 45° (maximum) toward the target. If you bring your casting hand to a position between your eyes, as Dot Vogel did, one line overlaps the other and you have the best shot at hitting the target. As you move your casting arm and hand away from the eye/target line, you form a triangle with the two lines starting from different positions but ending at the target where they will intersect. The narrower the base of the accuracy triangle, the easier it is to be accurate.

ACCURACY: LINING UP

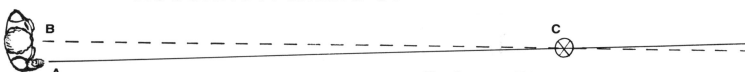

The Accuracy Triangle
A-C Hand/target line
B-C Eye/target line

BETWEEN THE EYES

Overlapping the eye/target line and the hand/target line is a foolproof technique for short-line accuracy.

Lining up, between the eyes, limits your stroke length and is a short-line tactic. I use it automatically whenever being accurate is particularly important at close range. The power snap puts the rod between my eyes, on the backcast, and I drift up, above head level, from where I begin the forward stroke, knowing that the eye/target line and the hand/target line are overlapping to give me the best chance for accuracy.

Even with beginners who are, as yet, unable to handle the drift move, I find that making them end the casting stroke between the eyes helps to "sculpt" their casting motion, angling the stroke upward and forcing the use of the forearm and just a little wrist on the backcast. (Too much wrist would make the rod hit the forehead.) Also, this position keeps the elbow where it belongs in relation to the shoulder. Try it with casts up to twenty-five or thirty feet. It is very effective!

It is natural to think you might be hit by the fly if you bring your hand to your face, but you will not be hit if, (1) you lift the line by lifting your arm with a straight wrist in the loading move and then, (2) lift your elbow during the power snap.

This combination will keep your rod hand and the fly line on parallel paths angled backward/upward. If you end the power snap as the fly leaves the water and not a fraction of an inch later, the fly has to go upward over your head. It can come *at you* if your backcast stroke is backward only, with no lift.

In this between-the-eyes position, you will need more room for the casting stroke as you lengthen line. Add body motion as a first tactic and, when that is insufficient, move the arm off center toward the outside of your body, still keeping your forearm in line with the shoulder for a relatively narrow base to the accuracy triangle.

To stay lined up, on the backcast, the power snap should end where you can see your rod hand, even if only peripherally. Body motion will help you do this so that on your longest overhead strokes, your hand, at the end of the power snap, will be in front of, or just above, your shoulder. During the drift move, your hand can go out of your vision but your elbow will still be in it. On the forward loading move, the elbow starts forward, bringing the hand in sight once more for the power snap and follow-through.

Staying lined up through the casting stroke as described above should keep you from getting a sore casting arm. Your muscles may tire but they should be the muscles you feel contract when you make a fist. If your shoulder hurts, you are probably out of line on the power snap. Make it end in front of, above, or as close as possible to the shoulder.

Point Of Aim

You can unroll a line *to* the target or at heights above it. If your fishing technique is to straighten every inch of line and leader, as with a wet fly, unroll the line to the particular inch of water. If you are fishing a tiny dry fly on a long leader that is not only tapered but has a long, level tippet of fine diameter next to the fly, your point of aim might be higher to allow the leader and fly to land last, to put slack in the tippet for a soft and natural presentation. Experiment with different heights for your point of aim as you change the character and length of your leader and fly and the fishing technique.

Depth Perception

Depth perception is another factor to be considered. Even if everything is lined up—eyes, hand, rod, and target—you can still miss the target by under-shooting or overshooting, until you learn to adjust for your own failings. However, if you miss the target to either side, it means you were careless, forgetting to stay lined up throughout the cast. There's no excuse for that kind of miss.

Loop Control

Narrow loops, wide loops. How do we control the size and for what purposes do we choose one above the other? What causes tailing loops?

Loop size is relative and is the distance between the upper and lower levels of the unrolling line. A narrow loop pushes through the air with less resistance than does a wide loop. It follows that narrow loops are desirable, both for accuracy and distance. It is easy to cast a narrow loop with weightless flies but it gets progressively more difficult as the weight and/or air resistance of the fly increases.

Heavy flies have an energy of their own, once they are set in motion, and require relatively wide loops to travel smoothly to the target. A good fly caster will vary the width of his loops according to fishing conditions and the character of his fly. He'll use narrower loops to be accurate, to put a fly under an overhanging branch, to drive into the wind. He'll use wider loops when fishing with weighted nymphs, big streamers, salt water and bass fishing flies; or, perhaps, in trout fishing he'll use a very wide loop to make his leader land in a puddle to give him a long drag-free dry-fly drift.

As explained in the instruction for the forward casting stroke, the technique that produces a narrow loop is to carry the rod forward, in the loading move, until the rod shaft is positioned 90° on the hand/target line, then to power snap the rod through a turnover arc that is restricted to 45° maximum.

To make a wide loop, you must begin the turnover arc earlier, *during* the loading move, so that its total length will be closer to 90° instead of 30 to 45°. The stroke will end at the same place as the narrow-loop stroke ends.

Use a pencil to simulate a rod, and cock your wrist slightly backward. Then push the pencil forward with your thumb. This is the turnover arc and, with the forward extension of the arm, it makes up the power snap. It is done within the larger arc of the whole arm's movement. A move within a move. It changes the rod butt/underside of the wrist relationship. In the narrow-loop instruction, you moved through the loading move with the end of the rod butt away from your wrist until you reached the 90° position on the hand/target line. Then you pushed the rod with your thumb, through a 30 to 45° arc, toward the target, which brought the end of the rod butt up against the wrist in a quick snap.

To make a wide loop, start the turnover arc as you begin the forward stroke, pushing with your thumb at an even pace through the whole stroke as the stroke itself accelerates to a stop. The end of the rod butt will move evenly toward the underside of your wrist.

LOOP CONTROL

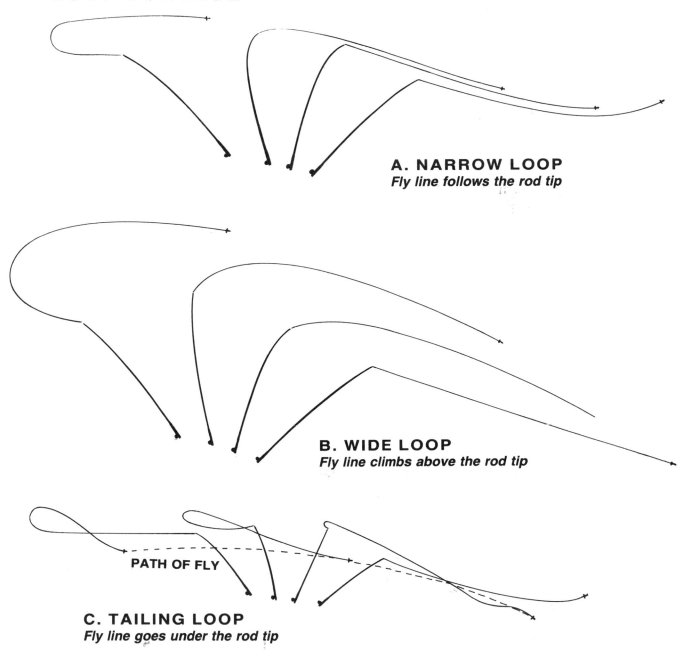

A. NARROW LOOP
Fly line follows the rod tip

B. WIDE LOOP
Fly line climbs above the rod tip

PATH OF FLY

C. TAILING LOOP
Fly line goes under the rod tip

The total turnover arc should be about 90°. It can be less but should not be more or the loop will just open up. At the end of the drift move, the rod shaft, above the grip, will be slanted backward at from 30 to 45° beyond vertical. The turnover arc will begin there, pass through vertical, and end at 45° maximum ahead of vertical, the same finishing place that you used for a narrow loop. The earlier-starting turnover arc raises the path of the line well over the rod tip, widening the loop.

HAND CONTROL

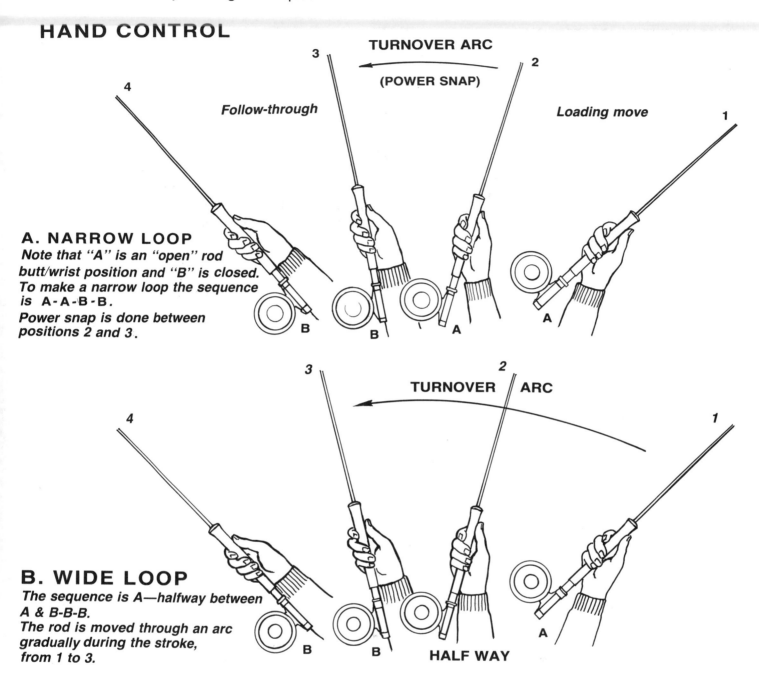

TURNOVER ARC

(POWER SNAP)

Follow-through

Loading move

A. NARROW LOOP

Note that "A" is an "open" rod butt/wrist position and "B" is closed. To make a narrow loop the sequence is A-A-B-B.
Power snap is done between positions 2 and 3.

TURNOVER / ARC

B. WIDE LOOP

The sequence is A—halfway between A & B-B-B.
The rod is moved through an arc gradually during the stroke, from 1 to 3.

HALF WAY

Another reference can be the elbow. The forward stroke starts with elbow movement. The elbow moves first, followed by the turnover arc. To make a wide loop, start the turnover arc *at the same time* the elbow begins to move, during what would normally be the loading move.

There is a way to *open up* a narrow loop if you are casting a heavy fly and feel the loop may turn out to be too narrow. After the power snap, immediately lower the rod tip. This will increase the distance between the two levels of unrolling line. It's an emergency technique; the cast may or may not turn out smoothly.

Trouble Shooting: Tailing Loops

A good loop, narrow or wide, unrolls with the two levels of fly line parallel to each other. If something goes wrong, and the end of the fly line, plus the leader and fly, hang down below the unrolling loop, this is a *tailing loop*. A tailing loop can collide with the line or make a "wind" knot in your leader. Wind knots lead to disaster, reducing leader strength by about 50 percent. One strand can cut the other under the pressure of playing a fish.

Tailing loops are common. Almost all anglers go through a stage of producing them without knowing why. The *single most common cause*, in my experience, is *lack of a loading move* when one is needed. Short casts (five to ten feet of line out of the rod tip in addition to the leader) do not generally require more than a power snap to execute the cast. As the line gets longer, the loading move ensures that the backcast has turned around smoothly and that rod and line are moving as a unit in smooth acceleration *before* the thrusting move of the power snap ends the stroke.

If you leave out the loading move and just power snap the line from its extended position (or worse, if it is still unrolling behind you) the line *closest* to the rod tip will follow it, but the move is insufficient to do anything but make the end of the line jump downward, then forward below the rod tip, crossing the line, to give you a tailing loop.

Another way to look at the problem is to think in terms of acceleration. The word "accelerate" means to increase speed. We do that in the casting stroke by building speed from the beginning of the loading move to the end of the power snap. Start slow and end fast. The opposite sequence, to start fast and end slowly—as must occur if you *start* the stroke with a power snap—produces a tailing loop.

C. TAILING LOOP

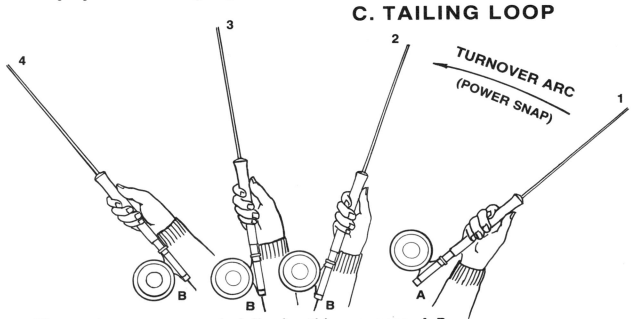

The most common cause is following this sequence: A-B-B-B,
in which the power snap is done between positions 1 and 2
instead of between positions 2 and 3.

Cause #2. *Too short an overall stroke*. The loading move and the power snap, in combination, are not long enough for the amount of line the rod has to move smoothly. This is common on shooting casts. You may need a longer stroke forward than was made backward, to increase line speed as you shoot. Too little room to make that forward stroke could be caused by the *lack of a drift move*. When drift is added to the backcast stroke, it creates the needed space for both a longer stroke forward and smooth acceleration. Another way to lose that needed space is to *drift forward* between backcast and forward cast instead of drifting backward. Drifting forward shortens the available space in which the forward stroke can be made.

3. *Concave path*. If, from its starting position, the rod is lowered on the loading move and raised again on the power snap, a concave path is created and a tailing loop forms easily. The solution is to move the rod hand on a *straight line* toward the target.

4. *Too much line carried on the backcast*. This is a cause I see in powerful casters who are casting long lines before they understand the limitations of "overhang" in the cast. Overhang is the distance between the heavy belly section of the fly line and the rod tip. In making long casts the maximum length of this overhang varies from individual to individual, depending on the rod's length and stiffness, and the caster's height, arm length, and acceleration technique. If the heavy section of the line is too far from the rod tip (too much overhang) for the given factors, the transfer of energy from the rod to the line cannot bridge the gap—through the lighter running/shooting line—to unroll the heavier line completely in the time available. The caster, sensing something is wrong, puts everything he has into the forward cast, in the right sequence, but the cast is already lost because of line position, and a tailing loop results. Start with short overhangs and increase them with care.

5. *Change from long rods to short rods*. You may experience tailing loops if you decrease the length of the rod with which you fish. Short rods require longer strokes and you will have to make them longer consciously and increase your acceleration to execute perfect casts.

It is widely thought that making the cast on exactly the same path for both back and forward casts will cause tailing loops. This is not true. It is easier to cast on the same path with short and medium-length lines than it is with long lines. The physical properties of both tackle and caster can determine when it becomes difficult.

Casting on one path, without the use of drift—which does change the paths slightly—requires precise timing on the unrolling of the backcast. You must wait for the line to unroll completely. Body motion, shifting your weight back and forward with the strokes, can be helpful, along with good line speed. There is no reason for the line to run into itself unless something is wrong in the cast.

It is difficult to eliminate tailing loops even after you know the reasons they occur. There is no better way to correct the problem than to understand and practice good mechanics. Otherwise it is "band-aid" doctoring and you may replace one cause with another. As you analyze your cast, look for poor mechanics; poor rod and line positions caused by hinging at the wrist or rotating outward from the shoulder; poor line speed (improper acceleration); strokes that are too short overall or are concave in shape.

If you cannot fix your tailing loops and see one passing overhead, you might eliminate it by quickly lowering the rod tip. It's only a band-aid fix, but it may save an important presentation. My Rx: Determine a hand/target line and accelerate to a stop along that straight path.

No Loop

If the rod and line are moved through a large arc—a convex path—with or without acceleration, you'll get what is called "no loop" on the cast. The line will follow the rod tip but will not project above the water long enough to unroll.

Hovering the Fly

William Taylor was a rod maker and a fine accuracy and distance caster. His style was distinctive, partly because of the action of his rods. He believed the rod should do most of the work for the caster.

After I had won my first national title in 1943, "Willie," as I irreverently called him, became my casting mentor. His first effort was directed at refining my false casting to the point of being able to "hover" the dry fly. He taught me that if I used extra power to unroll the line and leader on an inclined path, the fly would hover above the target for an instant, so that the accuracy of the cast could be seen. If it wasn't satisfactory, another false cast would adjust the line length or angle. When it was perfectly placed, a quick lowering of the rod, tip first (after the hover), would touch the fly to the water an instant before the leader and line.

"Taylor Made" bamboo rods were generally quite stiff, with a limber section at the very tip of about a foot or so. Narrow loops and hovering were easy with this design, but my dry-fly accuracy rod would have been a clumsy fishing rod, too stiff and heavy to cast all day. That rod action did help me to hone and sharpen my power snap and to hover my way to better accuracy. The hovering technique works beautifully with the fast-actioned graphite rods on the market today.

Hovering is a good dry-fly fishing technique: for accuracy, for helping the fly to land upright and lightly, and for head winds when the extra power that makes the fly hover also drives it through the wind. If you wish to aerially mend your line (alter the form in which it falls to the water) the hovering technique will let you see clearly the time in which to do it.

I witnessed a dramatic exhibition of the hovered fly against the wind, in 1945, at the USA casting nationals. Henry Fujita, of Cleveland, and Detroit's Harold Smedley were tied for first place in the Dry Fly Accuracy event. As the shootoff began, the winds in Detroit's Belle Isle Park were gusty and unpredictable. Defending champion Smedley was a fine caster and posted a high score, but the crowd watching was fascinated by the tactics of Fujita as his fly whipped around the targets in various planes, with Henry leaning his body or crouching as he parried the thrusts of the wind. His false casts unrolled completely and held the fly for an instant, for all to see, before he either retrieved it for another false cast or dropped it in the target. It was a memorable exhibition and the tactic won the event for him under those tough conditions.

The Mechanics

Your normal forward stroke consists of a loading move and a power snap, followed immediately by the follow-through. To hover a fly, separate the follow-through from the power snap by an instant, and make the power snap extra forceful. Do not follow through until after the fly has hesitated in the air, leader fully extended, and you make the decision to drop it.

In false casting a fly with this technique, when you eliminate the follow-through move you take away the space you would then use for a backcast loading move and so the cast becomes an abbreviated one. The backcast will include only a power snap and drift, and the forward cast will include a loading move and a forceful power snap.

Keep the forward stroke short, pulling the elbow backward as it starts down in the loading move and, then, make the power snap almost in place; try not to extend your forearm. Instead, push forward hard with the thumb, as you pivot the rod grip with the last three fingers of your hand, *pulling* the end of the grip backward/upward against the underside of the wrist. It is a powerful, abbreviated motion.

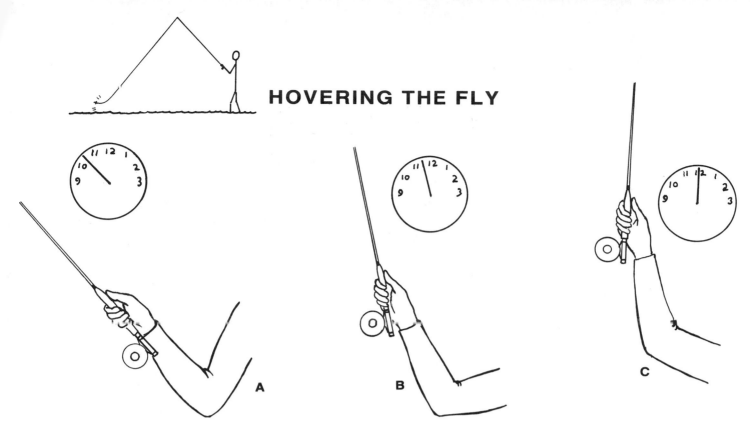

HOVERING THE FLY

Backcast: A to B—power snap; B to C—drift
Forward cast: C to B—loading/positioning;
B to A—power snap with extra force in the hand's action.

Angle of the Cast

A fly can land first only if the leader and line behind it are above it. The rod arc must be positioned to make the line unroll downward to the target. Drift on the backcast and the loading move on the forward cast can do this for you. Let me explain, using a clockface as a guide, with you standing at 6:00 o'clock, facing left. Use the rod shaft, above the grip, as a reference. Use a short line.
Backcast:

1. Start at 10:30
2. Power snap to 11:00 to 11:30
3. Drift to 12:00

Forward Cast:

4. Use the loading move to reposition the rod at 11:00 to 11:30 (90° from the target)
5. Power snap to 10:30

The first time you try this technique, do it with a little wind at your back. You can see it then, almost in slow motion, for an easy understanding of the mechanics. It doesn't work well with a yarn fly; use a fluffly dry fly on your leader.

A hovered fly, having discharged all of the extra power you gave it as it hovered, will land lightly and, usually, right side up, to improve your presentations.

Effective Length of the Technique

You can hover a fly in any plane but the effective distance will be limited by the design of your line and leader, the action of the rod, and your own casting strength. As the line length increases, it becomes difficult, if not impossible, to have the fly land first because of the change of angle on the cast. But the technique is still worth using, even if everything lands at once, because it will be a soft landing with line, leader, and fly fully extended.

A double-tapered line and a tapered leader with a relatively short tippet, on a fast-actioned rod, will hover best at the greatest distances. Weight-forward and triangle tapers will work at distances proportionate to the length of the line's full weight section.

Picking Leaves

The Pezon et Michel rod factory, situated in the town of Amboise, 100 miles or so southeast of Paris, did not have a casting pool on the grounds, in 1948. Visiting there at the invitation of Charles Ritz, after the French National Casting Tournament, A. J. McClane and I wanted to compare impressions of Charlie's parabolic-actioned rods. I wondered aloud where we could cast the rods; there didn't appear to be any open space. Al replied, "Right here," and cast between the branches of a great oak tree, the fly flicking individual leaves at his command.

Many years later I had two boys for students, ages nine and eleven, for a lesson on a lawn. When one needed special attention I feared for the safety of the fly rod in the hands of the unsupervised boy. As I was looking for a target on which he might practice, the lilac bushes reminded me of McClane at Amboise. "See if you can pick out a leaf and make your yarn fly touch it," I suggested. A little later, when I once more gave him my attention, I was really surprised. The challenge had pulled his casting motion together so that he now had a good line loop and his eyes were bright with enthusiasm as he really did put his fly on individual leaves. This exercise is now an important part of my instructional technique, and students agree that **picking leaves** really sharpens the eye/hand/target coordination and develops the power snap to perfection. In addition, it introduces the 180° spectrum of forehand and backhand casting that is possible from one central position and, finally, forces the caster to position the backcast directly opposite the next forward cast.

Anything can house your target series. If you don't have bushes or trees with low-hanging branches, cast at the knotholes in a fence, the individual bricks on a building face, or even made-up targets on your automobile (with a yarn fly, of course). Stand in one spot and cast in different planes to the left and right of vertical as well as at different levels.

Mechanics

Extend ten feet of fly line, no more, between rod tip and leader, to determine the distance you'll stand from the target area.

Do only the power-snap portion of the cast, false casting backward and forward, to make your fly touch the leaf of your choice. The movement of hand and forearm will be perhaps six to eight inches. The short length of the move should impress you. Don't just hinge at the elbow; lift and lower the whole arm from the shoulder as you do the moves, even though you could do them with just wrist movement. This will train your muscles for longer casts.

PICKING LEAVES

FC—forward cast, BC—backcast
By leaning your body you can cast from horizontal on the right to nearly horizontal on the left. To change targets, aim your backcast, by adjusting the position of your arm, to be opposite where the next forward cast will be.

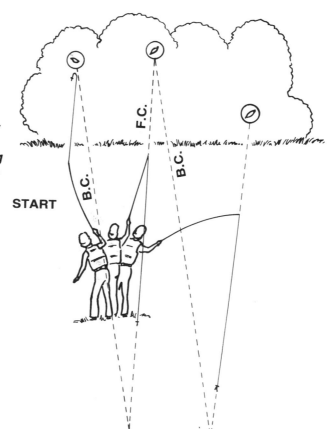

1. For your first target, choose a leaf that is directly in front of you so that you can overlap the eye/target line and the hand/target line and cast right in front of your face. Using the rod shaft above the hand grip for reference, end the backcast power snap at a position 90° or perpendicular to the eye/hand/target line.

2. Make the forward turnover arc, moving the rod shaft through a 30 to 45° total arc on the eye/hand/target line. If the rod shaft was at 90° from the target to start with, the angle of the rod will be no less than 45° from the target at the finish of the forward power snap. The smaller the arc, the narrower the loop that will extend to the target leaf. Rod length and action can affect the size of the turnover arc.

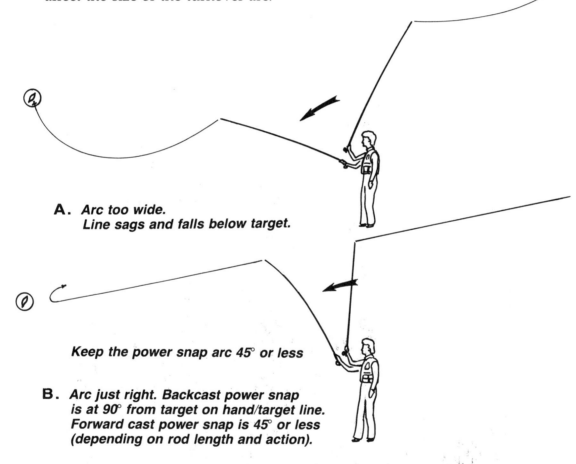

**A. Arc too wide.
Line sags and falls below target.**

Keep the power snap arc 45° or less

**B. Arc just right. Backcast power snap
is at 90° from target on hand/target line.
Forward cast power snap is 45° or less
(depending on rod length and action).**

The move must be crisp. Remember the screen door handle and really punch your thumb forward to keep the line loop from sagging. Change your target angle or level.

For targets that require a separated eye/target and hand/target line, you will have to *tilt* the rod shaft's 90° position to unroll the backcast directly opposite those targets. If the first target was at 12:00 on a clock you are facing, and the second is at 2:00, you will tilt your rod to put the backcast *opposite* that number 2:00 creating a hand/target line on which you will do the forward power snap.

As you false cast to leafy targets at different levels, position the rod shaft on each backcast power snap 90° from where the next forward cast must go. With the right sharpness of movement, the backcast will unroll 90° off the rod tip, just as the forward cast should unroll 90° off the rod tip, giving a total line movement of 180°, with no sagging of the loop. If your line sags or bellies, your arc is too large (keep your forearm from extending) or your force on the turnover is not sufficient or *directed* with enough sureness. A help might be to think of ringing an old-fashioned round-button doorbell with your thumb.

180° Spectrum

You can cast in any plane in the full 180° spectrum, from waist level on the right to waist level on the left, standing in one spot. All of the casting planes on the right, between horizontal and vertical, will be *forehand* casts, in which your elbow will be close to your body (and your hand will be well outside your body in the lower planes). All of the planes to the left, from vertical to horizontal, will be *backhand* casting and your elbow will be lower than your hand in the higher planes, and a little higher than your hand in the lower planes. Leaning your upper body to the right, or left, in coordination with the lower planes, will reduce the base of the accuracy triangle and will line up your eyes and rod hand as closely as possible with the target.

The hand/rod/forearm position stays the same through all of the angles. The forearm rotates sideward from the elbow and your palm will be facing *upward* in the horizontal planes on your casting side, facing *sideward* in the vertical planes, and *facing the ground* in the lower backhand planes.

High and low angles give you practice on the trajectory needed for short and long casts. The best long-cast trajectory is about 20° or more above a line parallel to the ground (at waist level), so be sure to aim at a target leaf that high.

Full Stroke with a Longer Line

Done correctly, this exercise will tire your casting hand rather quickly, because power snaps require force. There is not much resting time while so short a line unrolls. Once you see a noticeable improvement in your accuracy and your loops are narrow, add ten or fifteen feet of line and move back to cast this longer line to the same targets, now adding the loading and drift moves to your power snap.

With this longer line, the backcast power snap can end 90° from the target you have just touched and a drift move (or upper body motion) can reposition your rod hand to be in line with the next target, creating your new hand/target line. Another way is to anticipate where the next backcast will be, and to position the rod on the backcast power snap part way toward it, and then to drift the rest of the way. The width of the angle of an easy change of direction, in a backcast, is limited, and, if the angle is a large one, you must use both the path of the backcast and the drift move to get your rod positioned well for the new direction of the forward stroke.

With this longer line and full mechanics, the practice will be less tiring and the exercise will be closer to stream presentation. The improvement in the positioning of your backcast and in the control of your turnover arc should be noticeable.

four

ADD THE LINE HAND

The Line Hand

Shooting line adds a new dimension to your fly-casting capabilities. The most immediate change will be that, instead of stroking line through the rod and roll casting to extend it on the water, you will be able to start with a foot or two of line out of the rod tip (in addition to the leader and fly), and *extend line* by false casting, in order to reach your target area without having disturbed the water. At its most developed stage, the technique will let you shoot line on both back and forward casts so that you may reach your full distance-casting potential.

The **line hand** controls the flow of line for shooting, allowing inches or feet of fly line to slide through the guides at your command, and at a precise moment in the cast.

In addition, it does other routine line handling. The illustrations will show you some of its other duties.

1. Stripping line from the reel
2. Putting the line under a finger of the rod hand and stripping line in from behind it
3. Readying the line for shooting
4. Holding tension on the line during the cast
5. Releasing line for shooting and stopping the flow.

Line-Hand Tension

The main reason for asking you to put your line hand in your pocket as you learned the casting mechanics was that the line hand could not have helped but could have hindered or confused you. By using a constant length of line, you were working with a constant weight load. Whenever you add inches or feet to the amount of fly line that is out of the rod tip, you are adding increments of *weight* and you must adjust your stroke length, your timing, and your power application on the following stroke. This is the reason why the line must be added after, not during, the stroke.

Line-hand tension is preliminary to shooting line. It means that the line hand, holding the line to the left of the rod grip, should keep the weight load constant through the cast, by moving in conjunction with the rod hand, on a parallel path.

Strip three or four feet of line from the reel and hold it as shown in the illustration, twelve to fifteen inches to the left of the reel and a little lower. Hold the line between thumb and forefinger and become aware of the line

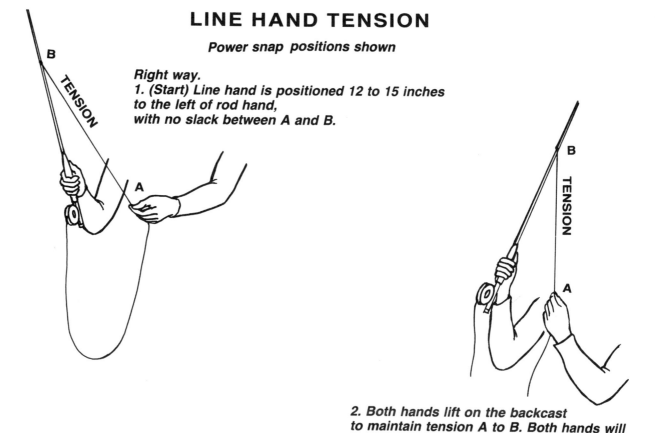

LINE HAND TENSION

Power snap positions shown

Right way.
1. (Start) Line hand is positioned 12 to 15 inches to the left of rod hand, with no slack between A and B.

2. Both hands lift on the backcast to maintain tension A to B. Both hands will lower on the forward cast.

between where you hold it and the first guide on the rod. This is the section of line that must be kept under tension. It won't be violin-string tension—just tension enough to keep the slack out of that portion of the line. As you make a backcast and forward cast, focus on that section of line and move your hand in unison with the rod hand to keep it from *sagging*. The line hand does not have to move quite as much as the rod hand because of the angle and the distance between the hands. It may help to think about maintaining a *triangle* between the rod hand, the line hand, and the first guide.

If you do not move your line hand and, instead, keep it in one spot, the rod will slide on the line (up and down or back and forth). When it slides up, the length of line outside the rod tip will be lessened and you will feel one particular weight of line tension. When it slides down, the line will be lengthened, for a different weight. *Or*, the line will sag between the first guide and your hand, creating *slack* that will take away all feeling of weight, for a second.

In keeping this tension, the hand holds the line at an angle from the first guide that will keep it well away from any part of the rod shaft, the grip, the reel, or your body and clothing, during the cast. As you cast in different planes or at different angles, the line hand, in order to maintain a parallel path to the rod hand, must adjust the angle of the fly line between itself and the first guide.

Wrong way
1. Start.
2. Rod hand lifts while line hand is stationary. There is tension from A to B but that line has lengthened.
3. Slack may be formed on the forward stroke as the rod hand lowers on the forward cast and the rod slides on the line that was added in #2.

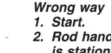

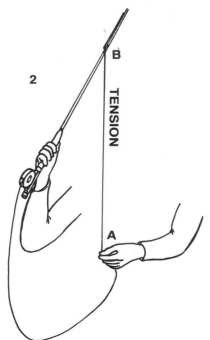

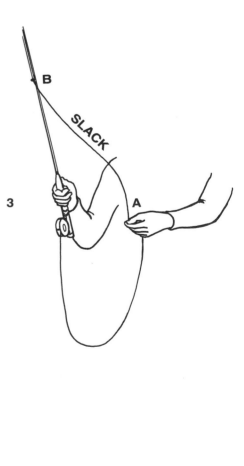

If you have already tried single or double hauls without success (or perhaps with success), you may find it difficult to move both hands in the same direction because of the desire to haul in opposite directions. Force yourself to move your hands parallel to each other even if you have to exaggerate the movement to begin with and lift the line hand quite high. As you get used to it and enjoy the feeling of a constant, instead of a variable, weight load, you will be able to lower your line hand to waist level, where it is less obtrusive. You'll feel and look more professional then and the technique of shooting line will be easy to master.

Shooting Line

The mechanics of shooting line on the forward cast are quite simple, using line-hand tension. You will make a backcast stroke, then make a forward stroke through the power snap, and then immediately release the line: (1) power snap; (2) release line. The loop you have formed with the power snap will unroll, carrying the extra line behind it during the follow-through time. Your point of aim should be a little higher than it would be if you were not shooting line, to allow time for the extra line to unroll before it lands on the water.

Backcast Power and Line Speed

To make shooting line easier for you, *overpower* the backcast a bit, without making your power snap any longer, and let the line unroll completely. That overpowered backcast should be called "extra" powered, just enough extra to increase the line speed so that, when the line unrolls completely, the shock of it straightening has flexed the rod more than on a normal backcast. I relate it to a stretching elastic band. The greater line speed keeps the fully extended backcast suspended for an instant (straight off the rod tip) and it feels stretched out, pulling on the rod tip. With the rod starting forward under a deeper load, any extra power needed on the forward cast can be added smoothly and easily.

Backcast Timing

You have learned that if you maintain a constant length of line, you will start the forward cast while the last bit of line and leader is still unrolling behind you. When you plan to shoot line, the backcast timing will change, even though the length of the line will not change. As described above, you will extend it *completely*, with extra power, and you will wait an instant longer for the line to pull on the rod tip. You won't have to guess how long. You'll feel it, especially if you drift with the rod.

These rules are not set in stone. With experience you can shoot line with a backcast that is not fully extended; but in order to do this, you'll need an extra-strong power snap and a longer-than-normal thrust of your forearm on the forward stroke. This can work with relatively short lines but is not as efficient a method as fully extending the backcast with extra speed.

Here are three exercises to develop your shooting-line skills on basic casts and false casts. You may change the order to suit yourself.

Exercise #1:

Shooting line on the basic cast. Take the line off the water and lay it back down on the water.

1. Extend line, in any way that you can, to make a cast of thirty feet. Put the line under the third finger of the rod hand, and clamp it against the grip.

2. Strip three to five feet of line from your reel, stretching your line hand back toward the outside of your left thigh. Drop the line.

3. Reach up and take the line from behind your rod hand's third finger and move it to the left twelve to fifteen inches and slightly lower than the rod hand. Keep the line pinched tightly between your thumb and forefinger.

4. Using line-hand tension, lift the line from the water, adding a little extra power on the backcast. Make the forward cast, releasing line immediately after the power snap. If all of the line disappears through the rod, and the line "slaps" against the rod shaft, everything is right. Try it again.

Reach forward of the rod grip to grasp the line and pull line in toward you as you pass it under the rod hand's line-holding finger. Then strip in (from behind the rod hand's third finger) the same three to five feet of fly line you shot out. Take the line from the rod hand and move it to the left. Make the backward and forward cast and shoot the three to five feet again, after the forward power snap.

SHOOTING LINE

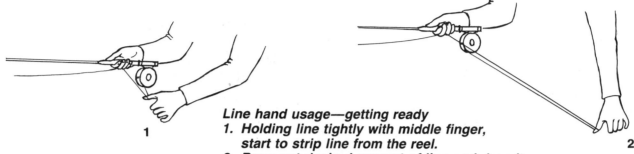

Line hand usage—getting ready
1. *Holding line tightly with middle finger,*
   start to strip line from the reel.
2. *Draw out desired amount of line and drop it.*
3. *Reach up and take line from middle finger.*
4. *Separate hands 12 to 15″. You are ready to shoot line.*

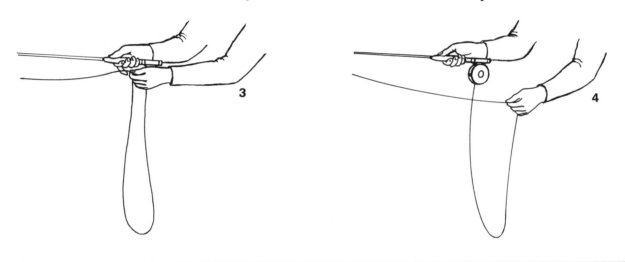

1. *Make backcast,*
   lifting both hands
   to maintain tension A-B.
2. *Make forward cast,*
   maintaining tension A-B
   through forward power snap.
3. *Release line*
   immediately after
   power snap—when
   you can see fly line
   ahead of the rod tip.

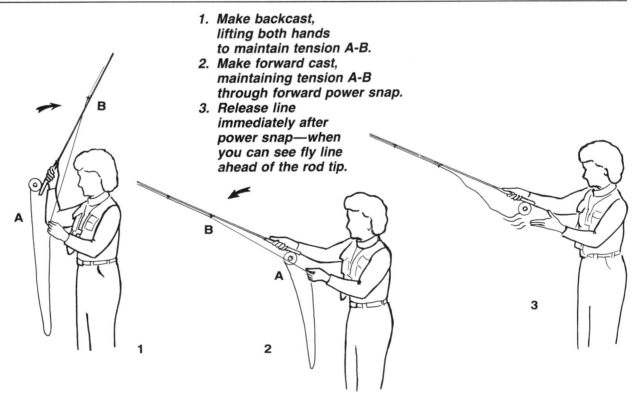

By stripping in and shooting out the same length of line, you will define, and perhaps refine, the amount of power, the timing and the stroke length needed to make the cast efficiently. Don't shoot on a given cast unless you are really ready and concentrating on the rod hand's mechanics. Make "dummy" casts until you are sure of the stroke length and can identify the moment when you will release the line.

When you have mastered one length of line both for pickup and shooting, work with another length until the feeling of different lengths and weights is familiar and you can adjust the variables without having to think it all out each time.

Troubleshooting

If the line doesn't shoot, look first to your line-hand tension. Then look to the power snap. If you release line *during* the power snap, you will destroy the loop that the power snap was to have created and your efforts will dissipate in the spread-out line. It is better to be late than early with the release. If your point of aim is fairly high, you can have a late release and still shoot effectively.

A bad backcast will keep you from shooting line. A common fault is to anticipate the shoot by taking your arm and the rod farther back than on a non-shooting cast. It's a developed response, like taking your hand farther back if you are going to throw a ball a greater distance. In fly casting it is the *flex* of the rod that's going to cast the line. A deeper flex contributes to a longer cast. Don't change the length of your backcast stroke prior to shooting line.

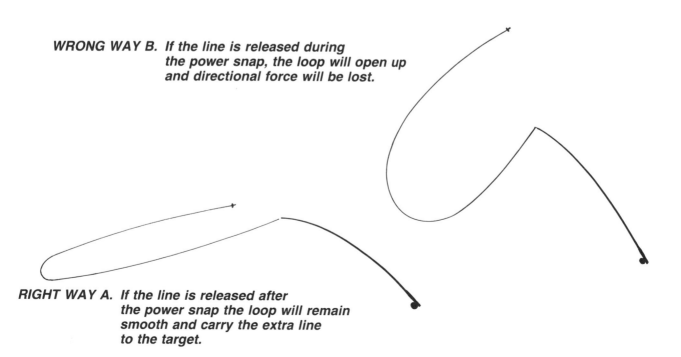

WRONG WAY B. *If the line is released during the power snap, the loop will open up and directional force will be lost.*

RIGHT WAY A. *If the line is released after the power snap the loop will remain smooth and carry the extra line to the target.*

You might try this adaptation of Exercise #1:

Bypass the use of the line hand and shoot line from beneath the third finger of your rod hand. Because the rod hand must keep a strong grip *through* the power snap, you are less likely to release the line early. You should make the power snap with all fingers gripping the rod, then the third finger can pop open to release the line. This technique works for students whose line-hand discipline is not sufficiently developed. If the shoe fits . . .

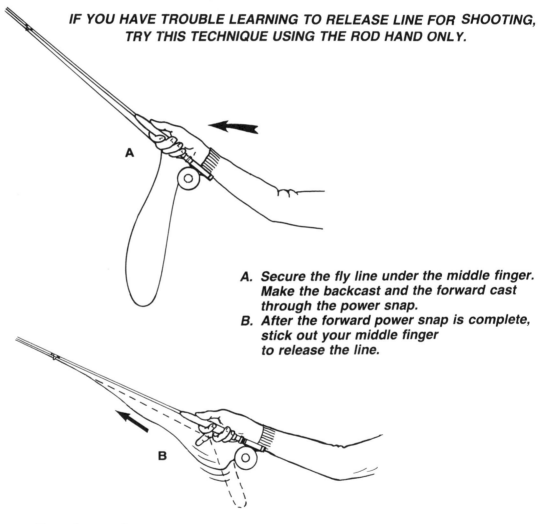

IF YOU HAVE TROUBLE LEARNING TO RELEASE LINE FOR SHOOTING, TRY THIS TECHNIQUE USING THE ROD HAND ONLY.

A. Secure the fly line under the middle finger. Make the backcast and the forward cast through the power snap.
B. After the forward power snap is complete, stick out your middle finger to release the line.

Exercise #2:

Shooting line while false casting.

Start with twenty feet of line and leader (combined) on the water, and with ten feet of line stripped off the reel and lying on the ground near your left foot.

Hold the line in your line hand only and start to false cast, moving the hands in unison to maintain tension and to help you feel, surely, this beginning-weight load on the rod tip.

When you are ready to shoot, release line after the forward power snap, opening your thumb and forefinger. Don't change the hand's position but keep the line cupped so that you may pinch off the flow when you see the leader starting to unroll. Make the next backcast remembering to adjust, slightly, the length of your stroke, the timing of the backcast, and the power application on both back and forward casts.

As the line lengthens you will be able to increase the amount of line you can shoot on each cast. You should be able to shoot this ten feet of line in three or four casts the first or second time you do it, and, eventually, in a maximum of two casts.

Strip the ten feet of line back in and go through the exercise several times, until you know that you are in control of the line additions. Then add five or six feet of line to the original ten and go through the same routine.

Extending the Stroke Length

You will find, as you increase the amount of line you false cast in the air, that you must extend your forearm, farther than was necessary with short lines, in the forward follow-through move, to create enough space for the longer backcast to come. As your line unrolls forward, extend your forearm, lowering it slightly at the same time, so that you have that space for the backcast loading move. Following through, and lowering at the same time, helps to keep everything in place throughout the mechanics. Body motion, forward and back, can be a real help to extend the length of your stroke, taking the place of much of the arm movement on the back and forward loading moves. Try it.

If you increase the speed of your stroke as it lengthens, you can comfortably end the longest strokes no farther back than the line of your shoulders.

Exercise #3:

Starting from scratch—stripping and shooting.

Reel in the line until there are only two or three feet out of the rod tip. Hold the fly in your hand. Release the fly and make a false cast, while at the same time reaching up with your line hand to grasp the line, forward of the reel. Strip line from the reel on this short backcast (it won't be much). Shoot it on the forward cast and strip on the backcast; shoot on the forward cast, over and over, until you have out the line length you want.

To start with, the strokes will be short—only a wrist snap long—and so will the amount of line you can shoot. It is almost impossible to get a feeling of line weight in those first short casts because there really isn't any. You can use only a power snap until you start to feel the line weight. Then add a loading and drift move, and *slow down*, to make the casts smooth and beautiful.

The given line weight for any rod balance is based on the first thirty feet of its length, so at ten feet you aren't going to feel the loading of the rod quite as easily as you will at thirty feet and you won't be able to shoot as much line at ten feet as at thirty. It takes weight to shoot weight.

Line Design

The design of the fly line has a lot to do with *ease* of shooting as well as the distance you can shoot. A double-tapered line, with seventy feet of heavy diametered line, will not shoot as easily as a forward tapered line once the weighted section of the forward taper, the first thirty feet, is out of the rod tip. The weighted section is backed by small-diametered running line that allows you to shoot more line for the same effort as you would a double taper. The ideal length of line held out of the rod tip for maximum shooting capability, without single or double hauls, will be the full thirty feet of the forward taper line. If you have a typical triangle taper line, it will be forty feet. Check any line you use, to see where the heaviest section ends; the manufacturer may vary them according to their designated uses.

Single and Double Hauls

A **haul** is an acceleration of the line by the line hand, independent of the rod's movement of that line. It is coordinated with the power snap.

The haul pulls line in through the rod, opposite the rod's directional movement. If the rod moves up, you haul down; if it moves backward/upward, you haul forward/downward; if it moves forward, you haul backward and if it moves backward, you haul forward. Hauling is the action that loads the rod more deeply than can be done with just the rod hand alone and it pays off in high line speed when it unloads. Additionally, it shortens the stroke (and reduces the power) needed by the rod hand, making the cast easier to execute.

SINGLE HAUL ON THE BACKCAST

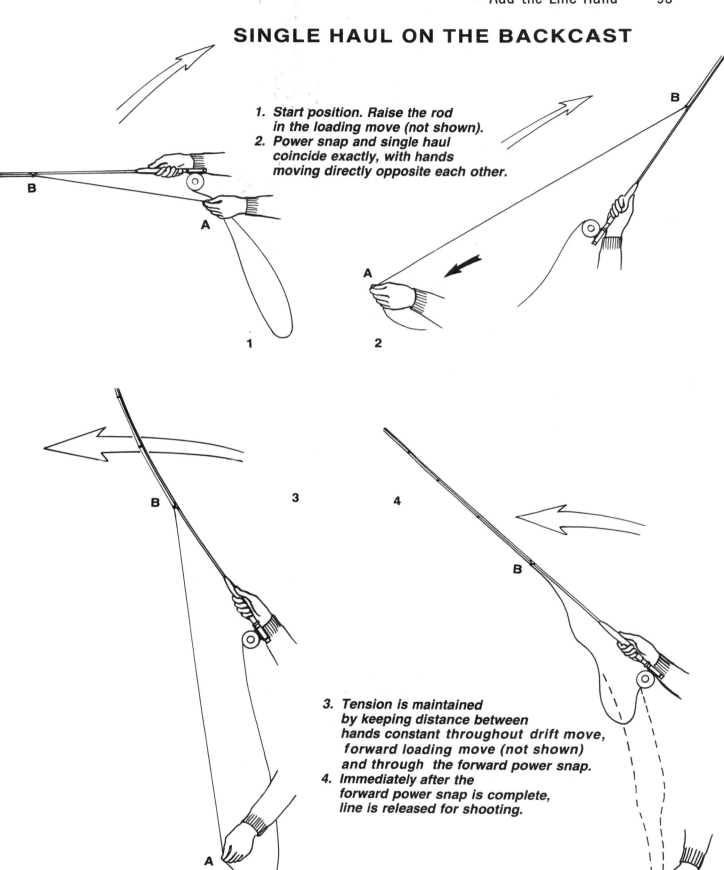

1. Start position. Raise the rod in the loading move (not shown).
2. Power snap and single haul coincide exactly, with hands moving directly opposite each other.

3. Tension is maintained by keeping distance between hands constant throughout drift move, forward loading move (not shown) and through the forward power snap.
4. Immediately after the forward power snap is complete, line is released for shooting.

A **single haul** is one-directional (line is hauled *in*) and it can be used on the backcast or on the forward cast, or, literally, on both casts. A **double haul** is a two-directional movement (after the line is hauled *in*, it is *let back out*). A double haul can be done on either the back or forward cast but is normally done on both.

When you practice hauls, be sure to have two or three feet of extra slack line hanging from between your line hand and the reel so that your haul, in its movement, does not inadvertently pull line from the reel or is not restricted in its length.

Single Haul: on the Backcast

On the backcast a single haul fills an easily recognizable need to help take line off the water.

1. On the loading move, as the rod hand lifts the line to the line/leader connection, the line hand starts to pull line in through the guides, in coordination.

2. On the rod hand's power snap, the line hand hauls, a short, sharp move *opposite* the rod's directional movement. *The power snap and the haul begin and end at exactly the same time.*

You have pulled line in, through the rod, reducing the weight load on the rod tip.

3. To complete the single haul, maintain that reduced line length/ weight load with line-hand tension, throughout the drift move of the backcast, and the loading move and power snap on the forward cast.

4. Release the line.

You must keep tension, between your line hand and the first guide, by moving the line hand parallel to the rod hand's motion. The distance between the hands must remain constant. After the power snap/haul, as the rod hand moves backward/upward in the drift move, the line hand moves forward/ upward. On the forward stroke, the line hand moves downward and back in toward the body, as the rod moves forward and away from the body. The hands *see saw* in their relative positions and the line do not move in or out of the rod. After the forward power snap, the line can be released for shooting. To sum it up, a single haul is made in coordination with the backcast power snap and then tension is maintained through the rest of the cast until the forward power snap is completed—at which time the line can be released.

Single Haul: on the Forward Cast

A haul on this part of the cast is usually used in conjunction with a slow-speed backcast, caused, perhaps, by limited space behind the caster.

To do the single haul on the forward cast only, use line-hand tension—move the line hand parallel to the rod hand—during the whole backcast. Coordinate the single haul with the forward cast power snap only, releasing line afterward.

Single Haul: on Both Strokes

Because the single haul is one-directional, the second haul will begin where the first one ended. They must both fit in the available space created by the full swing of your arm from the shoulder socket.

1. Do the loading move.

2. Do the backcast power snap and the single haul, in opposite directions.

3. Maintain line-hand tension during the drift move.

4. Maintain line-hand tension during the forward loading move.

5. Make the second single haul on the forward cast power snap.

6. Release line for shooting.

When would you use two single hauls in one cast? In a backwind, this technique can be better than a double haul with large, air-resistant flies.

With the double haul, when you attempt to "give back" the line you've pulled in on the haul, an air-resistant fly may *lag* against the wind and create slack in the leader, ultimately affecting the smoothness of the cast. With two single hauls, you avoid this possibility but can still effectively increase your line speed with a single haul on each stroke.

If you do wish to use only one single haul in the cast, under windy conditions, use it on whichever stroke moves the fly against the wind.

You may find that a single haul is harder to learn than a double haul because of the line-hand tension element. The key to making it easier is body motion; you can *see saw* your hands by moving back and forward from the waist or by shifting your weight from one foot to the other (with one foot dropped behind the other).

Double Hauls

Most fishermen know of the double haul only as a distance-increasing technique. They will say, "I don't need the double haul. I catch fish at forty feet or less and I can cast far enough without it."

The double haul has much more to offer than just added distance. When it has become second nature, you'll find yourself using it whenever it makes the casting easier—which may be more often than you think.

The double haul (1) adds speed to the line and (2) makes the rod hand's job easier by way of a shortened stroke length, because the line hand actually *moves* line. In addition to using the double haul for long casts, you'll use it in headwinds, backwinds, quartering and side winds, and for turning over long leaders in tight spots. Under any conditions you'll make more casts in a day's fishing and be less fatigued because both hands share the work.

When someone asks how far he must be able to cast to be a really good fisherman, my answer is "fifty feet under all conditions, to cover the fly fisherman's world." It may take you a lifetime, as it takes most of us, but the double haul will help you reach that goal. If you can cast fifty feet under difficult conditions, you'll cast seventy or eighty feet, or more, in good conditions. You will need that capability to fish successfully for salmon, steelhead, tarpon, and perhaps a few more species. Lots of big trout rivers require fifty-foot casts under tough conditions. It is true that most fish are caught at forty

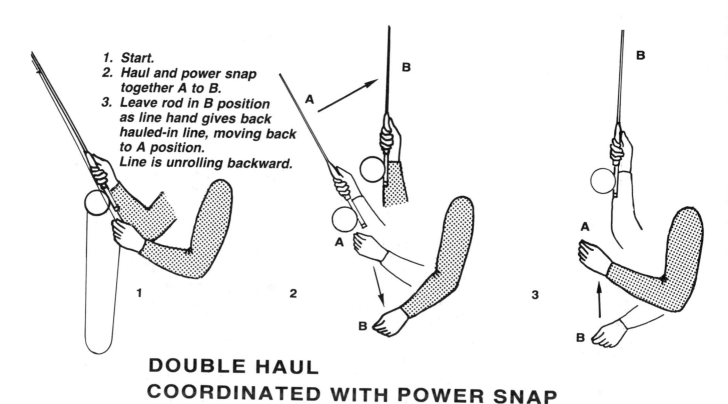

1. Start.
2. Haul and power snap together A to B.
3. Leave rod in B position as line hand gives back hauled-in line, moving back to A position.
   Line is unrolling backward.

**DOUBLE HAUL
COORDINATED WITH POWER SNAP**

feet or closer, but the heavy use of our waters leaves the "unreachable fish" to the presentations of the relatively few good casters who consider the double haul a necessary technique.

Fly Line Design

Because the design of weight forward and triangle taper lines is that of a *weighted section* backed by small diameter shooting line, either of these tapers is desirable to work with as you learn or sharpen your double-hauling skills. Work with the weighted section just outside of the rod tip. If you must use a double-tapered line, use twenty-five feet of line outside of the rod tip.

The Mechanics

I will offer you three practice patterns of the double haul and an adaptation. We all learn differently and the same words conjure up different mental images. Perhaps one of these patterns for learning will click for you, or, perhaps, they will all help.

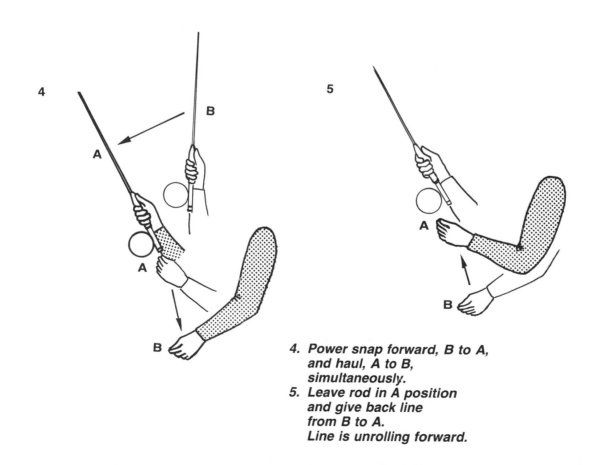

4. Power snap forward, B to A, and haul, A to B, simultaneously.
5. Leave rod in A position and give back line from B to A. Line is unrolling forward.

Double Haul #1

When you have mastered the double haul, your line hand will move in conjunction with all of the rod hand's moves, but, to start, I want you to isolate the haul as it coordinates with the heart of the cast, the power snap. The cast will consist of just the power snap portion of the stroke, without drift or a loading move.

False cast the line to the suggested length, then reduce the moves to just a power snap. It may be taxing to false cast this much line until you add the haul. The difference should be noticeable. (If it *is* too much line, reduce it gradually, until you find the optimum length.)

The power snap should be limited to just a short arc—45° on the hand/target line, once you have aerialized the cast. (Just as you did in "Picking Leaves.")

On the backcast, the line hand pulls the line in on the power snap and gives it back while the line is unrolling backward.

On the forward cast, the line hand pulls the line in on the power snap and gives it back as the line unrolls forward.

Yes, you "give it back" during drift and follow-through time, but, for this exercise, just keep the rod stationary while the line unrolls.

In terms of weight load on the rod tip, you reduce the load with the haul then increase it by the same amount as the line slides back out. You should feel the weight being added, as the line unrolls.

The illustrations show the separate paths of the rod, and of the line hand. On the backcast power snap, the rod moves from A to B while the line hand hauls from A downward to B. While the line unrolls, the rod remains stationary in its position and the line hand moves upward from B back to A.

On the forward cast power snap, the rod moves from B back to A as the line hand hauls from A to B again. At the end of the power snap, the rod remains stationary, as the line unrolls forward and the line hand moves upward/forward, from B back to A, where it started.

Speed and Force

When the line hand is moving the line from A to B, it is accelerating to a stop, just like the rod hand's motion. With the two moves coinciding exactly, an instant of great tension is achieved because the rod hand and the line hand have moved in opposite directions, exerting pressure to end the stroke. This is the action that *loads* the rod more deeply than can be done with just the rod hand alone, and it pays off, when the rod unloads, in high line speed.

From point B to point A, the line hand just rides up toward the first guide, giving back what it pulled through the rod, but at a *slower* speed, the speed of the (lower level) of the unrolling line loop. It reminds me of a yo-yo. Effort is made downward to make the yo-yo reach the end of the string with enough force to ride up again. The haul, downward, ends sharply; the line hand then relaxes as it moves up, just like the yo-yo action.

The hauling arm must never stiffen at the end of the hauling move but must remain flexed, in order to reverse direction and move up without hesitation. The motions are continuous although the level of force changes in them. You might make up some words like "PULLandgiveback" or "HARDandeasy" or "INandout" or "DOWNandup" to indicate in which part of the haul moves you use force and where you relax. Another bit of help may be to think of the movement of the line hand in reversing direction as being a recoil. Not a full one, just partial.

Double Haul #2

This is the method with which I have had the greatest success in teaching the technique one on one. The action of the hands and the response of the rod and line can easily be seen. This casting will be done in the horizontal plane, on grass, using the principles outlined in "Getting the Whole Picture" as the base. The line hand will be used in coordination with all of the rod hand mechanics, not just the power snap. Put out targets, at 90° from the rod tip and review the original exercise and check list to remind you of the parameters, the sidward stance, and the positioning of the mechanics in this plane. Remember to rotate your casting arm 90° to the right so that your palm is facing up throughout the whole cast.

Start with the fly line stretched out to your left target with the belly of your weight-forward line two or three feet out of the rod tip. Position the line hand slightly forward of the rod grip and to the side, with two or three feet of slack between it and the reel.

Hold the fly line firmly in your line hand and don't shoot line until later in the exercise. Shooting line slows you down because you have to pull the line back in each time, and it breaks the rhythm of learning.

HORIZONTAL DOUBLE HAULING ON GRASS

BACK CAST

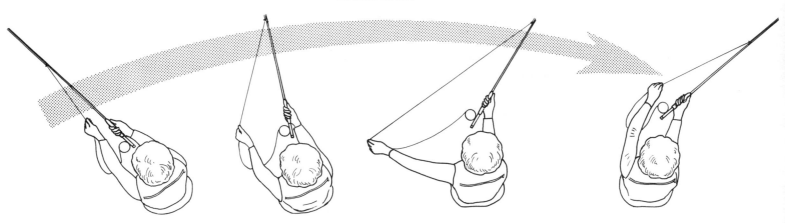

1. Loading move.   *2. Power snap/haul.*   *3. Drift/give line back*

TARGET SET-UP

FORWARD CAST

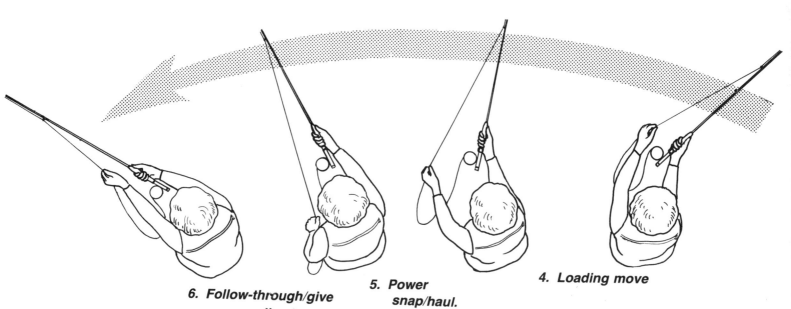

6. Follow-through/give line back.   *5. Power snap/haul.*   *4. Loading move*

ROD HAND MOVES	LINE HAND MOVES
Backcast: to the right	
1. The loading move.	1. Starts to pull in line, coordinating with the speed of the rod hand.
2. The power snap (to the target).	2. Hauls, in the opposite direction from the rod hand.
3. Drift and let the line land on the grass.	3. Gives back the line.

RELAX BETWEEN THE CASTS

ROD HAND MOVES	LINE HAND MOVES
Forward cast: to the left	
4. The loading move	4. Moves at the same speed to keep slack out of the line between the hands.
5. The power snap (to the target)	5. Hauls, in opposite direction from the rod hand.
6. Follow through and let the line land on the grass.	6. Gives back the line

Continue to work this way, letting each back and forward cast land on the grass. Make sure you watch every inch of the line unroll on both strokes to see *timing* and *line speed*, plus perfect *stroke length*, to make the fly land on the target. Use a weight shift on each stroke. It's a lot to do, but there's no hurry. Check the illustrations for the line hand position on the haul in this horizontal plane.

False Casting Horizontally

The next step is to keep the line off the ground and false cast horizontally, double-hauling to beat the band, but resting as the line unrolls. Let your sense of timing, your feeling of the line weight and the bending rod tip guide you in your efforts to make it all smooth, except for the end of the hauls. They should be *sharply* smooth.

It's difficult, on paper, to tell or show you how fast and sharp the haul might be. But I can share an experience I had in Ft. Worth at the 1948 Nationals. I had just been introduced to Jack Sparks of Waco, a former Distance Fly champion. He gallantly offered to ghillie for me in my Distance Fly practice session. After he had spread the shooting line on the platform, he knelt, back and to the side of my position, to be ready to take in the line, once again, after I had made the cast. He was six inches too close. I hauled on the backcast, with my hand angled forward. I hauled on the forward cast, with my hand angled backward, and caught him on the forehead to send him tumbling backward. He got up, shaken, and looked at me with new respect, saying he had had no clue that a woman of my size could generate such force. If I had hit him in the eye, a raw steak would have been in order. Be sure your haul generates some force!

Shooting Line

When you are ready to shoot line, strip ten or fifteen feet of it from the reel and let it lie on the ground at your feet. Remember that line is released for shooting after the power snap, with or without a double haul. If the cast, and the haul are made well, you'll feel the fly line's tension on your line hand signaling that you have generated enough line speed to shoot. On the presentation cast, don't skimp on that last haul; your hand may need to travel beyond your left thigh before you release the line.

Retrieve the line, each time, to position the end of the *belly* the same distance from the rod tip. A black mark on the line, at this point, would make it easy. (See "Marking Lines.") This distance, between the end of the belly and the rod tip is called "overhang."

Try shooting some line on one or two of the false casts in addition to shooting on the presentation cast. Make it your goal to shoot all of the line in just two casts.

When you are comfortable double-hauling in the horizontal plane, move upward toward the vertical plane, making a few casts at some of the levels in between. When you reach vertical, move your casting arm inward to line it up with your shoulder, then change the angle of the cast so that the backcast is inclined upward (the angle will be relatively shallow with this much line). Unroll the forward cast three or four feet above the ground until you make the backcast before the final shoot, at which time reposition your rod hand slightly lower, on the drift move, so that you may angle the forward cast upward at 20° or more above horizontal, the best trajectory for long lines.

If there is any wind blowing as you practice, cast into it; you'll feel the backcast's unrolling more positively.

The next step is to work on water, casting in the vertical plane, but, if you ever have a problem with the double haul, go back to horizontal casting where you can get the whole picture.

Double Haul #3

When you take line off the water, the surface tension will help you feel the loading move very easily. Using the double haul, you'll find that everything will happen more quickly because both hands contribute to the movement of the rod and line. Your stroke length will be noticeably shorter than without the hauls and, to test this, take a given length of line (thirty-five to forty feet) and pick it up with just the rod hand, noticing how much effort it takes, how long the stroke must be and how fast you have to move to get the fly out of the water. Then add the haul. There should be a noticeable difference. You'll be reaching the end of the loading move sooner with two hands moving the line. The power snap will be shorter and take less effort because of the help you get from the haul.

Line Hand Position

Here you can get a good look at the line hand's response to the rod's directional movement. If you start to move line, with the line hand, during the loading move, as you should, you will be pulling it in toward you at a slightly downward angle as the rod lifts upward. On the power snap, when the elbow lifts, your line hand will change direction about 90° and move *forward* to keep the pull on the line, opposite the rod's move.

DOUBLE HAUL: Shooting line or not: one cast, off the water and returned.

1. Start position. The line hand reaches ahead of the rod grip.

2. The line hand keeps slack out of the line as the rod is lifted in the loading move.

5. Drift move by rod hand. Line hand lifts line to keep it clear of the reel and rod butt, and keeps slack from forming

8. Halfway through the forward power snap and the second haul . . .

(All photos in this sequence by Allan Wulff.)

3. **The end of the loading move/beginning of the power snap.**

4. **The end of the first haul and power snap.**

6. **During drift move, the line hand moves up and starts to give back the hauled-in line— then releases line for shooting, if desired.**

7. **The rod hand begins the loading move as the line hand stops moving upward.**

9. **The end of the power snap and haul.**

10. **Rod is lowered on the follow-through.**

This seemingly crazy pattern results because, while the rod hand moves on an inclined, straight path, the rod shaft moves through an arc. Your line hand responds to the position of the rod shaft where the line is last encircled by the first guide.

The position of the line hand is traditionally thought of and illustrated as moving down toward the left thigh and back up again during the double haul, when casting in the vertical plane. But that downward path is not always the best one. Part of the line hand's job is to keep the line from fouling on either the tackle or on some part of your clothing. If you make a fairly long backcast, its angle will be fairly low, say at 45° off vertical. If your hauling hand ends up behind your left thigh, the fly line will be curved, across your chest, touching your clothing. Instead, the line must be hauled to a spot that is clear of obstructions and that will be *opposite* the rod hand's move, in the same plane. If the backcast is close to vertical, the haul will be opposite it, pretty much in a downward direction. If the backcast is beyond vertical, the line hand's haul may be a chest-high *forward* move to stay in line with the rod shaft.

The Length of the Haul

"How long should a haul be?" gets the same kind of answer as "How long should a stroke be?" There is no answer in inches or feet. The length of the haul, like the length of the casting stroke, is variable according to the length of the line, the length of the rod, and even the length of the caster's arms. A short person has to make a longer stroke and a longer haul with given rod and line lengths than does a tall person with longer arms. Lee used to chide me for making too long a haul compared to his until I pointed out his eight inches in height above me and the disparate length of our arms.

The length of the haul, whether three inches or three feet, must be accomplished within the time limit of the rod hand's power snap. On short casts, both the haul and the power snap will be short; on long casts, both will be longer and done with more speed, but beginning and ending at exactly the same instants.

It is more common, when learning this double haul technique, to make the haul too long rather than too short. If there is any flaw in the rod hand's mechanics, the addition of the haul will usually make you move both hands twice as far as is necessary. Remember that when all of the moves are done right, the haul should reduce, not increase, the length of the stroke.

Don't just move your hands mechanically! There must be an *instant of tension* at the end of the haul/power snap. Try to feel it but also look for it. Focus your attention on the fly line, between the line hand and the first guide on the rod. That's the area in which the tension can be seen at the same time it is felt. When it occurs, it signals the end of the haul. Be sure to have made the haul with a flexed arm so that you may give back the line you hauled in, without hesitation.

The Speed of the Move Upward—Giving Back the Line

The fly line cannot literally pull your line hand upward but, if *you* move the hand upward too quickly, you'll create slack. The speed with which the line hand moves toward the first guide is that which keeps slack from forming between the moving hand and the first guide. No faster; no slower. It is at the speed of the unrolling cast. Pay close attention to make sure that your *line hand does not pass, or reach above, the rod hand*.

Slide Loading—The Adaptation

This is the way the double haul has developed for me. There was a time when I had a little "gray area" every time I demonstrated the double haul, as to what the line hand was doing during drift time backward and the loading move forward. I knew I wasn't doing what the accepted version was, which is what I have explained to you thus far (moves three and four in horizontal casting), that the line hand ends its giving-back-the line move at the end of the drift move, and then comes forward with the rod hand, at the same speed, in the loading move. Finally, slow motion film of my compadre, the late Johnny Dieckman, another of Bill Taylor's pupils, showed me exactly what I was looking for.

The line hand and rod hand work as described through the power snap backward. Then, in the time it takes for the rod hand to move backward in the drift move and make the forward loading move, the line hand, following up toward the first guide at the speed of the unrolling line, is still moving upward as the rod hand is moving forward. They are *moving toward each other, during the forward loading move*. This means that the rod is sliding forward along the line, while the line is still unrolling backward. Startling isn't it? The hands come together just in time for the forward power snap.

While I haven't been able to prove to myself that this method gives me more distance under low-water wading conditions, it gives me as much as the standard method, but feels a thousand times better. When the rod slides forward, the weight of the line comes to be felt suddenly; in fact, the rod slides forward *until* it is felt. **Slide loading!** At that point, in the stroke, the angle of the rod shaft, just above the grip, will be at 90° on the hand/target line, ready for the power snap.

In deep-water wading conditions, I feel that I can get a maximum loading of the rod on the final backcast—unattainable without this technique. More on this in "Shooting on the Backcast."

Slide loading came about naturally for me, as I'm sure it does for others, once my mind was free of the mechanics and I trusted my feeling of the rod and line's interaction to guide me in making the motions smoothly. And it may happen the same way for you. This is "dancing" rather than just doing steps. It gives a feeling of completeness that is a high point of fly casting.

five

LONG CASTS

Certainly the tennis "serve" is not unlike the overhand pitch and these skills share such common principles as accounting for the summation of the forces, developing the highest possible linear velocity at the end of the lever, and anticipating the tangential path that will be taken by an object released from a circular path.

CHARLES SIMONIAN, from *Fundamentals of Sports Biomechanics*

Making Long Casts

Harold H. Smedley's book *Who's Who and What's What in Fly and Bait Casting in the United States* quotes noted angling author, Dr. James A. Henshall, as saying (in 1880), "The longest cast with the single-handed rod, I ever saw, without 'loaded' flies, was eighty-one feet and I believe the longest on record is Seth Green's eighty-four feet. At the last tournament held by the New York State Sportsman's Association, seventy feet won the first prize."

Man's ability to cast a fly a long way has greatly improved since Dr. Henshall's day, not only with the design and materials of the rods but with the skills of the casters themselves. In 1864, rules for single-handed distance allowed rods as long as 12½ feet, and up to a pound in weight. Today's rules limit the rod length to 9' 6"; the casting line (the shooting head) cannot weigh over 1½ ounces and must be no less than 50 feet from point of taper to the holding line. The line weight restricts the rod weight.

The old timers didn't know about the double haul. Marvin Hedge of Portland, Oregon, first used the technique in 1934, breaking Chicagoan George Chatt's existing record of 125 feet (in the Trout Fly Distance event) with a cast of 147 feet. Three years later, Californian Dick Miller cast a fly 183 feet.* The

History of the Sport of Casting: Early Times by Cliff Netherton.

double haul was here to stay and, fifty years after its introduction, Californian Steve Rajeff set a new national record, in the Single-Handed Fly Distance event, casting his fly 236 feet. His average distance, of the three longest casts in five minutes of casting time, was 219 feet. Rajeff's tackle:

> **Rod:** Sage, Graphite II, 4¾ oz., 9 feet long and rated for a #17 line.
> **Line:** 51 feet of a double tapered #11 line, Scientific Angler's Hi-Speed Hi-D sinking line.

Steve explains that if the fly line were to be weighed at the first 30 feet it would be a #11, but the weight at 51 feet would be 640 grains or a #17. If you think about this for a moment you'll realize that, when you cast a double taper, a long-belly weight forward, or a triangle taper line, all of which contain more than 30 feet of weight, you are casting a larger number of grains than that specified by the rod manufacturer's suggested line weight. It suggests that there may be a need for a more precise definition of the line weight/line length ratio for each rod.

> Rajeff's Holding line: .022 monofilament, 20 feet
> Shooting line: .010 Maxima monofilament

The casting was on grass, not water, and at ground level. In international competition in 1986, Rajeff cast a fly 241 feet.

Tournament casting is the research and development lab for the sport fishing field, in both tackle design and in casting techniques. Over the fifty years of my observation, the tournament events have not all been clearly related to fishing, but some of them are, and if you look at the rest of them as only "exercises," they bring out the best in the caster and the tackle, defining what can be expected of each.

The number of active clubs and casters has diminished over the years but the American Casting Association can direct interested persons to active clubs. Write to:

> A.C.A.
> Zack Willson, Executive Secretary
> 786 Hyatts Rd.
> Delaware, OH 43015

Long casts in the real fishing world will never come close to Rajeff's tournament feat. A fisherman must meet different challenges from those a tournament caster finds on a casting platform in five minutes of casting time.

1. You must be able to fish all day and make hundreds of casts.

2. You must carry, in loops in your hand (or in a basket at your waist) all of the shooting line that you need, beyond the belly of the fly line.

3. You must be able to cast your maximum distance in water perhaps as deep as you can wade.

When Lee and I fish near each other in the deep-wading conditions of most Atlantic salmon rivers, our marked lines tell me that he casts about 10 feet farther than I do, in the circumstances of casting as far as we can, consistently, cast after cast, through the whole fishing session. Lee casts between 80 and 83 feet with his short, light graphite rods (less than 7 feet, weighing less than 3 ounces) and I cast between 70 and 73 feet with either a 6' 10" or an 8-foot graphite. We both use #6 or #7 weight lines. (Lee, by the way, though he is 8 inches taller and 50 pounds heavier, chooses light tackle, for the challenge and the pleasure it gives him.)

Longer, stiffer rods (which would have more weight) would cast a slightly longer line for me, but the weight factor keeps me from using them in fishing that requires continuous casting. Each of us must determine our tools. Whatever your tackle, these are the key factors that will give your long casts consistency.

1. Good body stance and body motion for long stroke potential.

2. The double-haul technique added to good rod-hand mechanics.

3. Marked lines for visual recognition of maximum pickup length.

4. Tangle-free shooting of coiled line, from your hand.

5. The shooting of line on both back and forward casts to attain maximum loading of the rod.

Casting Stances and Body Motion

The length of your stroke can be affected by the way in which you stand; your casting **stance**. You can stand almost any way to make short casts but, as your line is lengthened and your stroke must lengthen too, body position and motion become all important.

There are two basic body stances. I call them *closed* and *open*. The closed stance is the one used in vertical plane casting in which your body remains facing the target through short and long casts. The open stance turns your body, 90° from the target and your casting plane is 40 to 45° off vertical.

Closed Stance

The body faces the target, shoulders square to it. The casting arm moves in front of the shoulder, forearm in line with upper arm, so that, except perhaps for the longest casts, the rod butt and rod hand are within your vision (sometimes it is peripheral) as you look at the target area. The bent arm moves in the area between the center of your head and the outside of your casting shoulder, laterally, and from just above the shoulder to just above your head, vertically. The casting motion, in this closed-stance position, is much like hammering a nail or chopping wood. Your feet are positioned next to each other for short casts (short strokes); the foot on the casting side drops back for long casts (long strokes), with both remaining pointed toward the target.

If the fly starts to come close to your head, perhaps because of wind conditions, you need only tilt your rod hand outward from the elbow, an *inch* or *two*, to tilt the rod tip a *foot* or *two*, which can take the path of the fly to the outside of your body without dramatically changing the position of your upper arm. There is a strong tendency among new fly fishermen, to swing the arm out from the shoulder in these circumstances and, of course, the shoulder will block the stroke. The resulting rounded path of the hand/rod butt will move the fly line through more than 180° between back and forward casts (it will be closer to 270°), thus affecting your overall control.

Closed Stance: Long Strokes and Body Motion

For long lines, you can extend the effective casting arc to its maximum by dropping the foot on the casting side back and using body motion with the stroke.

Backcast

When you pick up a long line from the water, lean forward to start, and raise your upper body with your arm and rod frozen in the starting position instead of a *loading move* with your arm. Your body movement will do it for you. It's much less work and is especially helpful when you are deep wading.

Shift your weight to the back foot during the power snap and continue the movement by leaning backward from the waist during the drift move. At the end of the power snap, your rod hand should be above, but not beyond, your shoulder. The drift move will take the rod hand out of your peripheral vision to a position behind, and above, your shoulder. Your bent elbow should still be in that vision. Leaning backward helps to keep the rod hand's position always within an area of strength from which you can push or pull weight. (In this case it will be to pull weight forward.)

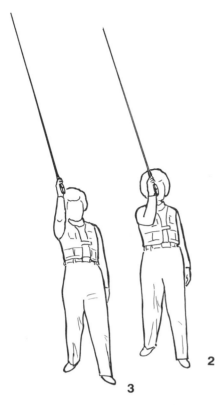

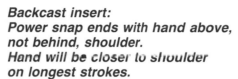

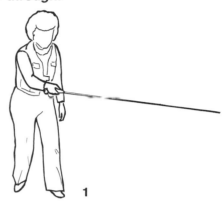

Back cast:
1. Start
2. End of power snap.
3. End of drift move. Note change in arm position

Forward cast:
3. Start.
2. End of loading move; in position for power snap.
1. End of follow-through.

Backcast insert:
**Power snap ends with hand above,
not behind, shoulder.
Hand will be closer to shoulder
on longest strokes.**

3

2

1

CLOSED STANCE—VERTICAL PLANE CASTING

Forward Cast

Start the forward loading move by shifting your weight forward and you'll find that you won't have to move your casting arm very far. Your body move will start the bent arm forward, leading with the elbow, and a minor retraction of the forearm and hand will position your rod shaft for the forward power snap. In this closed-body stance, your upper body remains facing the target during the weight shifts. It is a particularly good stance for accuracy and short to medium casts with any length rod. It is good for long casts if the rod is relatively long and fast actioned.

If your rod is short or soft actioned, you'll do better on long casts to use the open-body stance. You can tell, by the path of the fly, or how much work is required to make long strokes, when you should shift from one to the other. You can start with a closed stance for short casts and switch to an open stance for longer ones.

On a long line pickup, it is a common fault to end the power snap move as far back, relative to your body, as the drift move should have ended. If your line touches the water behind you, this may be the cause. The solution, in addition to starting the cast with the rod tip close to the water, is to increase your acceleration to get the line lifted and the fly out of the water in the allotted space your rod hand can move—no farther back than *even* with your shoulder.

OPEN STANCE—OFF-VERTICAL CASTING

Forward cast:

3. Start for loading move.
2. Start of power snap.
1. End of follow-through.

Backcast:
1. Upper body twists toward front for start.
2. End of power snap. Upper body has swung toward rear. Hand ends outside— but in line with—shoulders. Forearm muscle touches upper arm muscle. Rod is tilted 40 to 45° off vertical.
3. End of drift move. Palm is up, arm is flexed, rod, line, leader, and fly are in line with shoulders. Turn head to see it all.

Open-Body Stance

This is the more versatile stance for rods of different actions and lengths.

Your body faces *sideward* to the target (90°) and your feet are placed, one ahead of the other, left foot pointing at the target, right foot dropped back and turned out 90°.

Your rod hand and arm, and, of course, the rod, will be angled outward, about 40 to 45° off vertical. (Just rotate outward from the elbow.) The path of your rod hand will be outside the shoulder line.

Backcast

Start with the rod tip low to the water, with no slack, as usual, with your upper body turned toward the target area just for the loading move. On the power snap shift your weight backward and open your shoulder *rearward* to accommodate the rod hand's straight path, *keeping the elbow close to the body.* The rod hand will end the stroke outside the shoulder. Extend the arm on the drift move in a continuation of the stroke, moving your elbow away from your body, to the right rear. The palm of your rod hand should be UP at the end of the drift move.

You can actually see your backcast in this stance; it is not behind you. Just turn your head and notice that your shoulders, the rod, and the extended line, leader and fly, are all in line with each other at the end of the drift move.

If they are not easily seen, you have curved the backcast stroke instead of keeping it on a straight line.

Forward Cast

Use a weight shift to start the loading move (remember to keep your rod hand's palm up) bringing your elbow back in toward your body, to position the rod shaft for the coming power snap. Finish the weight shift on the power snap and follow through as usual. The casting motion, in this open-body stance, may remind you more of throwing a ball than of chopping wood.

The open body stance, with the rod angled 40 to 45° off vertical, will let you handle rods as short as six feet for long casts. The lowered path of the line and fly will be safely away from your head. You can make long strokes more easily in this stance than you can in the closed stance, especially when using body motion.

More on Body Motion

Body motion will give you longer, more effective casting arcs than you can manage with just lifting your arm. Body motion should be as much a part of fly casting for distance as it is for throwing balls. It makes the casting easier and better. Some fishing situations may preclude shifting your weight from one foot to the other, but you can usually bend from the waist, without rocking the boat or disturbing your footing in the stream. Use it when you practice long casting, even though you may have to restrict it when fishing.

The Woman's Angle

I *count* on body motion for casting long lines. I am 5' 5" tall, normally strong, but not powerful. And I am a woman. According to a *Newsweek* magazine report in 1983, I cannot expect to have the same strength, pound for pound, as a man of the same height and weight. Now that women have joined men in the physical exercise programs of the military, it has been determined that they are not equal physically; that women have only 55% of the strength of men. (Oy!) Conclusions such as this one are never absolute but, relating it to fly casting, it means that if you don't have great strength, you had better have everything else going for you. Good mechanics, and practice to develop your muscles, are fundamental, but body motion could make the difference. Moreover, if you do have height and strength and good coordination, the same things that help those of us with physical limitations can put *you* at the top of the game.

Marking Lines for Distance and Weight

Have you ever made a really long cast (defined as longer than usual) and wondered exactly how long it was? Have you had a friend boast of casting sixty to eighty feet regularly, in an area where you think you are casting to the same fish at fifty to sixty feet? Each of us has a different perspective on distances and even that can be altered by whether we are casting from a knee-deep position or a chest-deep position in the water. There is only one way to know how far you are casting and that is to *mark* your lines.

Lee introduced me to marking lines for distance and I introduced him to marking lines for weight. Marked lines are a valuable tool in all fishing but especially in Atlantic salmon fishing. If a fish rises and doesn't actually take the fly, it usually goes back to where it was before you made the cast. You will want to make *exactly the same cast* again. If your line is marked at particular lengths, say at thirty, forty, and fifty feet, you will know exactly how much line you had out by relating one of those marks to the rod. Perhaps the forty-foot mark was two feet out of the rod tip when the fish rose. If you stand in the same place and cast in the same direction, that cast can be duplicated. If you decide to let the fish rest, you can cast for other fish, and always come back to the original fish's lie by putting the forty-foot mark two feet out of the rod tip again. You could even leave the pool and, as long as you marked the spot in which you stood, you could cover that fish's lie on your return.

In the Wulffs' workroom, we mark our lines at thirty, forty, and fifty feet with quick-drying black paint or an indelible laundry marker. We put a one-inch mark at thirty feet, two one-inch marks at forty, and three marks at fifty feet. By adding the known lengths of the rod and the leader, one has no doubt about the casting distance. It helps in another way. If our level of performance falters, the marks remind us to "get it together" again.

The third benefit will help you to make an efficient "long cast sequence," (not more than two full casts). The thirty-foot mark on a forward taper line, or the forty-foot mark on a triangle taper line, is the end of the weighted section of the fly line. It is the section you want out of the rod tip when you begin your long cast sequence. Positioning a mark is a lot easier than guessing. It may save you a cast.

Marking lines for *weight* classification will tell you what you want to know if the identifying tab, the one that line companies provide to put on the reel, disintegrates, or if you change a line from one reel to another and forget to identify it on that reel. One of the frustrating things about owning more than one fly line is that you can't tell the weight for sure just by looking at it. You can tell if it is floating or sinking by putting it in water. You can tell its

MARKING LINES

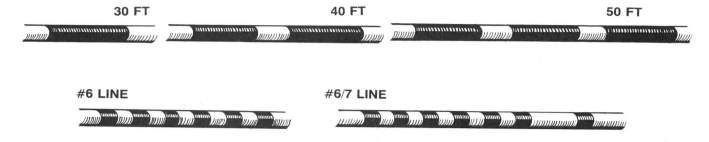

design—level, double-tapered, or whatever—by stripping it off the reel and comparing diameters. But the weight can be a mystery. Solve the problem with the same paint, this time *dots* of it, at the end of the front taper. Six dots for a #6 weight line, nine dots for a #9 weight. Perhaps the day will come when the line companies will include this marking for weight in the manufacturing process.

Holding Coils of Line

Inherently, fly line has a tendency to tangle and, even when you are fishing for tarpon or bonefish from a skiff, and lay the line in neat coils on the deck or bow platform, you'll be lucky if it doesn't find a protruding ring or anchor chain to catch on, as it lifts off the deck on the cast. The wading fisherman, who must hold all of his shooting line in coils between casts, needs to put some thought into how to make tangle-free deliveries a sure thing.

The secret is to form loops of different sizes, in a sequence that puts the holding point of the biggest loop at the back end of your hand and the smallest at the forward end. The hand must never move erratically (even though it may double-haul) to cause them to overlap or twist. Because the gradation is from smaller loops to larger ones as they come off your hand, they should not tangle.

The first loop you will make is for the river. You can let a loop lie on the water if it is not so long that it would get pulled downstream in the current too far. On the presentation cast, the "river loop" goes out last and the surface tension of the water, from which it lifts, slows it down enough to keep that final bit of line from wrapping around the rod shaft on the shoot even though you let go of it completely from your line hand. Additionally, the river loop puts slack between your line hand and the reel, which keeps you from inadvertantly pulling line from the reel, while stretching to make loops, or while doing hauls.

COILING LINE YOU WILL HOLD

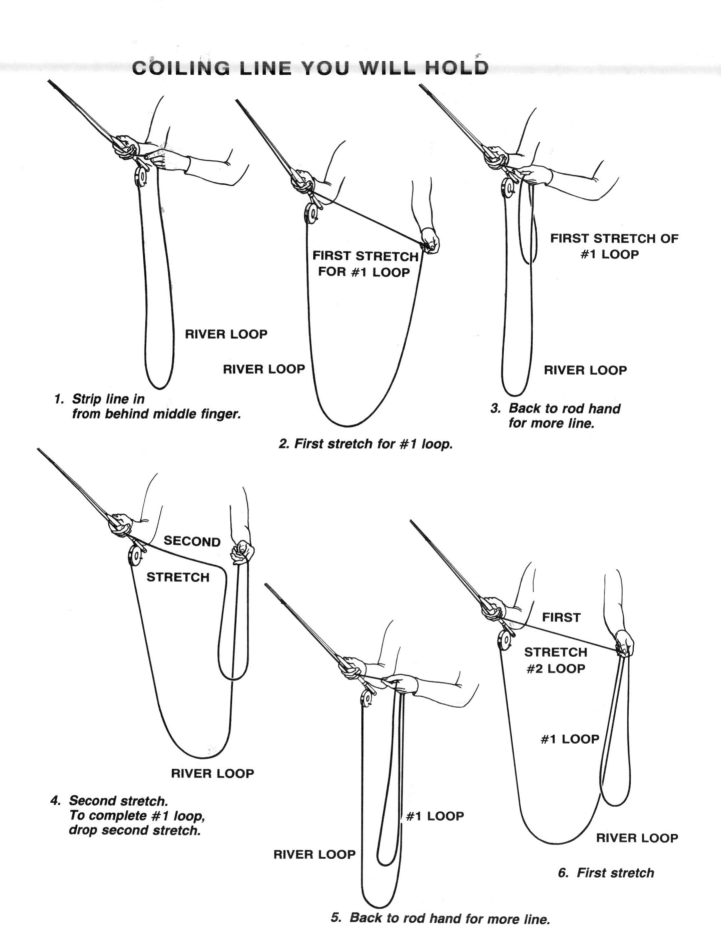

FIRST STRETCH FOR #1 LOOP

RIVER LOOP

RIVER LOOP

1. Strip line in from behind middle finger.

2. First stretch for #1 loop.

FIRST STRETCH OF #1 LOOP

RIVER LOOP

3. Back to rod hand for more line.

SECOND

STRETCH

RIVER LOOP

4. Second stretch. To complete #1 loop, drop second stretch.

RIVER LOOP

#1 LOOP

5. Back to rod hand for more line.

FIRST STRETCH #2 LOOP

#1 LOOP

RIVER LOOP

6. First stretch

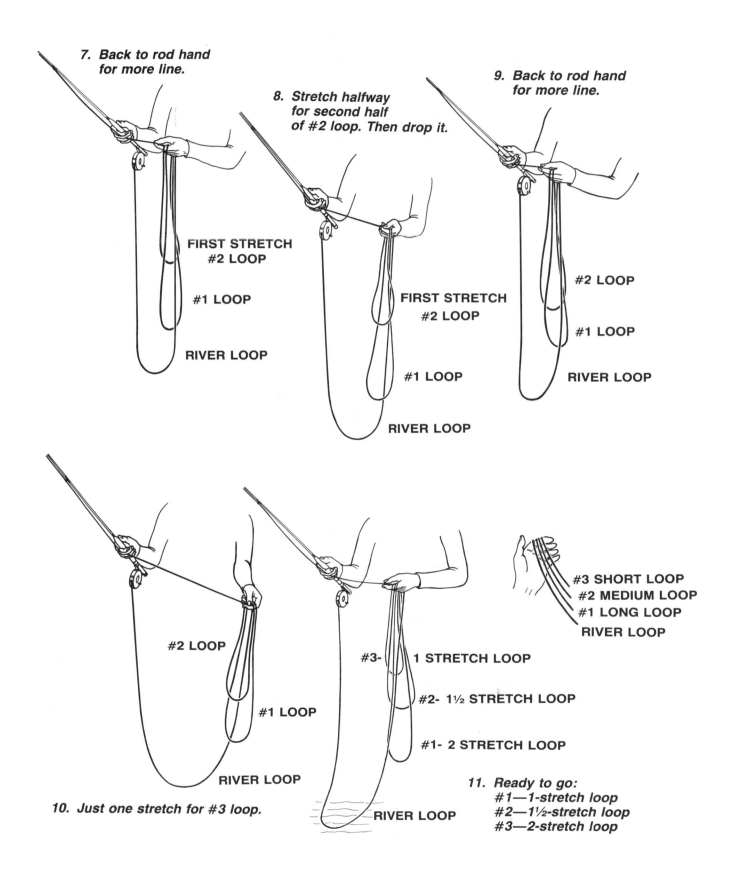

7. Back to rod hand for more line.

FIRST STRETCH
#2 LOOP

#1 LOOP

RIVER LOOP

8. Stretch halfway for second half of #2 loop. Then drop it.

FIRST STRETCH
#2 LOOP

#1 LOOP

RIVER LOOP

9. Back to rod hand for more line.

#2 LOOP

#1 LOOP

RIVER LOOP

#2 LOOP

#1 LOOP

RIVER LOOP

10. Just one stretch for #3 loop.

#3- 1 STRETCH LOOP

#2- 1½ STRETCH LOOP

#1- 2 STRETCH LOOP

RIVER LOOP

#3 SHORT LOOP
#2 MEDIUM LOOP
#1 LONG LOOP
RIVER LOOP

11. Ready to go:
#1—1-stretch loop
#2—1½-stretch loop
#3—2-stretch loop

That is the end of it. The loop that was two stretches large is on the bottom, the one-and-a-half loop is next, and the last, just one stretch, is on top. This sequence is a guide you may choose to alter. If you can carry more line than this will give you, add another one-stretch loop or change the second loop to 1¾ and the third to 1¼ before you get to the one-stretch loop. As long as you diminish the size of the loops, it should work.

If you are tall, you will have longer loops automatically, but, even if you are short, you can add another foot to each loop by reaching above the rod grip to start the stretch backward, being sure to run the line under a rod-hand finger to maintain control as you stretch back, in the way already described.

If you are carrying this length of line, you will surely need to double haul. Do it smoothly and keep the holding position of your cupped hand constant.

These loops should be thought of, not only as line lengths, but as line-weight segments. A hypothetical example would be that your line load weighed one pound at the pickup point. On the first forward cast you would add a length that amounted to a quarter of a pound, on the final backcast one-half of a pound, and on the final forward cast it wouldn't matter. You will try to release these lumps of weight in the same manner, each time you do the sequence, to have consistency in your casts. Each lump of weight requires an adjustment of stroke length, power, and timing, by you, as they are added.

No matter how many times I make long casts from these coils, I never take anything for granted and must make sure that the loops are exactly the same in length and number (give or take one small loop) *every time* or I won't have the precise control over how much weight is added on a back or forward cast. It is probably critical for me because of my size, but if things don't go well for you on long casts look to those lumps of weight you are adding. Don't do it haphazardly.

Shooting heads are (usually) thirty-foot fly lines to which you attach monofilament shooting line (behind them). If you use one, you will either have to hold the mono or put it in a "belly basket," made for the purpose. The shooting head is used for distances that are not easily reached with conventional tapers, so the amount of shooting monofilament that has to be held is considerable. If you must hold it without a basket, it is efficient to hold some of the loops in your mouth.

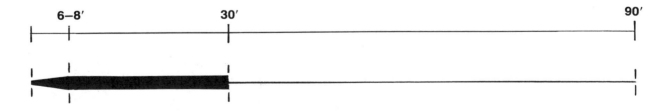

Make a river loop and perhaps one more loop for your line hand to hold; make two or more loops for your mouth to hold (resting them lightly between your teeth) and one or two more loops for your hand again, with slack line for hauling. The timing of the release from your mouth is easy—if you don't try to release the loops one at a time. Just kidding! Open your mouth after the power snap.

Long Cast Trajectory

The Seesaw

With long lines, the angle above the water, on which the backward and forward casts are made, is like a seesaw. As you lengthen the line, by shooting, the backcast angle lowers and the forward cast angle raises. The backcast is not thrown downward, it is thrown above horizontal (even if it is as little as "half and inch") to fight gravity but, as it unrolls, like the seesaw, it will drop below horizontal to be opposite the projected forward cast. When you are ready to make the *final*, presentation cast, the forward cast trajectory should be aimed at 20° or more above horizontal.

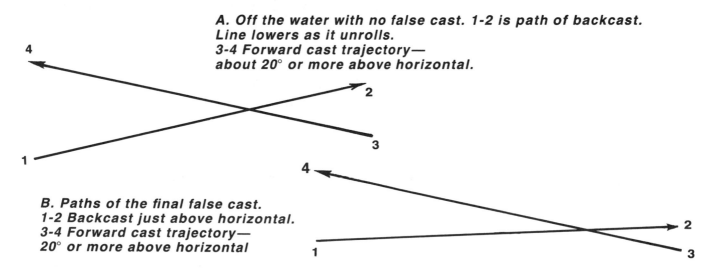

**A. Off the water with no false cast. 1-2 is path of backcast.
Line lowers as it unrolls.
3-4 Forward cast trajectory—
about 20° or more above horizontal.**

**B. Paths of the final false cast.
1-2 Backcast just above horizontal.
3-4 Forward cast trajectory—
20° or more above horizontal**

Rod Hand Movement on the Backcast

Taken off the water, the angle of the backcast can be seen, for any length line, when the fly line has been lifted to the line/leader connection. Short casts are made at relatively steep angles, and my instruction for them has asked that you lift your whole arm on the power snap to extend the rod arc *upward*, at the same time maintaining the angle.

The longer the line, the lower that backcast angle. For your longest casts, body motion will help to lengthen the stroke and extend the arc through which the rod moves, and the rod hand's path will be just above the shoulder. Your arm need not lift until the drift move, when it extends to follow the path of the unrolling line.

Long Cast Sequence

Never forget that good casting serves the purpose of keeping your fly on the water instead of in the air and that to minimize air time on long casts you'll use the double haul and shoot line in both directions with the goal of completing the presentation sequence in a maximum of two full casts.

It is relatively easy to shoot line on the forward cast because it is natural for us to throw things forward, and the extra power needed for shooting is easily applied in this direction. To shoot line on the backcast requires the same extra effort in both the casting stroke and the double haul. Contrary to

On the forward stroke, with long lines, the elbow will lift up, but not lock, during the relatively broad power snap. It may extend fully immediately *after* the power snap.

forward cast shooting, where we can use our eyes to help judge how much line to shoot, we must judge, by feeling alone, when we have added enough line on the backcast. It is relatively easy to determine when you are in error, because of the results.

Overhang

As suggested, mark your line so that you can easily see where the end of the weighted section of your fly line is. Then determine how far out of the rod tip that mark must be for a comfortable pick up in the long cast sequence. I will suggest that you start with three or four feet. This distance, between the rod tip and the end of the line's weight, is called **overhang**. How much overhang can be handled at pickup time and through the cast must be determined on an individual basis. Line speed is the big factor. Three or four feet of overhang to begin with allows for the line-haul movement, which will move the heavy portion of the line *toward* the rod tip on the backcast pickup, but not bring it into the guides.

One Full Cast

If you do not have to change direction dramatically between pickup and presentation, you can often eliminate false casting and make one pickup, shooting on the backcast, and shooting the rest on the presentation cast. The friction created by the surface tension on the fly line as it comes off the water, helps to load the rod perfectly and—with a little extra power to add line speed on the backcast—you can shoot what is needed, to fully load the rod for the forward cast. There can be an advantage to eliminating false casts. If the tackle is fairly heavy for you, false casts can diminish the speed of the cast rather than enhance it. When I had to cast a 6¾-ounce rod for tournament distance

On the backcast, line can be shot after the power snap, while the line is unrolling. If you use a double haul, release line for shooting as the line hand moves toward the rod hand in the "giving back" portion of the haul.

fly, I was unable to cast as far when I used false casts. My long cast of 161 feet was made "off the water," with a pickup with line shot on the backcast and the rest on the forward cast. Just one full cast.

If you use a triangle taper flyline, the forty-foot length of the tapered part (up through the eight and nine weights) gives you ten feet more of line (than a standard forward taper) *already in the air* when you pick it up. Perhaps this can eliminate a false cast for you. You will not have to shoot as much on the backcast and, in fact, you may not be able to overhang this design as far as the standard weight forward, but you'll cast just as far, perhaps more easily, because of the forty-foot length. (Tournament casters use fifty feet or more of working line weight.)

Two Full Casts

If you need more than one cast to reach your longest distances, you should be able to make the presentation in two full casts, *four strokes* over which you can spread the shooting of line and building of speed.

The sequence I use is this:

1. Take the line off the water with the predetermined overhang but do not shoot line on that backcast.

2. Make a false cast forward, shooting line.

3. Make a final backcast on which you shoot all the line that you and the rod can hold up . . . maximum loading.

4. Make the final cast, forward, shooting the rest of the line.

LONG CAST SEQUENCE

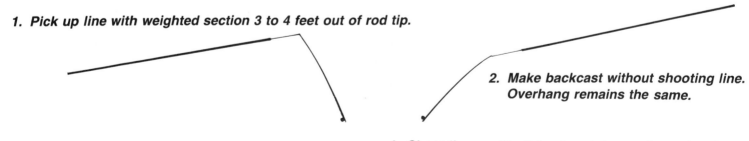

Overhang

1. Pick up line with weighted section 3 to 4 feet out of rod tip.

2. Make backcast without shooting line. Overhang remains the same.

4. Shoot line on (final) backcast for maximum loading.

3. Shoot line on the forward false cast.

5. (not shown) Shoot the remaining line on the presentation cast.

Line is shot on three moves out of a four-move sequence.

The reason I do not shoot on the backcast pickup is that when I need two casts instead of one, it is usually because I am changing direction and it is awkward to do both on the same backcast. I know that I can shoot all of the line I need in the remaining three moves and so my original pickup assures me that all is well and establishes the feeling of the base line weight to which I will add, from the coils in my hand.

Shooting Line on the Final Backcast

A full load on the fly rod gives it the perfect flex, making it possible to cast the maximum distance the rod was designed for (that is, in your hands), but the loading has to be done at the right time in the sequence . . . the final backcast. Shooting line on the final backcast is the key to ultimate distance on the following forward cast. You will increase the overhang of the line's weight from the rod tip, to a length that you would be unable to handle if you shot that much line on a forward cast and then had to throw backward and forward again before you could release it. *Maximum loading can happen only once in the cast.*

Slide Loading

The technique described as **slide loading**, under "Double Hauls," will take care of perfect timing and loading on this backcast. Your rod hand will end the drift move and start forward. At the same time, the line hand will be moving toward the first guide, still releasing line, bringing the hands toward each other and making the rod slide forward along the fly line until you can feel the maximum load of the fly line extending behind it. Then it is *power snap* and *haul* forward, and just watch it go and *go* and GO!

On the final backcast of a long cast sequence, in order to overhang the line weight more than a few feet, increase the acceleration of both the rod hand's stroke and the line hand's haul, to keep the line from falling too fast as it unrolls. It requires a maximum effort, compared to the other three moves.

SLIDE LOADING: Line is shot on the backcast

1. End of the loading move.   2. End of the power snap and the first haul.

4. The rod hand shows slight forward movement
as the line hand moves toward it, still releasing line.

3. The rod hand drifts as the line hand releases line for shooting.

5. Still feeding line, the line hand reaches its uppermost position as the rod hand has ended the loading move by sliding forward along the line—in time for the . . .

6. . . . not quite finished power snap and second haul.

(All photos in this sequence by Allan Wulff.)

The slide loading puts the rod hand in power-snap position before the backward extending line has time to drop. If you loaded the rod just as completely but your rod hand was farther back on its path, by the time you moved it forward—to its 90° on the hand/target line—the line weight overhanging from the rod tip might have dropped too far. The length of your rod and how deep you might be wading would be factors, as well as line speed.

Try slide loading to see what it can do for you.

This long-cast sequence takes only seven or eight seconds of time and your level of performance must be high through it all. You'll be taking the tackle to the edge of its performance limits. And the reward? A perfect cast that fulfills your distance casting potential.

six

VARIATIONS ON THE THEME

Curving Power Snaps

If you should be limited to straight-line casting for the rest of your fly fishing life, you'll get by but you may not have the answers to all of your questions. Rounded or circular casts have a definite place in solving problems in the field. You'll want to break some of the rules of straight-line casting and become master of both styles. Before I introduce you to the "oval" cast, made famous by Lee, let's break the rules on the power snap.

The heart of the circular cast, like the heart of the straight-line cast, is the power snap, but *this* power snap, in itself, must **curve**. It can be curved in an underhand or in an overhand fashion.

Try all that follows in an open-body stance, casting horizontally, to start, so that both back and forward casts will be completely visible. Use a short line for just a power-snap stroke.

An underhand curving power snap, on the forward cast, will "hover" your fly quite easily. The leader and fly will extend upward as the fly line unrolls, hovering the fly for an instant to give you an accurate, light-as-thistledown presentation.

129

Underhand Curves

1. Make straight-line power snaps, in both directions, noticing the form of the unrolling line. It will pass *over* the rod tip.

2. *Curve* the backcast power snap by "dipping" your forearm and hand to make a half circle. Keep the ends of the half circle on the same level. That will be your backcast and the line will pass *under* the rod tip. Make the forward power snap in a straight line. Practice this new move until you fully understand what is different about the path that the line follows and its form.

3. Make a straight-line backcast, then do a *curving half circle* on the forward power snap.

VARIATIONS ON THE THEME
CURVING POWER SNAPS
UNDERHAND CURVES

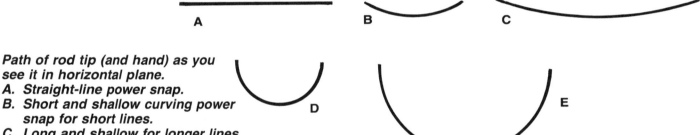

Path of rod tip (and hand) as you
see it in horizontal plane.
A. Straight-line power snap.
B. Short and shallow curving power
   snap for short lines.
C. Long and shallow for longer lines.
Add depth for slower line speed.
D. Short and deep.
E. Long and deep.

When you curve the path of your hand, you curve the path of the rod tip and, where the rod tip leads, the line will follow. An **underhand curve** will move the line under the rod tip and the path of the leader and fly will be slightly below the body of the line—until it is time for them to unroll. Then they will extend upward.

The curving power snap, on the backcast, combined with a straight-line forward cast, is the base of the circular casting style. Try it in different planes, tipping the half-circle curve to get a higher backcast.

COMBINATIONS

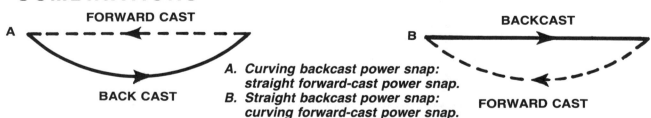

A. Curving backcast power snap:
   straight forward-cast power snap.
B. Straight backcast power snap:
   curving forward-cast power snap.

Overhand Curves

The **overhand curve** or **roll** is usually used on the forward cast after either a straight-line or curving backcast. Instead of making a downward dipping half circle, which moves your line under the rod tip, roll or rotate your hand and arm "overhand" in the half circle, making the fly line move well *above* the rod tip. You can do a 180° move, but a quarter circle roll of 90° will make the line unroll higher. Whether the line unrolls completely before it touches the water or hits the water halfway will be determined by how much roll you use (from 90° to 180°) and the stroke length, acceleration, and power of the cast. Experiment to find out.

OVERHAND ROLL

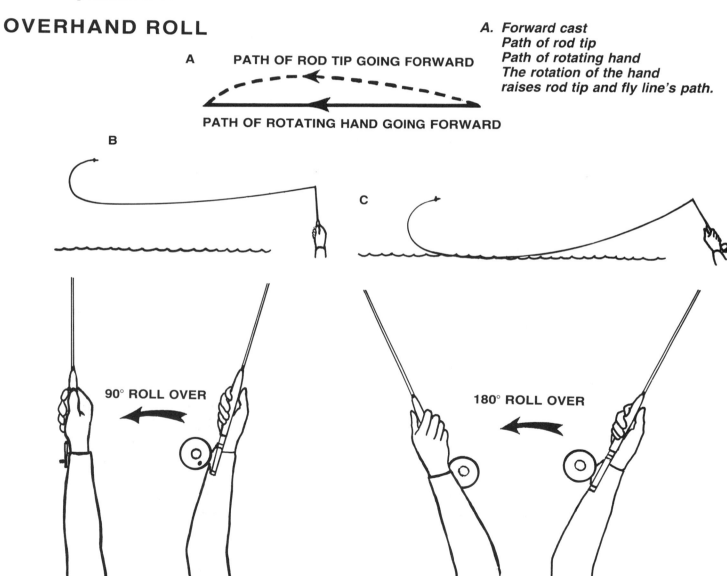

A   PATH OF ROD TIP GOING FORWARD

PATH OF ROTATING HAND GOING FORWARD

A. Forward cast
   Path of rod tip
   Path of rotating hand
   The rotation of the hand
   raises rod tip and fly line's path.

B

C

90° ROLL OVER

180° ROLL OVER

B. Start is palm up.
   Power snap is 90° roll-over.
   Line will unroll above the water.

C. With 180° roll-over, line will
   land before it is unrolled.

These underhand and overhand curving power snaps are the base of the oval cast (in an off-vertical plane), air rolls (shortened backcast technique), and slack leader presentation casts. You will probably think of additional uses as they become a part of your inventory of techniques.

Circular Casts: The Oval

In casting literature, there is reference to the "Belgian" cast as being circular. In 1948 I met Belgium's finest distance caster, Albert Godart, at the French National casting tournament. I believe that he was a proponent of this style but it was a missed opportunity. I never saw Godart cast. I have film of other Belgian casters and they used the straight-line technique.

The circular cast, in the form of an **oval**, hit me with a bang in 1967. Lee was famous for fishing with six-foot rods and had developed circular casting to a fine art with his oval, although he knew nothing of the Belgian circular cast. Both short rods and the oval were completely foreign to me, but I welcomed the lighter weight of his wedding gift, a Lee Wulff Ultimate bamboo rod. It was six feet long, weighed less than two ounces, and was made by Farlow in England. I was sure that I could fish it with my straight-line casting style. Lee suggested I might need longer strokes and greater line speed with the short rod and I responded by rocking my body back and forth, and moving my casting arm as fast as I could. It was hard work but I thought I was doing all right until I looked up or downstream at Lee. He was making beautiful, lazy-looking oval-shaped casts with seemingly little effort. He swept the line in low on the backcast then raised his arm and made a vertical-plane straight-line forward cast. After the second day of hard fishing I committed myself to learning the oval. Not able to analyze the backcast as being based on a curving power snap, at that time, I just said the word "Back" to myself and used the mental image of setting up for a roll cast with speed added to it, to keep my programmed rod hand from moving *up* on the backcast as it had, with long rods, for the previous thirty years. It took two days to train my muscles so that I could stop saying "Back!" on every cast and I came to love the oval.

Although Lee's films and writings seem to wed the oval technique to short rods, the style is valuable with any length rod and should be a part of your repertoire for handling heavy flies, for fishing with limited backcast space, and, because the backcast never crosses its own path (as does the figure-eight form of straight-line casting), the oval may help you to eliminate wind knots or tailing loops.

The oval uses an underhand curving power snap on the backcast and a straight-line power snap on the forward cast. As you do the loading move on the backcast, be sure to keep it straight. Just as the loading move positions the rod shaft 90° on the hand/target line before the power snap, in straight-line casting this backcast loading move must lift the line clear of the water to position the rod shaft for the curving power snap. There will be a change of direction in the rod's path, between the loading move and the power snap, of roughly 90°. When you false cast with the oval there will be a 90° outward rotation of your hand and forearm at the beginning of each backcast.

The drift move is an integral part of the oval, connecting the widely separated paths of the backcast and forward cast. As the arm repositions the rod upward for a vertical forward cast, the end of the line, the leader, and the fly line up behind the rod like a puppy-dog's tail, to be 180° from the projected path of the forward cast. The forward cast is a standard, basic-discipline cast, with a straight-line power snap.

The Mechanics

Use an open-body stance and, in the early stages of learning, watch your backcast. Angle the backcast off-vertical. The forward cast can be made in the same plane or changed to vertical. Try it, first, by changing to vertical.

1. Do a loading move to lift the line from the water with the rod angled slightly outward.

2. Do a curving power snap, tipping the curve to end a little higher than it began.

3. Drift upward to reposition for the vertical forward cast.

4. Do a loading move and power snap in a straight line to the target.

On the backcast the height of the line's path above the water can be adjusted by the *depth of the curve* and the *angle of the tipping* of the power snap's half-circle form. You can adjust stroke length, power, and timing as you are used to doing, and coordinate single and double hauls exactly the same with this form of cast as with the straight-line cast.

There is something about the mental image of an oval that makes one move follow another very easily. You'll like the *constant pressure* feeling of completeness with this circular form of casting.

THE OVAL

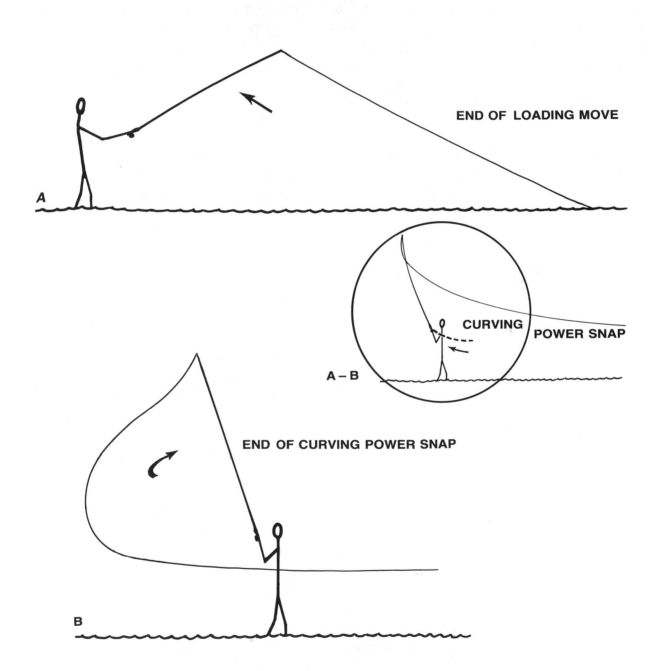

END OF LOADING MOVE

CURVING POWER SNAP

A – B

END OF CURVING POWER SNAP

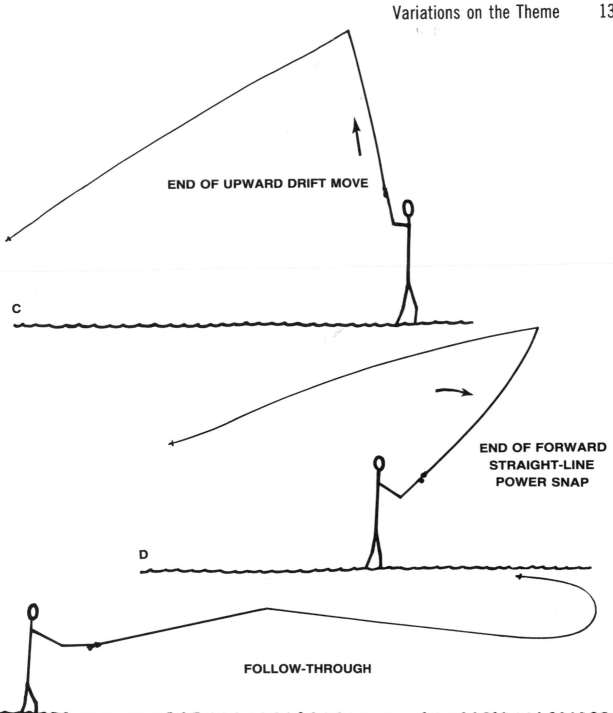

END OF UPWARD DRIFT MOVE

C

**END OF FORWARD
STRAIGHT-LINE
POWER SNAP**

D

FOLLOW-THROUGH

E

Aerodynamically, the oval's rounded backcast is susceptible to more air resistance than a straight-line stroke. You won't be able to generate quite as much line speed as you would with a straight-line cast. You can make up for this, when you need to, by adding a little *length* to the forward stroke to get the line speed up to par. The backcast drift move is the key, extending the arm both backward and upward as you reposition for the forward stroke. Be sure you do not drift forward or you will cut down on your potential stroke length.

Heavy Flies

The oval is an excellent technique for casting heavier flies. With straight-line casting, the turning around of a heavy fly requires perfect timing because the loop is relatively narrow on the backcast and the fly's direction must be reversed through a short space. With the oval, the paths of the leader and fly, and the main body of the line, are well separated, allowing lots of room for the turning around. Try it with heavier flies.

Short Rods

The oval is particularly well suited for casting long lines on short rods. You already know that as the line lengthens, in a straight-line backcast, the trajectory flattens and the line falls below the rod tip as it unrolls. If you are wading deeply and using a short rod, you can hardly manage such a maneuver because there is so little space between the unrolling line and the water. With the oval, the body of the line unrolls roughly parallel to the water, and the path of the leader and fly *lifts upward* at the end of it. The drift move then raises the rod tip and the line near it, once more lining everything up for the forward stroke.

Whenever I have been fishing for Atlantic salmon, no matter what the length of my rod, the oval has saved my flies from being emasculated on rocky shores behind me. The deeper I am in the water, the higher I tip my curving power snap to make the leader and fly *lift* at the end of the backcast. Another advantage is that the oval need not take up quite as much room as a fully extended straight-line cast and so I am less likely to get wind knots from starting the forward cast too early, by being worried about hitting rocks.

The more I use the oval, the easier it is to understand how the form must have developed for Lee, who was stimulated to perfect his casting style on the stream, where backcast room is often a problem.

seven

FISHING ADAPTATIONS

The Full Spectrum: Changing Direction

Backhand Casting

For a right-handed caster, any plane to the left of vertical in the 180° spectrum is **backhanded**. My first attempts looked like the illustration. I brought my hand back to my chest with the elbow low. On longer casts, I kept my body upright and brought my rod hand over my left shoulder. The positions were uncomfortable and it was difficult to be accurate. I looked and felt as if I were choking myself.

For the planes just to the left of center, no dramatic change of arm position is necessary. Center your arm on your body and tilt the rod to the left by tilting the forearm and hand (the elbow will move outward and upward). A two-inch tilt of the hand will be magnified through the rod to become perhaps 30° to the left of center for the path of the rod's tip and the line. This angle is effective if wind is blowing from your casting side.

As you use lower backhand planes, perhaps to present the fly under overhanging branches, both the arm and body positions should be altered to accommodate the unusual angles. *Lift your elbow* higher as the rod plane lowers and lean sideward from the waist, bringing the rod hand above eye level. Eye, hand, and target can be lined up in a stance that is both comfortable and productive of accurate casts.

137

BACKHAND CASTING

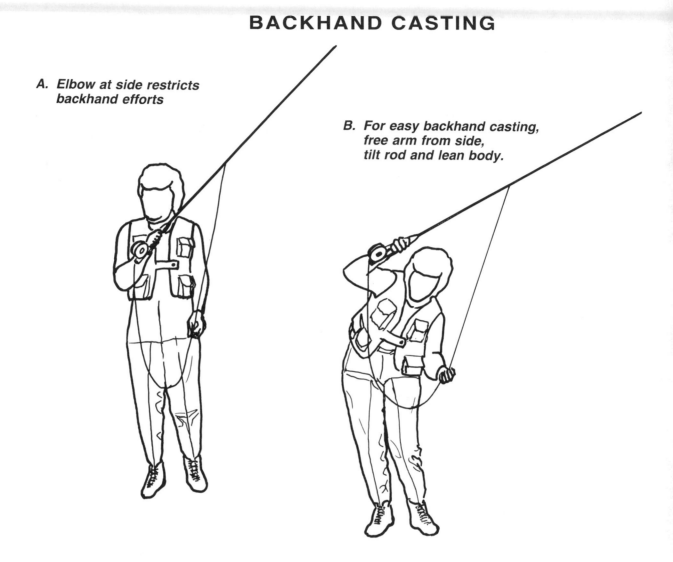

A. Elbow at side restricts backhand efforts

B. For easy backhand casting, free arm from side, tilt rod and lean body.

Double hauling could be necessary on longer backhand casts. Because the position of body and arm restricts the move somewhat, lean back and make your backcast on an inclined path, upward, so that your hauling hand can move forward, opposite the rod hand. On the forward cast, the backward haul will be made in the usual way.

Changing Direction with no Backcast Limitations

Whenever you present a fly in moving water you must change direction between the pickup and the presentation. The angle of change can vary from a few degrees to almost 180°.

STANDARD FISHING PATTERNS
REQUIRING CHANGE OF DIRECTION

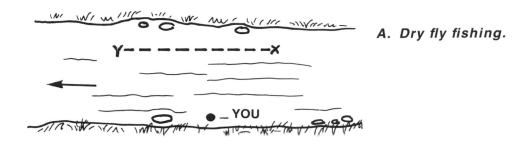

A. Dry fly fishing.

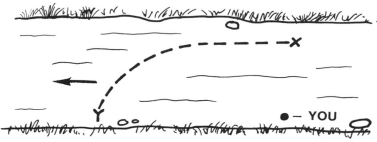

B.
Unweighted nymph fishing.

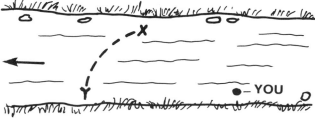

C.
Wet fly, streamer, and nymph fishing.

Fly travels from X to Y and requires
change of direction between presentations.

False Casting

The easiest way to change direction is to false cast, keeping your feet where they are but rotating your body a little on each cast, until you are lined up with the new target area. The backcast angle is changed a little at a time, the ideal way to keep out of trouble.

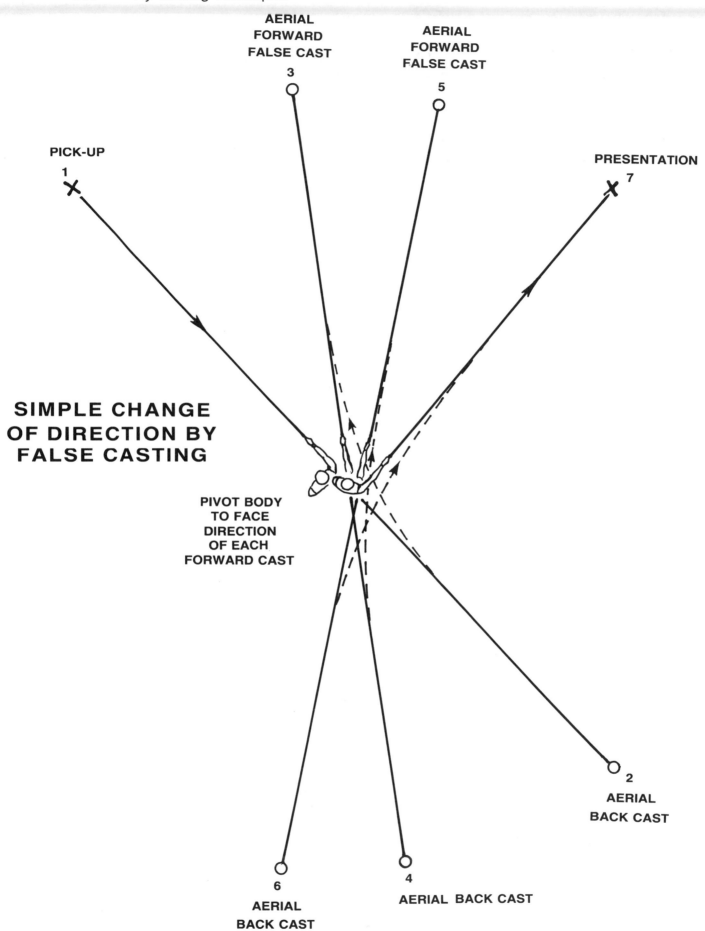

AERIAL
FORWARD
FALSE CAST
3

AERIAL
FORWARD
FALSE CAST
5

PICK-UP
1

PRESENTATION
7

SIMPLE CHANGE
OF DIRECTION BY
FALSE CASTING

PIVOT BODY
TO FACE
DIRECTION
OF EACH
FORWARD CAST

2
AERIAL
BACK CAST

6
AERIAL
BACK CAST

4
AERIAL BACK CAST

Roll Pick-up

If you have slack in your line when you are ready to make the pickup, you can get into the false casting with an *aerial version of the roll cast* to remove the slack.

Try this technique the first time, without changing direction.

1. Start in the roll cast position.

2. Roll the line forward, *above* the water by four to five feet, instead of *on* the water, to make it a false cast.

3. Make an aerial backcast.

4. Present the fly.

CHANGING DIRECTION WITH ROLL PICK-UP

1. Start in backhand roll-cast position.
2. Aerial forward cast, turning upper body upstream.
3. Aerial backcast (on right side),
   turning body farther.
4. Presentation cast.

If you decide to use this technique to change direction, the stream's flow will determine whether you'll begin backhanded or forehanded. Pretend the stream is flowing to your right, and you are right-handed. At the end of your fished-out cast, the line can be at an angle to the current or directly downstream with the current. Either way, you'll begin with a forehand roll cast, with the rod hand starting in front of your right shoulder, body and rod positioned in anticipation of the upstream direction of the next presentation cast.

1. Make the forward cast into the air well above the water and aimed upstream of where you started from.

2. Make the backcast while you turn your body a bit more upstream.

3. Make the presentation cast.

If the stream were flowing to your left, you would start with a backhand roll off the left shoulder, into the air, and then, as your upper body swung upstream, you could make the aerial backcast centered on your body or off your right shoulder. Only the beginning roll would be backhanded.

This **roll pickup** technique will be one you'll use whenever you have slack, changing direction or not. Use a single haul with it when the length of your line makes it necessary, to keep from "ticking" the water between the forward roll and the aerial backcast.

Changing Direction Without False Casting

The more intense we become as fly fishermen, the less time we want to spend with the fly in the air, and we try to make our changes of direction without false casting. If a false cast is necessary we limit it to one.

The literal change of direction begins with the pickup. On the backcast, you'll send the fly to a point that is roughly opposite the projected path of the next forward cast, in order to help *bridge the angle of change* you will effect when you reposition your rod hand to line up with the new target. The change is made with both the angle of the backcast and the repositioning of the rod hand (drift). You must think it out ahead of time, make a mental diagram, and follow it.

To solve change of direction problems, use alone or in combination, these techniques:

Straight and curving power snaps
Tilted rod angles—backhand and forehand
Rotation of the forearm and hand, or the whole arm
Movement of the arm from the shoulder, up, down, and sideward
Body motion—shifting your weight backward or forward or side to side
  and/or rotation of the body with the feet kept still

For easy reference, the illustration shows the full 180° casting spectrum as a clockface. The planes from 12 to 3 are forehand planes and from 12 to 9 they are backhand planes. Changes of direction often require a combination of forehand and backhand strokes.

The *size* of your angle of change—from where your line is to where you want it to go (in addition to the length of your line)—will determine the pattern through which you might move your rod. Here are some examples.

ANGLE OF CHANGE

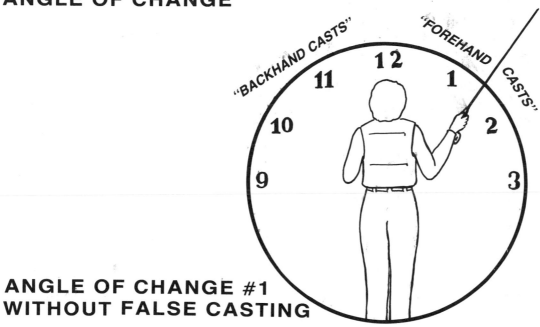

ANGLE OF CHANGE #1
WITHOUT FALSE CASTING

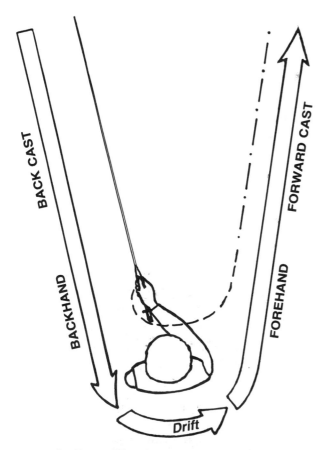

A. Reposition rod hand sideward, from backhand to forehand, during drift time.

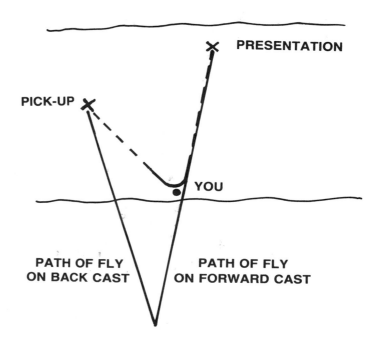

B. On backcast, send fly to a point central between where it was and where it will go next.

PICK-UP

PRESENTATION

YOU

PATH OF FLY ON BACK CAST

PATH OF FLY ON FORWARD CAST

Angle of change #1

Up to 90° (or perhaps more with short lines) the change can be accomplished with a form that resembles the letter "V". The fly, on the backcast, is sent to a point central between where the line was and where it will go.

Understand how this works. To change the path of the flyline, your rod hand will move to its new position (through arm or body motion) during drift time, taking with it the line that is closest to the rod tip. The angle of change at the far end of the line must necessarily *be less* than at the rod tip.

Try these changes:

Backcast	Forward Cast	Backcast	Forward Cast
12	1	11	1
1	3	10	1
2	12	10	11

When the angle of change gets so large that the path of the backcast plus the drift move cannot bridge it, the pattern must change. Long lines on big water can be the reason.

Angle of Change #2

To change direction, say 90°, you'll go the long way around to move the rod through 270° of change. The backcast and forward cast will be straight-line casts, but the rod hand's total move with drift is semicircular and your body will lean from the waist to help. Try these, moving the rod through the large arc:

Backcast	Forward Cast	and in the other direction	
9	2		
11	3		
		2	10
		3	11

The first time I was ever aware of a change of direction problem with this kind of solution was on New Brunswick's Upsalquitch River. On one of its lovely salmon pools, I found myself wading as deep as I could, right at the edge of the current, which was running to my left. I had to make my longest-possible casts to reach the other side of the current and was using an eight-foot rod. The angle of presentation across the current was nearly 70° from where the line had to be picked up, directly below me.

If I had had to make the cast only once or twice, I would have false cast my way to the 70° change, but because I had to make, perhaps, two dozen casts in this pool, it was worth working out a two-move (one full cast) change.

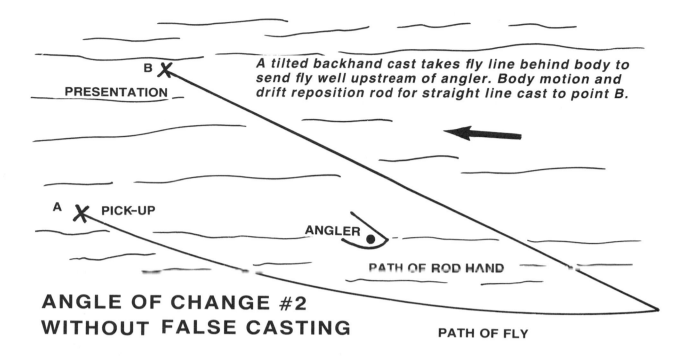

B X
PRESENTATION

A tilted backhand cast takes fly line behind body to send fly well upstream of angler. Body motion and drift reposition rod for straight line cast to point B.

A X PICK-UP

ANGLER

PATH OF ROD HAND

ANGLE OF CHANGE #2
WITHOUT FALSE CASTING

PATH OF FLY

Because the line was directly downstream to my left, and I am right-handed, the pickup had to be backhanded.

1. Leaning my upper body in the downstream direction and with my casting arm well extended, rod tip low,

2. I picked up the line in a *tilted backhand* cast to take the rod tip and line behind my body, but above my head, and to send the fly to a predetermined spot upstream, which was as close as possible to being directly opposite the presentation area. My rod hand was above, but not behind my head. The tilt of the rod lessened the angle the rod would have to bridge in the drift move.

3. To follow the path of the unrolling line, I drifted my arm and the rod, and leaned my body in the upstream direction, then lowered the rod angle to keep the rod tip even with the line as it lowered in the air.

4. The presentation started at just about shoulder level and the cast was made quartering across and downstream.

I used the double haul on the backhand backcast and shot line on both the pickup and the presentation. Double hauling backhanded requires a leaning body to ease its potential awkwardness as you haul forward. The leaning of the body, from facing downstream to upstream, then to cross stream, made the whole 290° change work smoothly. The pattern worked, saving false casting time, and now I use it regularly, mentally referring to it as my ''Upsalquitch Pickup.''

Angle of Change #3 (Not shown)

The oval, with its curving power snap, is a good change-of-direction technique if the angle of change is not too large and is from left to right for a right-handed caster. Use the loading move to position the rod for the coming change and follow with the curving power snap, drifting to a new rod-hand position for the forward cast.

Angle of Change #4

This pattern is an open-ended figure eight with a curving power snap on the backcast. It moves the rod tip and the line through a long path to make a relatively short angle of change, this time in front of the body. It will be limited in its use by the length of the line.

Use this technique in a situation like this: The stream is moving to your left and the line must be picked up from directly downstream and presented across the stream in a 45° to 90° direction change. You'll use a horizontal pickup and a vertical presentation.

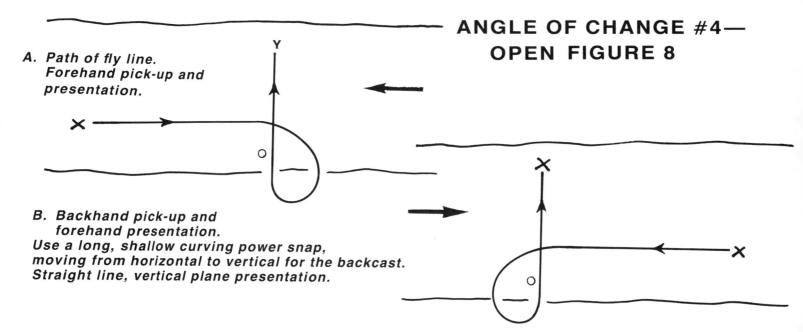

ANGLE OF CHANGE #4— OPEN FIGURE 8

A. *Path of fly line. Forehand pick-up and presentation.*

B. *Backhand pick-up and forehand presentation. Use a long, shallow curving power snap, moving from horizontal to vertical for the backcast. Straight line, vertical plane presentation.*

1. Lift the line from the water, beginning the 90° rotation of your arm in preparation for the power snap.

2. Use a curving power snap *tipped* to end the rod hand above eye level on the right side of your head.

3. *Drift* to line up with the target area.

4. Make a straight-line presentation.

The vertical stroke crosses the path of the earlier horizontal stroke. I use this technique often and consider it a variation of the oval.

If the direction of the current is reversed, (moving to your right), follow the same open-ended figure-eight form with a backhand pickup. The curving power snap will end above eye level, *left* of your head. You'll *drift* to line up with the target and present the fly.

Limited Backcast Space

Limited backcast conditions are all too common on good fishing water. But with a little thought you can often use the available space, even if it is not exactly where you want it to be. The angle at which you stand in a stream, by a degree or two, can often give you a good backcast. You can use the roll cast or (a new technique) the *air roll*. When there is open space down the middle of the stream and none at the sides, you can cast parallel to the bank and then present at 45° across the stream to the target. There are many possible solutions from which to choose, although only one may work with any particular problem.

The Air Roll

The **air roll** was developed by Lee as a refinement of the oval cast. With it you can extend the line fully behind you or extend it to any lesser degree according to the backcast room available and your control. The minimum extension would be comparable to the amount of line used in a standard roll cast.

The cast, at full extension is an oval. It consists of a curving power snap on the backcast and a straight-line forward cast, with drift connecting the two. The control for reducing the backcast extension is in the *depth* of the curving power snap and the *speed* of the backcast. The shorter you want the backcast extension to be, the deeper the curve you'll make and the slower the line speed should be.

A slow-moving backcast lets you feel the weight of the line, by which you'll judge how far you will let it extend behind you. *Slow line speed, curving power snap, drift upward*—then, because of the low position of the end of the line and the long path it must follow before it goes over the rod tip, make the forward stroke with a fairly *wide loop*. Make the forward stroke a long one

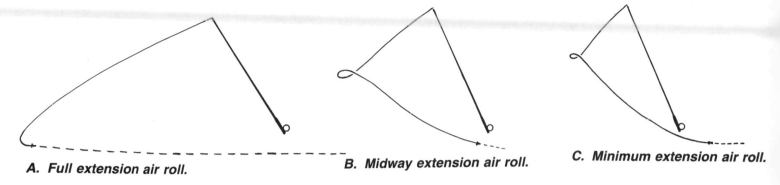

A. Full extension air roll.

B. Midway extension air roll.

C. Minimum extension air roll.

AIR ROLLS IN LIMITED BACKCAST SPACE

to provide the time and space in which to build a smooth acceleration. No part of the mechanics should be done too suddenly.

Air rolls require quite a bit of practice but, if you use an open body stance to watch the backward extension, you'll be surprised at how quickly you'll catch on. It is when you can't watch the backcast that the practice time pays off.

Lee is a master of slow backcasts from years of using them in tight quarters. One of my favorite mental pictures of him was taken on Montana's Gallatin River. He was sitting on a rock, about six feet back from the river's edge, casting his Scott Power Ply 6'10" graphite rod, for a #7 line, with about 20 feet of room behind him, as I came around the bend of the river. The fish were 50 to 55 feet across the river against the far bank and couldn't be reached from any other spot. I had tried. Lee was air-rolling beautiful casts, consistently reaching the holding water. The fadeout of the picture is of a 16-inch brown being released, a victim of the technique.

You'll cast parallel to the shore on these.

Figure 1: You wish to present to point A.

NO BACKCAST ROOM: PRESENTATION ACROSS THE STREAM

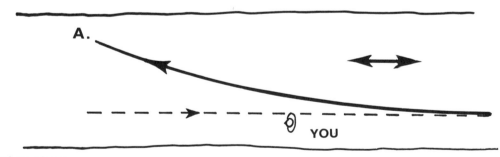

1A. Cast parallel to shore.
Turn upper body toward target for presentation.

Because your casting arm is on the river side, you can cast parallel to the shore and then turn your body toward the target area on the final backcast's drift time to present the fly. A long rod will be helpful.

Figure 2: You wish to present to point B.

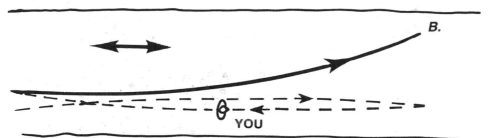

**1B. Cast parallel to shore.
Center backcast on body and tilt
forward cast outward for elliptical path.**

You can use a backhand cast to make this presentation and, on the last backcast, during drift time, turn your body to line up with the target. This is fairly easy with short lines.

If I am casting a long line and need to double haul, I find it awkward on two backhand strokes, so I use a combination of forehand *and* backhand strokes, making the form of the cast elliptical. (Shown.)

Your casting arm will be against the shore.

1. Make the backcast exactly vertical, between your eyes, ending the stroke with your rod hand above your head. (You may have to lean back from the waist.)

2. Drift to the left (toward the opposite shore) tilting the rod in that direction to

3. Make the forward false casts backhanded (just left of center).

The full cast is a narrow ellipse, with the backcast centered on your head and the forward cast tilted to the left to keep the line and your fly's path away from the shore. During the last backcast's drift time, turn your upper body toward the target area and make a forehand presentation, from the head-centered position.

Shallow Semicircular One Stroke Cast

The fly is below you in a stream and there is a little room between your body and an overgrown bank behind you.

    1. On the loading move, you'll break the rule of lifting the line only to the line/leader knot. Instead, lift the line, leader, and fly slowly and smoothly from the water, starting a shallow curving path behind your body.

    2. When the rod shaft is roughly 90° from where you want it to go on the hand/target line, rotate the forearm and hand in the direction of the target and finish the cast with a power snap and follow-through.

    If the cast is to be made from left of your body to the right, you'll begin backhanded and end forehanded. If the cast is right to left, you'll begin forehanded and end backhanded.

SHALLOW SEMI-CIRCULAR ONE- STROKE CAST

A. Pivot upper body.

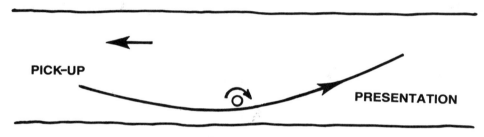

B. Rotate forearm/hand between loading move and power snap.

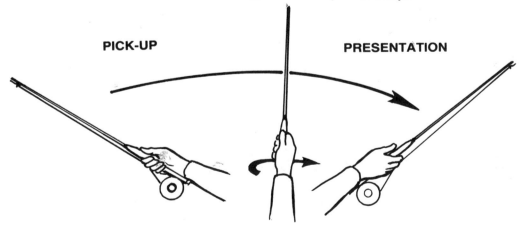

Reverse Casting: Facing The Backcast Area

Fish may grow to be trophy size and seem impervious to being caught because they have found a holding place that is "unreachable" to most anglers. A hypothetical place might be opposite a great fully-branched tree just waiting to catch your backcast.

You come to such a place, read the water as being perfect for such a fish, and look carefully at the big tree for a tunnel of space into which to put your backcast. There is one where part of a branch has broken off, but the odds are near zero if you are not watching the tunnel as you make the effort. The solution is *two forward casts*. Face the tree. Position your feet so that you can pivot between the strokes. Use an open body stance, with the foot on your casting side nearest the streambank. Put a forward cast into the tunnel of space and, during drift time, reverse your position to make a second forward cast to the target water. It often takes only one good presentation to fool a fish. Make the first one perfect.

REVERSE CASTING

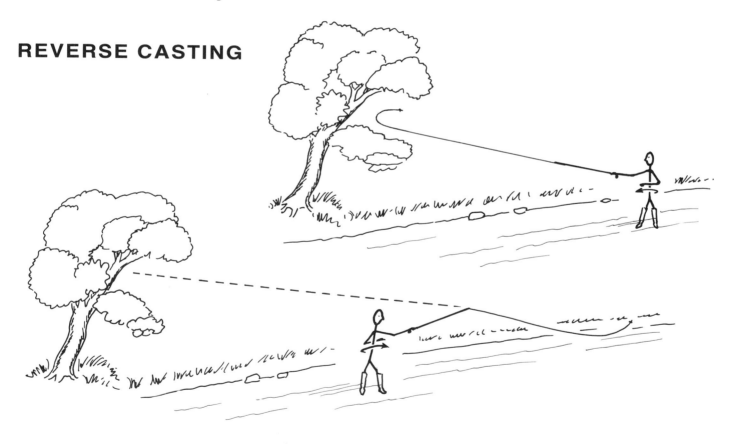

Spread feet apart, sideward to presentation area.
Rotate upper body to face backcast area
and make forward cast into space available. During drift time,
rotate upper body to face target and make presentation.

Pick-ups

A **pick-up** is line taken off the water. If there are circumstances that keep you from just picking it up straight, such as too much slack line, one or more obstacles in the path of the line, leader, or fly as it would come off the water, or, perhaps, the backcast area is too high for a standard backcast pick-up, one of these techniques may help. They are based on the truism that where the rod tip leads, the line will follow.

The previously-covered roll pick-up is the most commonly used technique to get rid of slack line or to roll line from a "messy" pile on the water.

Horizontal Waves

Move the rod from side to side as you raise it slowly. This could be used to pick line up from among obstacles or grasses. The length of the line will determine how wide the strokes must be and how fast you'll lift the rod. When you get to the line/leader connection or the fly, power snap. The stroking/waving is the loading move.

HORIZONTAL WAVES

Vertical Humps

This might be used with a fairly high bank behind you. The pattern is to make humps in the line, by vertical moves, as the rod is moved gradually from an *extended* arm's length in front of you to a *bent* arm's length in front of you, before the power snap. The rod moves both up and down and back toward

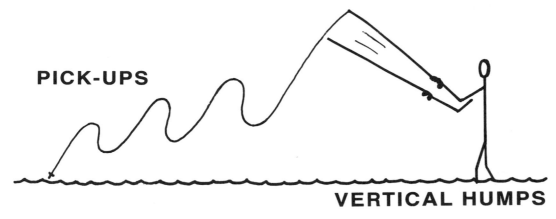

PICK-UPS

VERTICAL HUMPS

you. There is a rhythm of force and relaxation to it. Lift upward with a little force, drift down without it, lift again with force, drift down without it, all the while moving the rod back toward your body. When all of the line is in the air and you have built some acceleration, lift with a real power snap. It will send the line almost vertically off your rod tip, so it will only be useful with a fairly short line.

Loop Pick-up

I use this to take a dry fly off the water at a steeper than normal angle if I need to avoid an obstruction or to avoid dragging a dry fly through heavy water that might affect its floatability. Start with the rod tip low.

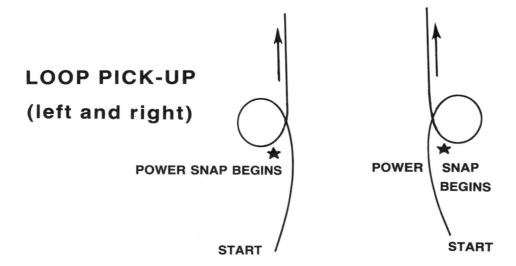

LOOP PICK-UP

(left and right)

POWER SNAP BEGINS

POWER SNAP BEGINS

START

START

    1. Flip the rod tip toward the fly, much like an underhand spinning or plug cast. The tip goes down then up.

    2. Keep on going *up* and form a circular loop to the left or right of the vertical path to lift line and leader, leaving fly in the water.

    3. Power snap the fly out of the water.

Your arm extends on the initial flip and stays extended until you know the fly can be backcast safely after the circular loop is formed. The loading move would last through the forming of the loop and then you lift with the power snap from there, pulling the forearm back and up.

Only certain of these techniques will fit your personal style of fishing. The rest may not be worth your trouble. If you do the ones that seem "far out" just as exercises, you will have a deeper understanding of the character and interaction of your rod and fly line, which might help you solve problems.

Pick-up to Change Flies

Changing flies takes away from fishing time. But it may be worth it, and you won't know until you've made the change. To cut down on the time it takes, you can make an uncompleted backcast and "catch the fly" in your hand. Every intense fisherman eventually works this out.

The object is to catch the leader in your line hand, as it passes you on a slow backward journey. To make the leader come to your hand, angle your casting arm to tilt the rod, lining up the tip with your left shoulder.

1. Lift the line in a loading move, followed by

2. a slow power snap, with your hand above eye level.

The line should be easily seen as it comes toward you (it will be higher at the rod tip and lower at the end you'll catch) to allow you to judge the taking spot. The leader and fly will be *climbing* on their path by the time they get to your hand.

3. Catch the leader and curl your fingers around it so that the thumb and forefinger stop its motion.

Turn your attention to the rest of the line. The main body has continued on, behind you, and will land upstream and drift down to tangle in your legs unless you move quickly.

4a. Make a forward (roll) cast to put that loop of line downstream where the current will keep it ready for your eventual return to fishing.

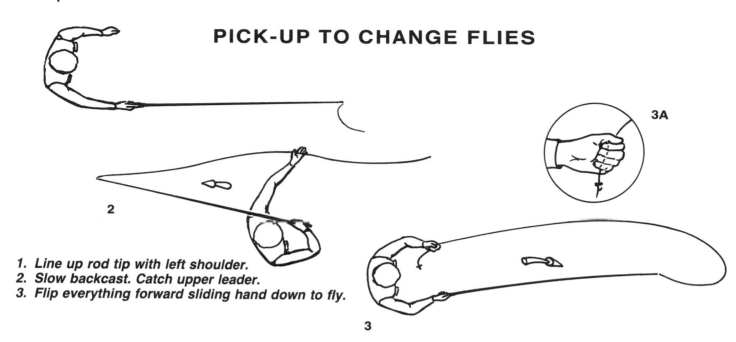

PICK-UP TO CHANGE FLIES

1. Line up rod tip with left shoulder.
2. Slow backcast. Catch upper leader.
3. Flip everything forward sliding hand down to fly.

4b. Your lightly clenched hand slides down the leader to the fly. (The leader and fly moved on up in response to the roll cast forward).

5. Clamp your hand before it gets to the hook.

You'll become familiar with the feeling of the tapered leader diminishing in size, to develop a reflexive clamping at the right instant. I have never hooked myself doing this pick-up but I have lost my hold on the small-diametered leader, by making the forward roll too sharply.

When you have changed flies (or taken out a wind knot), you can roll cast the fly out of your hand and false cast your way back to fishing territory, pleased with your shortcut. This technique is easier to do with thirty feet of line than with fifteen feet, because of the relatively greater air resistance. It will be impossible to do if your weight-forward or triangle-taper weighted line section is more than just out of the rod tip.

Presentation Casts

Presentation is the artful way your fly comes within the view of the fish. It is the placement, form, and sequence of the line, leader, and fly as they land on the water and can include any movement you may impart to the fly as it nears the fish.

A hangover myth, part of the fly casting mystique, is that the fly *must* land first, to fool fish. Many anglers think they are second class fishermen because they can't always make that happen. Others question the need to do so in all circumstances, and these anglers are right. Having the fly land first is a sometimes thing.

Leader design, and fly size, weight, and design, are the factors that determine, along with the cast, in which sequence the line, leader, and fly will land. The fly can land first, or everything can land at once, or the leader and fly can land last, with precise control being easier on short casts than on very long ones.

Unrolling the Line Above the Water

The basic discipline I've presented instructs you to unroll the line, leader, and fly above the water so that they all land at once. Actually, the *line* lands all at once. The design of your leader and the weight of your fly will determine how and when they land. If you cast a small, dry fly on a long, tapered leader with a long fine tippet, the end of the tippet and the fly will land last. If you are casting a wet fly with a relatively short, progressively tapered leader, they may all land at once, or the line will land an instant before the fly, because of its weight. It doesn't matter, as long as you understand that it is the way the line unrolls (which you control) through your cast and it is the design of the leader and the weight and fluffiness of the fly that determine in which sequence they will land.

In the hovering technique the line unrolls above the water and, if the line is a short one, you can angle the unrolling line to have the fly land first. As the line lengthens and the angle of the cast lessens, you can still hover the fly, but when you drop it, the line, leader and fly will all touch down at about the same instant.

PRESENTATIONS

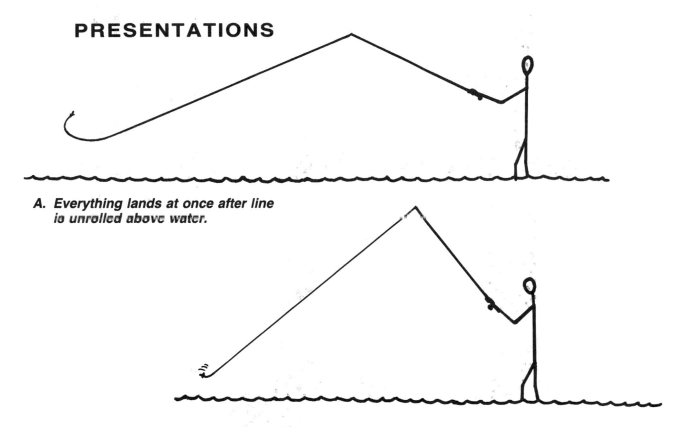

A. Everything lands at once after line is unrolled above water.

B. Fly lands first—hovering technique for short lines.

Line Unrolls on the Water

This technique changes the sequence. The line lands on the water, at about its middle, and then unrolls on the water from there, with the leader and fly definitely landing last. This is the way you probably cast naturally, before taking instruction to "make a straight-line stroke along a hand/target line with a short turnover arc, *to* the target."

To put the line on the water at about its middle, you'll need to use a wide loop and lower the rod as you execute the power snap. Another way

C. Line lands first, fly lands last.

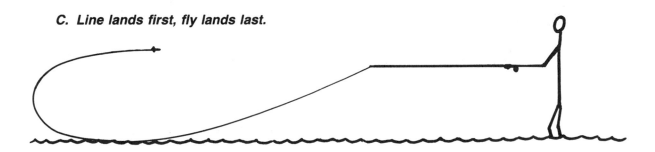

to say it is that the path of your hand will drop below the hand/target line, *after* the loading move. Wide loops, you will remember, are made by starting the turnover arc at the same time you begin the forward stroke.

This is a good technique for use with heavier flies, such as streamers or bass bugs.

Overhangs

The lovely places in which trout choose to lie often pose a challenge to the angler. Under overhanging bushes is one such place.

If the bush overhangs from your left, use a forehand horizontal cast. The leader and fly, unrolling parallel to the water, are less likely to hit the overhang than they would on a vertical plane cast.

Use an open-body stance in which your feet are lined up with the target. Rotate your hand and forearm 90° to a palm-up position in preparation for the coming power snap. Angle the backcast to end six inches, or so, above horizontal, to give the fly line room in which to unroll above the water, then drift the rod down to line up the tip with the target area (fly line following suit). Present with a straight-line cast. Good line speed should keep the unrolling line from touching the water.

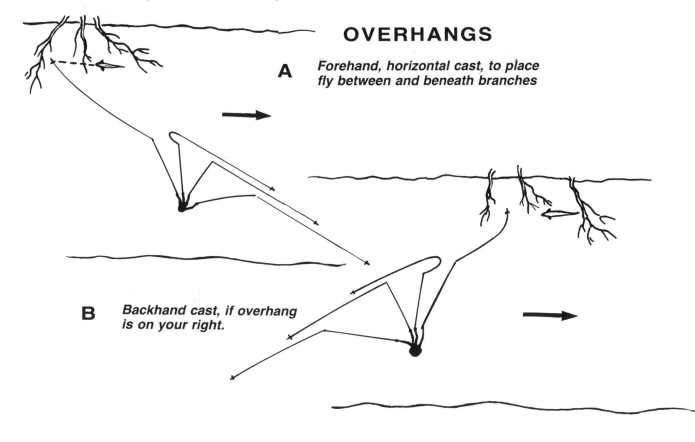

OVERHANGS

A *Forehand, horizontal cast, to place fly between and beneath branches*

B *Backhand cast, if overhang is on your right.*

C   *Use of curving power snap
on backcast.*

BACKHAND: If the overhang comes from the right, make a backhand cast close to horizontal, leaning to your left, with the rod hand above eye level.

I use a rounded backhand cast to solve this problem, with a use of the curving power snap that may yet be new to you. This time it is an *overhand* curving power snap on the backcast, made in a different plane from its use in the oval.

1. Start with the rod hand to the right of center on your body.

2. Do a short loading move in preparation for the power snap.

3. Make an overhand backward curving power snap that ends above eye level to the left of your head, having put the backcast off your left shoulder. This path, for the unrolling line, will be as close as you can make it to the optimum 180° from the projected path of the forward cast which is under the overhang.

4. Drift the rod hand downward a few inches, to line up with the target, for the forward cast.

5. Present the cast backhanded.

Your palm will be facing downward at the end of the forward cast. If you must make more than one cast (to false cast), at the end of the forward cast rotate your hand and forearm 90° to the right to begin the next backcast. A total rotation of 360° will occur from the beginning of one cast to the beginning of the next cast.

The Roll Cast

The roll cast will get you under overhangs if you adjust it a little. Tilt the rod to one side or the other so that the line unrolls in an off-vertical plane and is not as likely to collide with the overhang. Extend a little more length than you will need. Cut the forward stroke short by making it at a steeper angle than will take it to the target. (Aim below, or short of the target.) The power, unused to unroll the line, will put slack in the leader, showing as "squiggles" in the way it lies on the water. It sort of sneaks under the overhang.

Roll Cast #2

A *horizontal* roll cast can be effective if, on the forward stroke, the line is unrolled just above the water. The danger is that the fly will ride higher than the line and collide with the overhang. It is worth developing.

Slack Leader Presentations

Slack in the leader, near the fly, helps to ensure a long, drag-free float and is normally a better technique than putting slack in the fly line. One way to get effective slack is to use a relatively long leader and tippet and make the cast to let the line land first. You can refine it by making the leader pile on itself. This technique is called by many names, among them "puddle," "pile," or, as Lee calls it, "the *plop* cast." New students of fly casting call it "my normal cast" because the leader doesn't straighten out.

Technique #1—The Plop Cast

Determine your hand/target line. Using a fairly wide loop, angle the path of your hand to be below the target instead of to it, and underpower the cast. (Accelerate slowly and make the power snap soft). The still-unrolling loop should collide with the water near the end of the line so that the leader can pile up on itself.

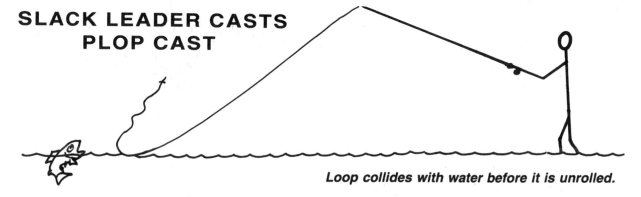

**SLACK LEADER CASTS
PLOP CAST**

Loop collides with water before it is unrolled.

Technique #2—High Angle Cast, Parachute Type

This is better for longer lines. Aim the forward cast higher than normal, so that the leader extends upward (instead of downward or parallel) to the target. Immediately after the power snap, lower the rod faster than the line is falling. You'll be able to see the extended line, leader, and fly, from its low position at the rod tip to its high position at the fly. The line will land first and the leader will fall back on itself to create slack.

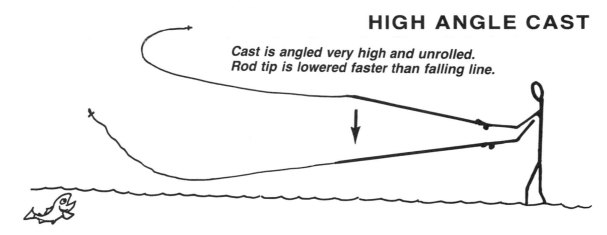

HIGH ANGLE CAST

Cast is angled very high and unrolled.
Rod tip is lowered faster than falling line.

Technique #3—Curving Power Snaps

This one uses an underhand curving power snap on the backcast and an overhand curving power snap on the forward cast, both in the horizontal plane.

1. Make a horizontal backcast with an *underhand* curve.

2. Drift up a few inches, keeping the palm of your hand facing upward.

3. Make a horizontal forward cast with a rolling power snap of 90° (rotate your hand and arm). The leader and fly will lag behind the line and land with slack.

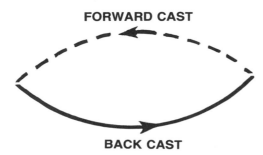

FORWARD CAST

BACK CAST

CURVING POWER SNAPS

Underhand curving power snap on backcast.
Overhand roll/rotation power snap on forward cast.
Illustration shows path of rod tip.

Curve Casts

The first time the great angler/author Joe Brooks and I stood on a casting platform together was between exhibitions of mine at the Philadelphia Sportsman's Show in the mid-fifties. I asked him to show me how to do a curve cast. He showed me. I made a few awkward attempts that failed, thanked him and left.

As I look back on it now I am sure that, if we had had a common casting language to explain the mechanics, I could have learned it in those few minutes, one on one. Let's see how you and I do.

Casting "around a corner" to avoid an obstacle or to place the fly so that it comes to the fish ahead of the leader, is a technique to practice at home, where you won't put down a fish or lose a fly on the obstacle.

A curve cast is based on one of two techniques. One *overpowers* the cast, using "recoil" to curve the leader and fly, and the other *underpowers* the cast so that the curve you have put in the line doesn't have time or space to straighten before the line lands on the water.

Technique #1:

Extra power and recoil. "Recoil" means "to spring back," and your rod hand will **recoil** from the power snap.

1. Make the cast horizontally, forehand or backhand, toward the target, with enough power so that, as your hand recoils, the leader and fly flip into a curve.

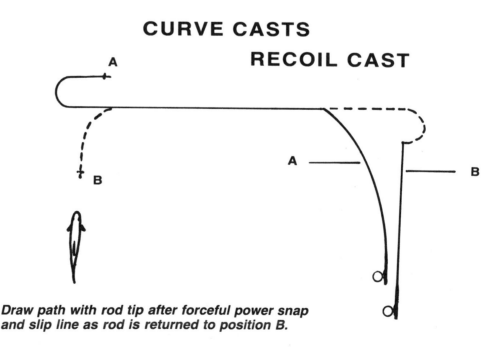

CURVE CASTS

RECOIL CAST

*Draw path with rod tip after forceful power snap
and slip line as rod is returned to position B.*

2. During follow-through time, draw, with your rod tip, the horizontal path you want the back end of the line to follow, slipping line through the rod from your line hand, to keep from shortening the cast. If the curve is to the left, and you are right-handed, it is almost like drawing a question mark with the rod tip.

Variation: I vary this technique, if there is no obstacle, by making the cast in a vertical plane, then dropping sideward to the horizontal plane, on the recoil *and* subsequent movement of the rod, at the same time slipping line.

The angle at which you do the curving cast might be affected by your depth of wading position, the height of an obstacle, or the length of the cast. Practice in different planes and at different lengths.

Technique #2:

Describing the curve with the rod tip in an underpowered cast.

1. Find the hand/target line for the forward cast.

2. Start your forearm and hand forward with a semicircular move, describing with the rod tip a wide curve the fly line will follow, to the right or left of the hand/target line. Make the semicircle at a fairly slow speed, lowering the rod as you do, so that the leading edge of the curved line is aimed downward toward the target area.

3. Follow through *at the speed of the falling line*, to keep it from having the time or space to unroll.

UNDERPOWERED CAST

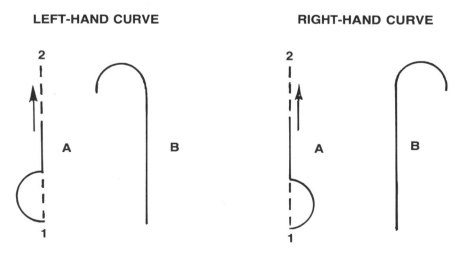

LEFT-HAND CURVE   **RIGHT-HAND CURVE**

1-2 is hand/target line
Draw semi-circular path with rod tip through loading move
and power snap (on downward angle). Thrust arm forward
at speed of line to keep it from unrolling. B. Finished curve.

The width of the semicircle will determine the width of the curve.

The line will move alongside the rod tip, instead of over it, and the leader and fly will be off to one side of the line (on the right for a right curve). By adjusting the acceleration, the power, and the angle of the line's path, you can land the leader and fly in a curve on the water. Because of the sloping angle of the fly line loop, this technique will be better used in open water, with no obstacles.

Variation: You can use this underpowering principle with a horizontal plane cast, by using less-than-normal force on the straight-line power snap, and pushing your arm forward to keep the line from straightening out before it lands, as you did in the vertical technique.

Casting Patterns for Stream Coverage

There are two kinds of motion that make an artificial fly attractive to fish. The motion within the fly (materials that simulate parts of real insects, like the gills or legs) and the motion *of* the fly, through or on the water. The fly tyer worries about motion within, and you, the caster, control the motion *of* the fly.

If you cast a fly upstream, to move freely on the surface or below it, it will simulate food, dead or alive, that is being carried with the current, and the motion within the fly will be the more important of the two kinds of motion. If you cast, quartering downstream, the fly will move across the current, appearing to be alive, and the materials within it will take second place, because of the speed of its movement. If you cast upstream and let the fly go with the flow until it reaches its full extension, it will then move across the current and you will have covered both approaches. Deciding how you want to bring the fly to the fish will determine the pattern of your casting.

Quartering Downstream

This is the best method for covering water, for putting your wet fly, streamer or nymph, within reach of any fish in the stream. If you are unfamiliar with a stretch of water, it is the ideal way to explore it.

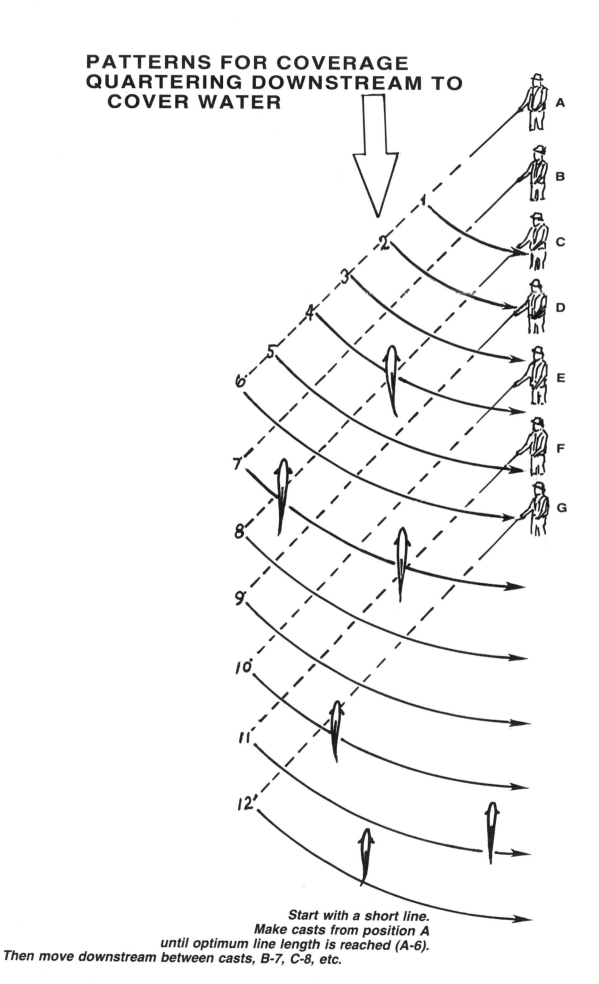

PATTERNS FOR COVERAGE QUARTERING DOWNSTREAM TO COVER WATER

Start with a short line.
Make casts from position A
until optimum line length is reached (A-6).
Then move downstream between casts, B-7, C-8, etc.

1. Starting with a line long enough to put your fly a few feet inside the current, cast, quartering downstream. Let the fly swim back to the edge of the current on your side of the stream.

2. Strip a precise amount of line from the reel, say, two or three feet, and make a second cast, shooting the line, at the same angle, from the same spot, and in the same direction. Let it swim back across the current.

3. Strip line from the reel again in your predetermined length and make a third cast. On each additional cast, continue to extend line until you have reached either the far edge of the current or your own distance limitations.

4. Keep that length of line constant and move yourself downstream the two or three feet at a time instead of adding more length to your line. You'll have uniform coverage of the water. Your fly will pass within the vision of every fish, by no more than half the length of each position change.

Dry Fly Use of This Pattern

One of the most exciting ways to locate big trout or Atlantic salmon is to cast a *skater*-type fly (like the Wulff Prefontaine, which has a snoot that gives it a tumbling action) on the surface, in the quartering-downstream pattern. In addition to the motion the current gives the fly, you can give free reign to your talent to make it hop and tumble and move upstream or drift down, in short spurts or long, to tantalize the hell out of a good fish. The strikes are usually, at the least, explosive, and sometimes they are more. There is a John Atherton painting of a salmon in a vertical leap that is well known among salmon anglers. Fish generally come out of the water vertically only after they are hooked or are free jumping. A few years ago, the best memory I took home from a salmon fishing trip was of two such vertical rises, as the fish tried desperately to catch the fluffy fly. (Because of the bulk of the hackle and the relatively small size hook, it is sometimes difficult to hook fish on a skater. *After* the rise, you switch to a conventional dry fly and dead drift it to the salmon's lie.) One of the rises (Lee's) was of an estimated twenty-pounder on Quebec's Grand Cascapedia and the other (mine) was a fourteen-pounder, caught and returned to the Restigouche River in New Brunswick. Those rises were heart stopping!

Upstream Coverage

When you fly cast you are always fighting gravity, and when you fish upstream you are always fighting drag. To put it simply, drag makes an imitation look as if it is connected to something. The placing of the cast on presentation, the angle of the line, and whether or not there is slack in the leader, all help to give your flies, above or below the water, drag-free floats.

The pattern for dry fly or unweighted nymph fishing is not directly upstream. The ideal angle is *across* as well as upstream, so that you are below the fish and your line and leader are off to the side as the fly floats over the fish. Picking up slack as it forms will be easy.

If you want to *cover* a pool with a dry fly you'll begin at the edge closest to you and then, on succeeding drifts, work your way across. Always let the fly go well beyond the possible lies before you pick it up. If you make a bad cast, let it float on through, even though you don't want to, so that your emotional response to "flubbing" doesn't cause the fish to be put down as you snatch the line off the water.

A drift that starts upstream can be extended to a downstream drift, and as you need more line, you can stroke it through the rod from your line hand's supply, as described earlier. Downstream drifts with unweighted flies can be very effective, and should be included in your bag of tricks.

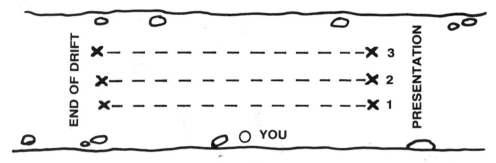

Weighted Nymphs on the Bottom

The fishing pattern most generally used for weighted nymphs is to position yourself a minimum distance from the holding water so that at the most effective depth the line is straight down from your rod tip.

You'll cast far enough upstream of the fish's lie so that the weighted fly will have time to sink to the bottom before coming within its vision.

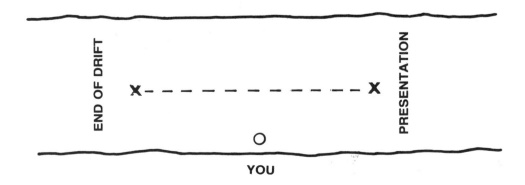

You'll keep your eyes on the line/leader connection or on a "strike in-dicator" or some portion of the line to check its speed, which should be that of the current. If it hesitates, if the speed of the moving line changes in any way, you'll strike! You may need to mend line with this method of fishing, to keep the fly moving freely with the bottom current. Weighted nymph fishing can be a highly developed art and a deadly one, once you get the hang of it.

The One-Stroke Cast for Weighted Nymphs

When using weighted nymphs you must lift the fly to the surface, either as a fishing tactic or as the beginning of your loading move, and then make a soft power snap to take the fly out of the water. If you do not need to false cast, you can make a one-stroke presentation.

1. From an open body stance, lift your fly to the surface, on the loading move, rotating your arm *outward* to place the reel upside down, as the fly comes to the surface.

2. Do a *soft* power snap upward and upstream to your point of aim, letting your body swing with it.

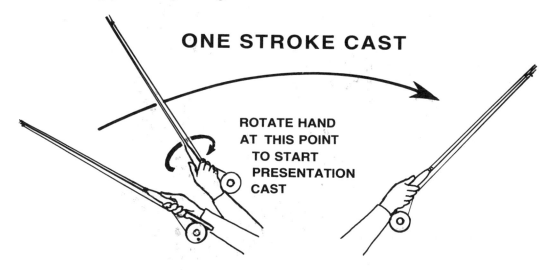

ONE STROKE CAST

ROTATE HAND
AT THIS POINT
TO START
PRESENTATION
CAST

False casting a weighted nymph can be dangerous. Make the moves non-violent. The best technique to use is an oval, to *round* the path of the heavy fly so that it doesn't cross itself. Use slow speed and accelerate smoothly. Once the fly is put into a flight path, it will keep going on its own momentum.

Line Control: Aerial Mending

The word "mending," in the fly fishing world, usually refers to moving a portion of the line against the current, as you fish the fly. **Aerial mending** means moving all, or part, of the extended fly line, as part of the cast, *after* the forward power snap and *before* the line lands on the water, in the time allotted to following through. Naturally, your point of aim must be high enough above the target area to facilitate the mend.

The reason for mending in the air is in anticipation that one or more of the many currents in the stream, between the rod tip and the fly, will belly or drag parts of the fly line, in turn dragging the leader and fly.

1. *A simple mend.* A simple mend is made with an overhand semicircular move in the upstream direction to move the portion of the fly line nearest the rod tip upstream while the front end of the line remains where you aimed it originally. The size of the mend is controlled by the width of your semi-circular move.

2. *Curves in the line.* To put curves throughout the line, make the cast, then quickly move the rod side to side, with a waving motion. The number and width of the moves you make with the rod will be reflected in the fly line as it lands on the water. You will need more than enough line to reach the target because you reduce the extension when you put curves in the line.

3. *Slack near the rod tip.* To get a rod's length of slack line near the rod tip, make the cast through the power snap, then raise the rod as if you were going to make another backcast, slipping line from your line hand with the rod's motion. It will slip through the guides to give you slack without having reduced the length of the line. You might want to use this technique at the beginning of a downstream dry fly drift.

4. *The Reach Cast.* When you present a dry fly you position yourself so that the fish cannot see you, by standing across from and slightly below the fish's lie (usually). As you present the fly upstream, a straight line cast will put the heavier portion of the line, coming off the rod tip, at the lowest downstream position of any part of the tackle. If there is any current that can affect it, you are in trouble. The technique publicized by Doug Swisher and Carl Richards as the "**reach cast**" can help you.

At the end of the forward power snap, as the line is unrolling to your target, move your rod arm as if it were an extension of the fly rod, from the shoulder, upstream, as far as you can reach. The fly line nearest the rod tip will go with it, of course, and the cast will be shortened unless at the same time you slip line from your line hand to replace the length you would other-

AERIAL MENDING REACH CAST

1. **Make a normal stroke through power snap.**
2. **During follow-through time, move arm and rod upstream, slipping line.**

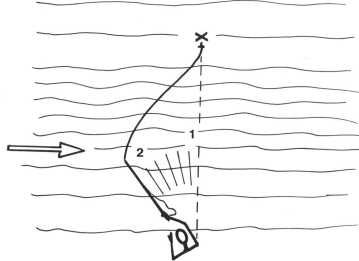

wise lose as you reach. The result will be that your rod angle will have put the heavier portion of the fly line upstream and the leader and fly will be angled downstream, although you have not changed your position to do it.

Good line speed is critical for aerial mending. Make the fly *hover*, then do the reach. The technique is good for both upstream and downstream dry fly fishing.

PUTTING THE MEND WHERE IT IS NEEDED

1. **Mend near rod tip is done late.**
2. **Mend farther out is done sooner.**
3. **Mend near leader is done as a continuation of the power snap.**

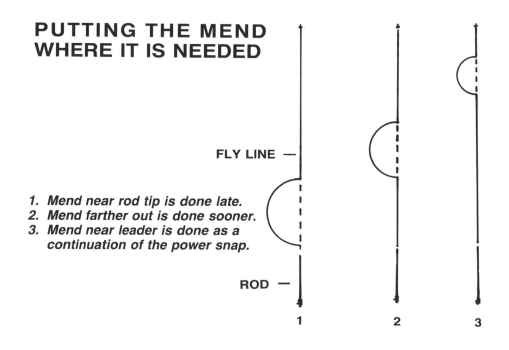

FLY LINE —

ROD —

1   2   3

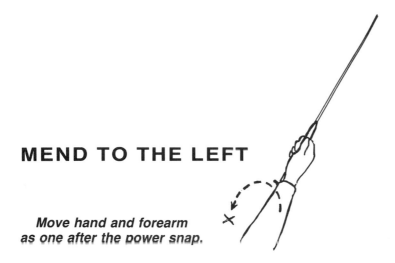

MEND TO THE LEFT

*Move hand and forearm
as one after the power snap.*

5. *Hand rotation mends.* This technique mends the line through hand rotation, placing the mend in any section of the line you choose, before the fly line lands on the water. The hand rotation follows the power snap and is made in the upstream direction. The later you do the move after the power snap, the closer the mend will be to the rod tip. To put a mend in the line farther out, the timing of the mending move becomes critical. The hand rotation must continue the forward thrust of the power snap so there is time for the impulse to travel farther out the line. It requires sharp moves, fast-actioned rods, high line speed, and lots of practice.

Line Control—Mending on the Water

Once the cast is made and the line is on the water, mending the line is useful, to prevent drag on a free-drifting fly or to slow down the speed of a fly moving across the current.

Mending the line, on the water, is accomplished by making a semicircular movement of the whole rod in a direction that is against the current's flow. The mends can be large or small, with either quick flips or slower, more deliberate moves, depending on which portion and how much of the line you judge can be moved. The speed of the current's flow will be a factor. Slipping line may be a useful tactic for mends closest to the rod tip.

The design of the fly line will determine, in part, how much line you can mend. The double taper design will allow a greater length of line to be mended than any other design, because of the length of the belly section. On the weight-forward designs, once the light running line is out of the rod tip, you won't have much control.

When you are fishing a fly across the current (downstream) the speed at which the fly travels can be very important. If the line bellies, the fly will lag behind and then whip around at the end of the swing at a speed that is incredibly fast. A lesson in the value of slowing down the fly was taught to me graphically one August day on Norway's Gaula River.

MENDING ON THE WATER

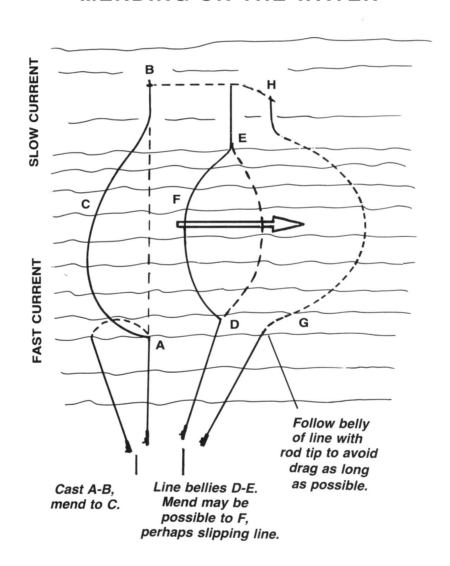

SLOW CURRENT

FAST CURRENT

Cast A-B, mend to C.

Line bellies D-E. Mend may be possible to F, perhaps slipping line.

Follow belly of line with rod tip to avoid drag as long as possible.

My host, Johan Abelsson, took me to a tributary where a narrow, fifty-foot-long tongue of turbulent water swept over rocks, then diminished suddenly into a deep, wide bowl of quiet water. It didn't look like any salmon river I had ever fished and my hopes were not high for action. I also didn't quite know how to handle the wild water when Johan told me to cast the fly right into it. I presented my Surface Stone fly down and across the tongue to the far edge, and the turbulence bellied the line, with the fly lagging behind but racing at top speed.

When a salmon flashed at the fly, my reaction was one of surprise at the appearance of what seemed to be a big fish in this small run of water. I cast again to the same spot, with the same length of line, to check on whether my eyes were deceiving me, and the salmon chased the fly, again failing to catch it. It was then that Johan whispered, "Mend it." I'm sure he felt like yelling, "MEND IT, DAMN IT!" as this was to be the third cast. I made the identical cast and mended against the current as soon as the fly line landed. I didn't see the fish move this time, because he took the fly close to his lie, not having had to chase it.

This twenty-three-pound fish was the best catch of the week. Johan was as happy for me as I was, but it was *his* fish in my mind. He gave it to me. I left Norway with a greater appreciation of "mending" for salmon.

There is another technique for controlling fly speed across the current, and that is in the angle of your fly rod. If you want to make the fly move faster, you can raise the angle of your rod. To slow the speed of the fly, lower the rod tip as it swings.

If you want to slow the fly through a particular area, pull line in through the guides in anticipation and then release it smoothly. A fly can sometimes be stopped dead, for a second, by the sudden release of slack line through the rod.

Adding Line Without Casting

The need may arise to add line to a cast already on the water, perhaps to lengthen the drift of a dry fly or to add new length to the line before pick-up, instead of shooting it after the pick-up.

Stroking

The same technique that you used as a beginner to stroke line through the rod, when you could not extend it in any other way, will work to add line on the stream. Keep the rod tip low and make small strokes, vertically or horizontally, with the rod hand. The line hand must provide the slack, from its supply of line, either loose or from the reel, to make the rod take it. All of the moves must be gentle ones. The reason for not just dropping the line, to let the weight of the extended line pull it through the guides, is that you'll need instant tension if a fish strikes, so the supply of line must be controlled.

Roll Cast

You can shoot line in a roll cast *above* the water but not *on* the water. To extend line without actually casting it, start with the rod tip low, after you have already made a roll cast. At the same time as you raise the rod to move it backward to the starting position, let line slip from your line hand to move through the guides; the rod will eat it up. You can add most of a rod's length of line this way.

Wind

Wind scares us all as beginning casters, and well it should if there is a hook on the end of the line. Most of us have been hit by a fly; it is one of the reasons anglers wear hats and sunglasses. Just train yourself not to set the hook when the fly collides with something other than a fish, and you'll save yourself pain and trouble. Casting in windy conditions is a part of fly fishing. To solve the problems it brings to you, you must determine where you want the fly line to go, the possible effects of the wind on it, and how your cast should vary from the norm in order for you to retain control.

You can change angles by tilting the rod; change planes between strokes; increase or decrease the power in your stroke; change the timing of your backcast's unrolling, and *drift*, or not, according to what you can judge of the wind's intensity and direction as it affects your cast.

WIND DIRECTIONS

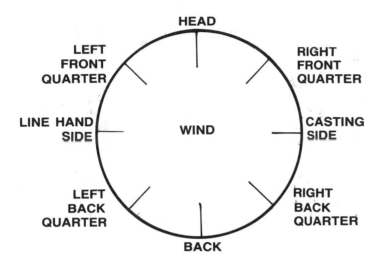

Headwinds

The lower you are in the water, the easier headwinds are to overcome. Wind is never as strong just above the surface of the water as it is higher up. Make your forward cast with great speed, driving into the wind at as low an angle as you can manage. Body motion will help. (Crouch!)

Heavier lines will move your fly through winds more easily than will light-weight lines at the same speed. I wouldn't want to be caught with anything less than a #7 weight fly line in heavy winds, but a #9 would do a better job.

I am reminded of my first trip to Iceland, in 1972. I had only glass rods in my caddy: a six-foot rod for a #7 line, a seven-and-a-half foot rod for a #7, and, in case the wind blew, I had an eight-and-a-half foot rod for a #9. The wind was blowing when we got there and I turned to the #9 weight immediately. The rod weighed five ounces and, along with the air resistance of its large-diametered cross section, it was a real chore to cast in the heavy winds. The seven-and-a-half foot rod didn't have enough stiffness in the butt to drive the line into the wind and that left me with the six-footer. It worked. The #7 line was heavy enough and the slim profile of the rod shaft cut through the wind like a knife, compared to the #9 weight outfit.

Over the years, the change in materials, from the relatively heavy glass to the light, strong, and small-diametered graphite rods of today, has made a real difference in the ability of fly fishermen to handle windy conditions.

Backwinds

Your line may not straighten in a backwind and you certainly cannot *drift* into one, so vertical-plane casting can be difficult, except for short lines.

Technique #1. Cast a short line upward with extra power and, as soon as the fly passes over the rod tip, start forward, letting the wind help.

Technique #2. The *oval* is a good technique because the leader and fly travel to the right of the body of the line on the backcast, and, on the forward cast, use an off-vertical plane to keep the line on your right.

Technique #3. The following two-plane technique is good with long lines and heavy flies, as in tarpon or salmon fishing. From an open-body stance:

1. Make a horizontal backcast as low as possible to get "under the wind." High line speed is necessary.

2. Drift up to an *off-vertical* plane. (A vertical plane will give you the fly in your back.)

3. Present the cast.

Technique #4. If all else fails, do the cast in which you reverse yourself between strokes. Use the open-body stance to cast *into* the back wind with a forward cast, and then reverse your body during drift time (it is literally follow-through time because this is a forward cast) and present a second forward cast, *with* the wind.

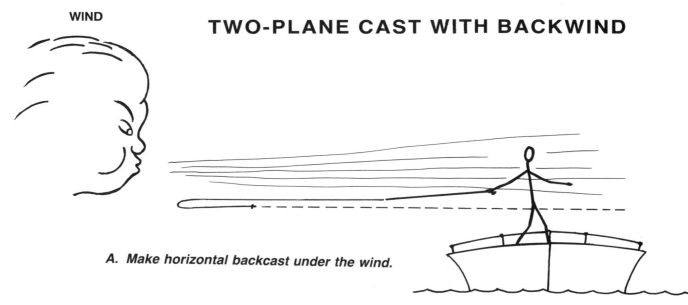

WIND

TWO-PLANE CAST WITH BACKWIND

A. Make horizontal backcast under the wind.

Wind from the Casting Side: Quartering-back, or straight from the side, wind.

You can use backhand casts on both strokes to beat these winds. If the line is long enough to require a double haul, you can use a combination to make the backcast hauling easier. Make the backcast pretty well *centered on your body* with the rod tip tilted leeward. Drift a few degrees to the left to separate the paths of the strokes. Make the forward cast backhanded. The shape will be elliptical and was described earlier under "Presentation Casts with Limited Backcast Room." The path described by the fly will keep it well away from your body.

Wind From the Forward Quarter on the Casting Side

Use a backhand cast. Tilt the plane of your cast to end up cutting across the wind at a 45° angle on the forward cast. Use either a one-path cast or an elliptical cast but it will be important to lean and crouch if the winds are bad ones.

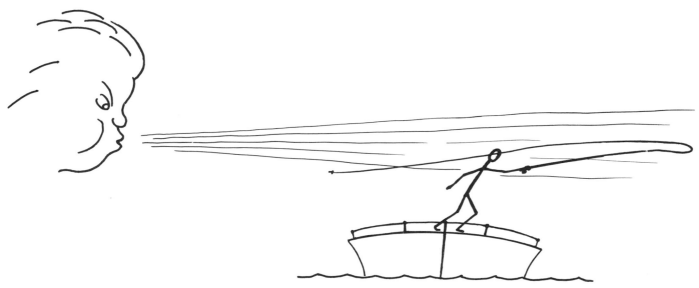

B. Make off-vertical forward cast with the wind.

Wind from the Line-Hand Side

This condition is relatively easy to handle. The wind will blow the line and fly to the right of your body. If the wind is heavy, make the backcast stroke very close to your body to minimize the sideward effect. Aim a little left of the target. If the wind is from the left front quarter, angle your forward cast to cut into it at 45°, using either forehand or backhand strokes.

Changing the Direction of the Cast in Windy Conditions

In the section on changing direction, I suggested that you use a clockface to practice the various *angles of change*, and to try to make the changes without false casting. When wind is a factor, at least one false cast can make the change easier.

Take into consideration where the wind is likely to blow the fly line on each stroke and choose between forehand and backhand casts to keep the rod from colliding with the line.

For example, if you have no wind and must change direction from left to right, you can keep the line on the left of the rod or change from left of the rod to right of the rod, between casts. If there is wind to contend with, blowing from the left, let us say, you will want the fly line to go to the right of the rod on the pickup and stay there through the sequence.

If the wind is blowing from the right as you change direction from left to right, you'll want to keep the fly line on the left of the rod during the change, which will entail the use of all back hand, or center-of-your-body, casts.

These rules are not cast in stone. In this same example of moving from left to right with wind from the right, you can often move the line from the

> Wind can truly cause knots to form in your leader if the cast is not perfectly controlled. The leader has no real weight and flies have *some* weight. Once the fly starts to move out of synchronization with the fly line's weight and direction, anything can happen. Heavy winds can blow the fly line, the leader, and the fly around in crazy patterns that produce real knots.

left of the rod to the right of the rod for your final cast, by rotating your upper body to the right for an open-body stance to get a long stroke in an off-vertical plane. The length of the line and of the rod will be important factors, as will the speed of your moves. Meeting the challenges of casting in the wind can be a stimulating exercise.

When winds are impossible, I cut down on how much I move from one angle to another. I eliminate the false casts, which the wind can catch so easily, and make off-the-water casts instead, one after the other, bridging the angle of change gradually. Only on the actual presentation cast do I shoot line. This may take a few minutes longer to execute, but the final results are more certain.

When wind comes in gusts, it is very easy to see it as a disturbing effect on the water's surface. Lee tells me that, as a seaplane pilot, he would time his touchdown to coincide with the very end of a wind gust, taking advantage of the calm behind it to settle the plane deeper in the water before the next gust began. You can use the same technique, timing your backcast to coincide with the end of the gust and making the presentation in the calm behind it.

My final thought to pass along to you is that, if all of your efforts fail and you know you will be hit by the fly, practice the art of "Ducking."

Getting Out of Trouble

Whenever you feel your fly touch something during a cast, for heavens' sake, don't set the hook! Stop the movement of the rod instantly. That's the rule. After you've snagged your fly a dozen times, relaxing instantly will become a reflex action. You'll look around to see if anyone saw what happened, and if no one has, then you'll work at trying to save the fly. You could save a lot of time and immediately break the leader and put on a new tippet and a new fly but sometimes it's a matter of pride. You try to save the fly by one of the following methods.

1. Jiggle the rod tip, hoping to shake the fly out of the snag in case the hook did not actually penetrate the obstacle. Keep this motion pretty light. The easiest way to break your rod is to bend the tip sharply a few times, under heavy pressure.

2. If the fly is on shore, behind you, you can walk in and retrieve it, providing the trouble spot is low enough.

3. Next you'll try the roll cast. Strip line from the reel so that you can slide the rod backward on it and put a bend in the upper third of the rod as you get your rod hand up in front of your shoulder to make the cast. Aim the cast right at the fly along the hand/target line, and, when the line passes beyond the fly, *snatch* the rod backward as if you were making a quick-starting backcast.

GETTING OUT OF TROUBLE ROLL CAST

Obviously, if the leader is wrapped around a branch, this roll cast won't work. But if it isn't, the idea is that by rolling with enough force to make the line go beyond the fly and then making a quick snatch, you might pull the fly out the same way it went in. And it works. One of my nightmare recollections happened, not on a stream, but in New York's Coliseum where 2000 people saw me catch my fly in overhead lights. There was a great silence as the emcee realized what had happened and I hoped I was dreaming; but I wasn't, and when I located the fly and moved to try the roll casting technique, the crowd held its breath with me. "Somebody up there was watching"— and the technique worked. Every fisherman in the audience would remember that trick.

If the roll cast doesn't work, you consider a few other things. Could you wade over there and then be able to reach the fly with your rod tip? Will you spoil the fishing ahead? How valuable is that fly, and do you have another just like it?

4. If the fly is above you no more than arm's reach and rod's length, you go to the place where it is caught, and wind up the line and leader until the tip guide on the rod can be wedged against the fly hook. Push with the tip, being careful not to do it so hard that you snap off four inches of the rod. Pushing with the tip works better than any other method. However, if you get snagged on a high backcast, you'll usually end up on tip toes in the stream, arms stretched as high as they will go, wondering if you'll fall on your face when the fly lets go. It can be the most adventurous solution.

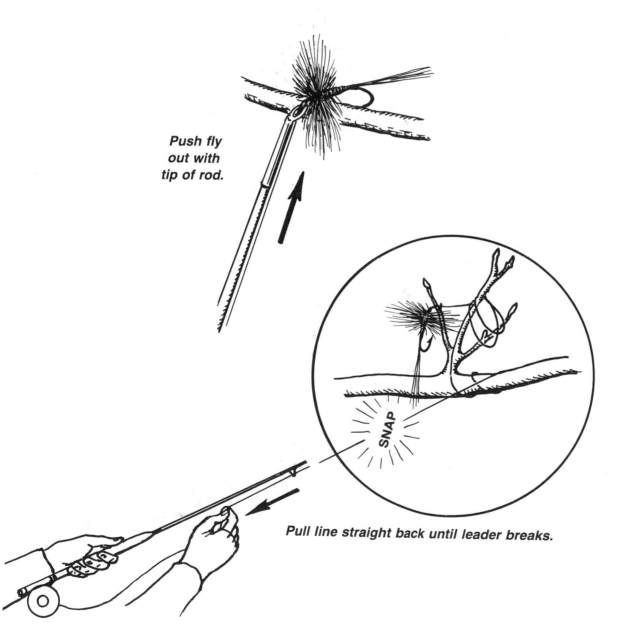

Push fly out with tip of rod.

SNAP

Pull line straight back until leader breaks.

5. "All else has failed." You've got to break it off. The rod now becomes inanimate. It's the line you concentrate on. Wind in line until you can make a straight pull through the rod but are not using the rod hand in any way. Reach up with your line hand, to just below the first guide, and wrap the fly line around your hand, pulling straight along the rod butt, until the leader pops. As it does, look to see if the fly is falling, so you can catch it. You still might save it.

The weakest link in the leader will break, first at a point of abrasion or in an overhand wind knot, then at the knot tied with the weakest monofilament, at the fly or at the tippet knot nearest the fly. If, when you get it back you examine it and think it broke at a wind knot which has only 50% strength, don't ignore the message. It could have happened on a fish.

If your fly is caught on a log above the water, the roll cast will usually work. If the fly is caught under water, get within reach and use the tip-pushing technique.

Another use of the *roll cast snatch* occurs when your fly is cluttered with surface weed or grass. Lefty Kreh showed me this trick one spring day in the sixties, when we fished in Florida's Flamingo Bay amidst patches of grass floating on the surface. Roll cast your line directly to the fly and snatch it as it gets there. The snatch drags the fly sharply through the water, ridding it of the grass.

eight

TACKLE

Fly-Fishing Tackle

Choosing tackle is a personal thing, based not only on the nature of the fishing but on the limitations of the pocketbook. My recommendations will be based on factors other than the cost. You should be able to follow them, at any financial level.

FLY-LINE STANDARDS OF THE AMERICAN FISHING TACKLE MANUFACTURERS' ASSOCIATION

Code	Weight/Grains	Range
1	60	54–66
2	80	74–86
3	100	94–106
4	120	114–126
5	140	134–146
6	160	152–168
7	185	177–193
8	210	202–218
9	240	230–250
10	280	270–290
11	330	318–342
12	380	368–392

Fly Lines

Choose the weight of your fly line before you choose anything else. Fly lines are designated by their weight, their design, whether or not they float, and their color.

The first thirty feet of the fly line is weighed on a grain scale and given a number designation. For each number, there is a limited tolerance that allows room for variation by the manufacturers. To you, it means that one manufacturer's #6 weight, for example, can be very close to another manufacturer's line weight on either side of that #6 (a #5 or a #7). The standards of the industry are not as tight as they might be as the technology advances. This may be important to you when you are looking for the perfect line weight to balance your rod.

These are the range of line weights generally used for different species of fish:

Trout:	#3 to #8
Bass:	#7 to #10
Atlantic salmon/steelhead:	#6 to #10
Bonefish/other "flats" fish:	#6 to #9
Tarpon:	#9 to #12
Ocean Fish:	#9 to #12

In the chapter, "You Start with the Line," the features of the various designs were covered, except for Shooting Tapers (see "Coiling Line"). Information about the design, the weight, and whether the line floats or sinks, is given as a code on the package.

Identification

L	Level	F	Floating
DT	Double taper	S	Sinking
WF	Weight-forward taper	S/T	Sink tip
TT	Triangle taper	I	Intermediate, floating or sinking
S/T	Shooting taper		

Here are examples of how they might read:

L7F   DT7S   DT6S/T   WF8S   TT4/5F   ST10F   WF7I

More About Design

Lines of the same basic design can differ between manufacturers. Not in the design of level lines, not usually in double tapers, but in *weight-forward* lines. You already know that you can buy special bass or saltwater tapers, but, in the trout category, there can be differences in the length of the front tapers and in the length of the belly section. Some even have long back tapers, though most are short.

For trout fishing, lean toward the longer front tapers and longer bellies, as these are the features of a double taper that are valuable for delicacy on presentation and in roll-casting capabilities. If you can have a long front taper and a long belly in a weight-forward line, you can have the best of both worlds. It is sometimes difficult to determine from the information on the box just what those dimensions are, but your dealer can tell you what you want to know. Once you own a line, you can tell with the naked eye how long the tapered and belly sections of the fly line are, by comparing diameters.

The **triangle-taper** design does not have a front taper and a belly, but tapers continuously from a small diameter to its maximum diameter in forty feet and is essentially a weight-forward line after that. Because the design is patented there is no variation within the basic category. The line comes in bass bug and saltwater versions in which the whole taper is only twenty-seven feet long to handle the bulkier or heavier flies in short casting sequences for longer distances.

The triangle-taper design is based on the oldest fly line design, a single taper, originating in Great Britain. Fly lines were braided of horsehair, starting with a few strands and with additional hairs braided in to thicken the line. Most of the casting technique was roll casting in those days and this was the perfect roll-casting line, with a heavier part always turning over a lighter section, which helped to keep the momentum from diminishing. It is said that with long two-handed salmon rods, anglers could roll cast one hundred and twenty-five feet, and with this design, I'm sure it was true.

Color

Fly lines, like lollipops, come in all colors. Light-colored lines will let you see your cast unroll. If you know that it is a good one, you'll have more confidence as you fish the fly. When visibility is less than perfect, because of low light or the coloration or size of the fly, the light-colored line is helpful in estimating where the fly is at all times.

It is true that light-colored lines show up more easily to the fish, but the fish doesn't necessarily have to see the fly line, at least not until after he has had his chance at the fly. Darker-colored lines may be effective in lake fishing if you are using a sinking line, but otherwise you will gain more than you'll lose with a light-colored floating line for surface fishing.

Sinking Lines

When is a sinking line better than a floating line? When there will be *time* for the line to sink the fly to the desired depth in still or slow-moving water. Sinking lines come in various densities that affect their sink-rate, and there are at least six densities on the market. They sink at rates from one foot per second to ten feet per second. There are sink-tip lines, with ten, twenty, or thirty-foot sections on otherwise floating lines. And there are intermediate lines that will sink slowly if they are not dressed with floatant and will float if they are, much as the old silk lines use to do.

Save the high-density lines for deep fishing in slow-moving water. For relatively shallow streams you are better off with a floating line and, perhaps, some weight in the form of split shot or lead wrappers near the fly (as in nymph fishing) to take it to the bottom.

Sinking lines are a little harder to cast, compared to floating lines, as the density increases. You will have to retrieve more line between casts for the pickup. For their weight, these lines are small in diameter and when put in motion travel like a bullet. Keep your rod tip angled to make the line travel well away from your head or body.

Fly Line Point

Until now you have been concerned with the weight and design of the fly line; it is time to focus your attention on the end of the fly line (where it will join your leader), and take a look at its diameter.

When fly lines are manufactured, there is margin for error allowed in the length of the flat sections that lie between two tapered lines, where they will be cut apart. Most manufacturers say that they give you *six* inches of flat section (the point) on a line, before it begins to taper. If you check your fly line (and you should check every one), you will often find that this flat section is longer than six inches. Six inches won't hurt the cast, but two feet may well affect it, and I have seen lines with three-and-a-half feet of excess flat line, as recently as 1984. You can check, without a micrometer, by comparing the *diameter of the point* to line farther up in the taper, using only the naked eye. By doubling it on itself, you can see when and where the diameters start to differ. Cut off all but four inches of the flat line and you will be ready to put on your leader.

Leaders—for Trout Fishermen

This section will be directed to trout fishermen. Leaders are more important to these fishermen than to others, because of the variety of fly sizes used in pursuing the species. The taper of the leader must be suited to the fly size and the fishing conditions, both of which can vary considerably.

The Connection

The line/leader connection is very important. The energy generated in the cast moves through the unrolling line to the leader and fly. The leader should be thought of as an invisible continuation of the fly line, as if they were one and the same.

The material in the butt section of the leader, nearest the fly line, will be comparatively stiff and of relatively large diameter to take the transfer of energy from the unrolling fly line and give *direction* to the base leader. The front end will be of finer and softer material, to prepare the fly to land gently.

The leader must cast well, be long enough and fine enough to fool the fish with the chosen fly, and its weakest section must be strong enough to play the fish well after it is hooked.

Whenever you change a fly, you use up a piece of leader. When you change from a small fly to a large one, or vice versa, you need a different thickness of leader next to the fly. Ready-made leaders don't solve the problem unless you constantly use new ones.

Let me present the basic leader system I use. It may or may not be the best one for you, but, by becoming familiar with it, you can understand the problems that may arise with any system. This leader will have a permanent base and an adjustable front end that will let you change whatever is necessary as the need arises on the stream.

The permanent part of the leader starts with a butt section attached to your fly line—to keep from using up the line's front taper. To the butt section is attached a 7½ to 9 foot knotless tapered leader (purchased as such), and, between the end of that leader and the fly, the taper is continued with pieces of softer monofilament, in gradually diminishing diameters.

TAPERED TROUT LEADER

#6 LINE .032	.023 BUTT	.021	KNOTLESS TAPERED LEADER	0X .011	1X .010	3X .008	5X .006	6 OR 7X .005 .004

7½'–9'

	12"–15"		IF THIS IS FINAL TIPPET:	8"–12" 12"–15"	8"–12" 2'–3'	8"–12" 3'–4'	4'–6'

Maximum length 19'3"
Minimum length 14'6"

Having trimmed off the flat line from the end of the fly line, look at its diameter. The tip end of a fly line will range from about .042 in heavy lines (#10) to perhaps .025 for the very light ones. Use material for the butt section of your leader that is roughly two-thirds of the fly line's diameter. If you don't have a micrometer, use, as a guide:

.021 for lines #4 and 5
.023 for lines #6 and 7
.027 for lines #8 and 9

Make this permanent butt section twelve to fifteen inches long and attach it with a needle knot. A coating of flexible contact cement, like Pliobond, will keep the knot from wearing as it passes through the rod tip when you are playing a fish. This permanent butt section should be good for the life of the line.

Let us say that your fly line is a #6. You will have attached a butt section that measures .023. (Diameters are given on the spools of leader material.) Next, tie on a knotless tapered leader of 7½ to 9 feet in length, with a butt diameter of .021 and a tip diameter of .011 or .010. This is the end of the permanent leader section.

For the front section, you will work with lengths of tippet material, designated by their diameter in the following code (this information is on the spool):

Size	Tip Diameter	Pound Test (may be different with various companies)
0X	.011	10
1X	.010	8.5
2X	.009	7
3X	.008	6
4X	.007	5
5X	.006	4
6X	.005	3
7X	.004	?
8X	.003	1.2

To add on to the base leader for whatever will fit the circumstances, add lengths of tippet material (8 to 12 inches, depending on whether there will be many or few) starting with 1X (.010) and reducing the diameter by .002 or 2 "X" designations with each piece, until you get to 5X. Then reduce it by 1 "X" designation because it is getting pretty skinny by then. Always make the last section of tippet material next to the fly longer than the preceding pieces.

How do you know what final size of tippet to use for each size of fly hook? There is a guide called the Rule of 4. Divide the size of the hook by the number 4 and it will give you an X recommendation. "Size 12 fly, divided by 4 is 3(X)," size 20 would use 5X tippet material. Whether the number comes out evenly or not, check your water conditions. If they are glassy, go lighter, and if they are rough, go heavier. It's only a guide. Experience and common sense will get you through.

The lighter the final tippet, the longer it should be. You might use one foot for the final 1X tippet, two or three feet for a final 3X tippet, three to four feet for 5X, and four to six feet for 6X. As the tippet material gets finer (and weaker), longer lengths will cushion the shock of striking and playing a fish.

If you think this imaginary leader is pretty long, you are right. It is set up for the tiniest of flies when it ends at 7X. You'll be able to cast it if you have a normally good cast because the taper of the leader will help you. The 4- to 6-foot front tippet will not straighten but will land softly, like a cobweb, for a good presentation of a tiny fly.

The length of the leader must suit the conditions. Leaders are your invisibility. Use length when you need it and shorten up when you don't. Heavy flies in turbulent water can be fished on leaders that are both short *and* heavy. A leader for a weighted nymph might taper from .021 to .011 in 6 to 7½ feet. Long, fine leaders are needed for smaller flies and to fool wary fish.

With this imaginary leader, if you must change from a #24 fly to a #12, you can break the leader back to the 3X tippet and save it, with the fly attached, rolled up in your pocket, for later use.

When you use this base leader system, you will always know which diameter tippet material you have tied to it, by the number of sections below the knotless taper. If you pick it up one day and see two sections tied on, you know they are 1X and 3X. If there are three sections, you'll be down to 5X. If instead, you *buy* a leader that takes you to 3X or 4X to start with (and they are available), either you will have to replace the front end after you change flies a few times, or you will have to add or subtract material to adjust to the different size flies you'll be using, or quite often you'll have to use a new leader and what will you do with the used ones? The base leader system deserves your consideration.

With this system, you'll carry spools of tippet material with you of, perhaps, 1, 3, 5, 6, and 7X, as I do, along with a few emergency knotless tapers, 9' 4X. Use a *barrel/blood* knot to tie monofilament to monofilament or the simpler-to-tie surgeon's knot. Make sure you don't combine different manufacturer's tippet material. They may not be compatible and may break easily at the knots.

KNOTS

Hold line, needle, and leader in place with thumb and forefinger.

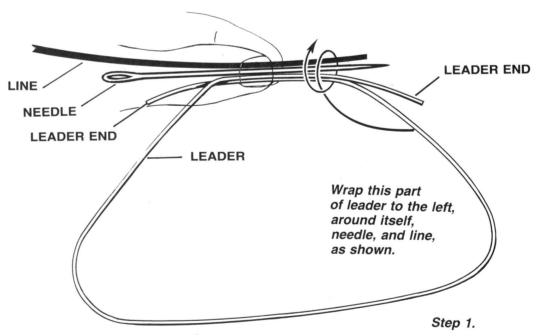

LINE

NEEDLE

LEADER END

LEADER

LEADER END

Wrap this part of leader to the left, around itself, needle, and line, as shown.

Step 1.

Needle Knot for Attaching Fly Line to Leader

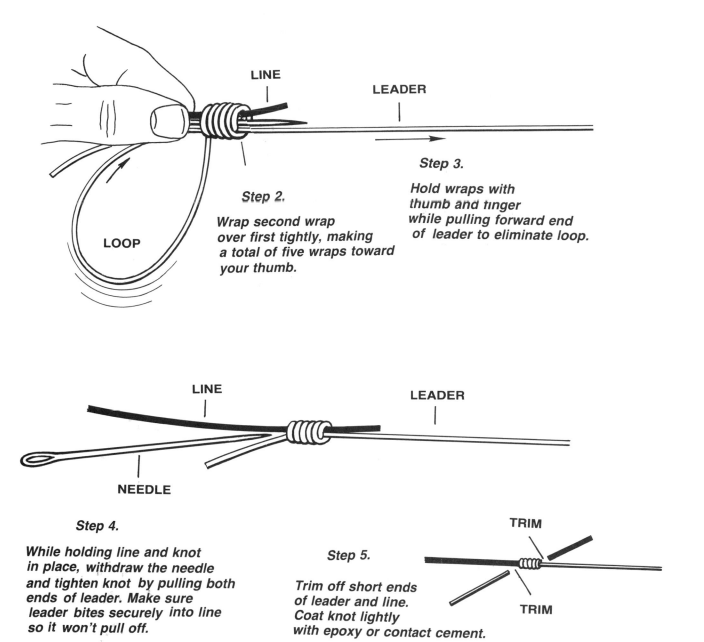

LINE

LEADER

LOOP

Step 2.

**Wrap second wrap
over first tightly, making
a total of five wraps toward
your thumb.**

Step 3.

**Hold wraps with
thumb and finger
while pulling forward end
of leader to eliminate loop.**

LINE

LEADER

NEEDLE

Step 4.

**While holding line and knot
in place, withdraw the needle
and tighten knot by pulling both
ends of leader. Make sure
leader bites securely into line
so it won't pull off.**

Step 5.

**Trim off short ends
of leader and line.
Coat knot lightly
with epoxy or contact cement.**

TRIM

TRIM

An option you have with this leader is to use interlocking loops to connect sections of the leader. You can loop different knotless tapers to the permanent butt, or loop various sections in front of the knotless taper, at .011. Loops are convenient but are more visible on the water than a good knot.

The leader is very important. Give some thought to how best you can handle the changing of the tippet size on the stream.

FOR TYING SECTIONS OF LEADER MATERIAL TO EACH OTHER

BARREL KNOT

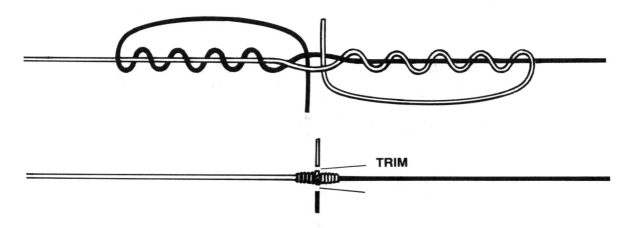

TRIM

SURGEON'S KNOT

Step 1. Overlap two strands of leader to be tied.

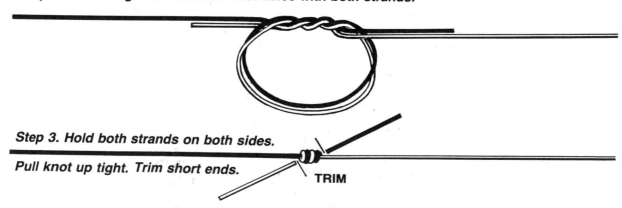

Step 2. Go through an overhand knot twice with both strands.

Step 3. Hold both strands on both sides.

Pull knot up tight. Trim short ends.

TRIM

Fly Rods

Tournament casting has always been the proving ground for rod design, because rod makers know that the design is more than scientific. The fine old company names like Hardy, Leonard, and Mills, all appear in tournament records of the past. Today's rod makers include casters of my generation, Jim Green of Fenwick and Jim Hardy of Great Britain. If the rod makers, themselves, do not compete, they have consultants who do. Charles Ritz, in his work with Pezon & Michel, had champion Pierre Creusevaut as his backup. Johnny Dieckman worked for Conolon, Jon Tarantino with Hardy, and today, Steve Rajeff is the tournament arm of Sage Rods.

Rod Action

No matter how many experts have input on the design of fly rods, you are the final judge. Choosing the right rod is such a personal thing that I equate it with choosing a mate. Feeling is the greatest factor in making the decision. A good fly rod, like a good marriage partner, becomes a part of you. Never buy a fly rod you haven't put a fly line on and cast.

You really choose a rod on the basis of your experience in knowing what to expect of yourself and what to expect of a rod. Your personality can influence your decision on rod action. Do you want to have it move slowly so as not to demand too much of you? Do you want it to be fast actioned so that everything you do is immediately shown as response in the fly line? Do you want it to move slowly and *then* give a sudden shot of power?

You don't have to think it out; just try several rod and line combinations and you'll find that you already know something, that you like one rod action over another. This is the beginning of making the decision: knowing how it feels in your hand and what it does for your casting.

If you have to feel a rod without a line on it, you can learn something about its action by *stroking* it, moving the rod through the casting stroke, forward and backward. At the end of the power snap you'll feel and see elements that will tell you if the rod recovers quickly or slowly from the cast, if there is a feeling of strength or weakness in the butt section above the grip, and how far the tip bends in the stroke. It can be a first step in deciding which rod, or rods, of a group, you want to put a line on.

As a last resort you can buy by catalog, but words on paper about work-manship and adjectives describing the action, may not do for you what you expected. Be sure you can return a rod you buy by mail. On the other hand, if you end up with a rod you are not sure you like, before you put it in a closet and buy another, try lines one size lighter and one size heavier, then you might try a different design (forward taper, triangle taper, double taper) and, perhaps, the line of a different manufacturer. You may come up with a winning combination.

ROD ACTION

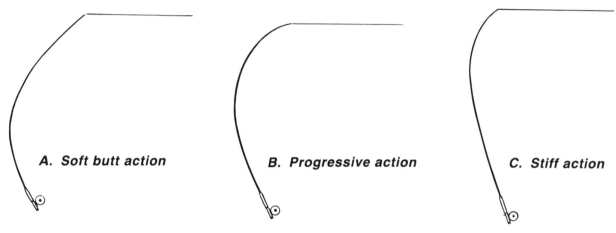

A. Soft butt action   B. Progressive action   C. Stiff action

Balance

Most fly rods come to you with a recommended line size imprinted on the butt section. Use this only as a guide. The tackle industry has traditionally *under*-lined their rods, in my judgment. Perhaps it is because they are double-taper oriented, and I use forward tapers. Use one size heavier than recommended, if you use a weight-forward line, but if you can try more than one weight on a rod, or the same weight by two different manufacturers, you'll know for sure that you are matching line to rod as well as you can.

Determining whether a given line is too light or too heavy for your rod, gets easier with experience, but I can give you some guidance. Lines that are too light do not flex the rod in the loading move and feel stick-like. There is no feeling of life in them. Lines that are too heavy make the rod feel soggy, bending the tip deeply even on slow casts without line hauls. The loop will fall as it unrolls, no matter how good your casting mechanics, instead of staying on a straight line off the rod tip at the end of the power snap.

I once had a solid-boron rod that the maker designated as a #4 weight rod. I didn't own a #4 weight line, so I put on a #5 and couldn't feel any action. The rod felt like a stick, although it did cast the line. I put on a #6 next and struck gold. It was a beautiful combination. I tried a #7 just for fun, fishing with it one evening on the Grand Cascapedia, and, just as I had decided it was too heavy and I would change back to the #6, a twenty-one-pound Atlantic salmon took the fly and made my day. *He* did not realize that the line was too heavy for the rod.

The term "balance" doesn't mean the ratio of reel weight to rod length and weight. It means the matching of the weight of the fly line to the action of the rod, to bring out the best in it. Once that boron rod was balanced with the right line for me, it gave me great pleasure to use it.

The casting mechanics you have learned will work for any kind of rod action, but you will have to adjust your timing and power intensity for individual rods, especially for soft, or slow-actioned rods. You can't hurry those. You may have to cast wider loops, wait longer on the unrolling, lengthen your stroke to make the power snap less of a shock, and, generally, slow down. You must adjust according to what you see and feel.

Materials

During the period of time that I have been fishing with fly rods, the materials have changed. Bamboo was followed by fiberglass, and today graphite and graphite-boron combinations dominate the market. There is a feeling generated in the casting of certain bamboo rods that may never be duplicated with space-age materials, but my choice for a fishing tool is graphite. The light weight and fast recovery of graphite give me ease of casting and excellence of performance that is more difficult to find in the other materials. This is, of course, a general statement, but the weight/performance ratio is what I look for, in addition to feeling. Boron is, for its weight, the strongest material yet known, but it is a little heavier than graphite. There are some powerful graphite-boron combinations available for heavier lines. If you consider the factors of weight and price, you can find the rod action you want in any material.

Rod Grips

The shape and size of the rod grip is more important for anglers with small hands than with large ones. The grip should not be so large that it prevents you from using full strength in a power snap when you need to make the turnover arc small. In the turnover arc, you'll pull the grip back up toward the underside of your wrist. Check that action when you choose a rod grip, to make sure it is not too fat for the last three fingers to move, *with strength*. If you determine that it is too large, you can use sandpaper to remove some of the diameter. Many women and children, having been made presents of rods with grips too large for them, are turned off to fly casting because their hand tires too easily and they don't understand that it can be the fault of a grip of the wrong size or shape.

Short Rods/Long Rods

Let's compare a long rod with a short rod.

Long rods: (9 feet)
> Relatively shorter strokes.
> Fewer false casts for long casts.
> Backcasts that can be higher above the water, especially helpful from a sitting position in a boat.
> You can move more line for the same effort when you mend line.
> The path of heavy or air-resistant flies will be higher above your head.
> Longer overhang for pickup on long casts, perhaps saving a false cast.
> More cushion in playing fish to allow for angler error.
> Makes long roll casts easier.

Short rods: (6 to 7 feet)
> The weight.
> Easier to handle in small-stream conditions.
> Much better control over fish when they are in close, which is where you are most likely to lose them.
> The challenge.

For all-day fishing, the big difference between long rods and short rods is weight. Before graphite took over the fly-rod market, 8½- to 9-foot rods weighed 4 to 4½ ounces for the effective line weights of #6 or #7. Just as I had moved to short rods because of their weight, so had a large majority of anglers. Graphite reversed the trend.

Callouses may develop at the top of the palm, or grip burns may develop on the heel of the hand if the rod grip is too thick or if the shape is incompatible with the shape of your hand.

Short rods are generally thought of, by the fly fishing public, as being too light to be effective or too stiff to be a pleasure. Neither has to be true, but unfortunately, there is not enough of a demand on manufacturers for short graphite rods in order for today's rod designers to spend time developing actions that have both the strength and the delicacy that the bamboo rods made by Wes Jordan (Orvis) and Farlow, in consultation with Lee, were wont to have.

The short graphite rod I use for all-around trout, Atlantic salmon, and, sometimes, bonefish, is a Scott Power Ply, 3-piece, 6'10" for a #7 line, made first for Lee by Harry Wilson. Additionally I use an 8-foot graphite for a #6 line. I fish for bass with a 9-foot rod and for tarpon with a 9 or 9½ for a #10 weight line. For bonefish and salmon I carry a 9 foot for a #8/#9 line as a spare when the shorter lighter rods won't do. I rarely use them.

Because short rods require more of you as a caster, you'll need longer strokes, more speed, and precise timing. To cast a short rod:

Technique #1. Use an open-body stance with the rod tipped *off vertical* 40 to 45°, as described in "Body Stances."

Technique #2. Use the oval cast.

I recommend that you learn to cast with the longer rods, but every angler who enjoys the challenge of good fly casting should, at some time in his life, own and master a short rod for the sheer pleasure of it.

And Finally

Don't buy a rod because someone else likes it. I've been fighting that battle all of my life, because I am a woman in what has been a man's field, but the advice might be valid even if you are a man. I am reminded of Charles Ritz, rod designer, angler, and author. Charlie designed rods for Pezon & Michel and was in his "parabolic action" phase when I visited France in 1948. He described, in ecstatic terms, an action that to my hand felt like a soft butt, a soft tip, and a lump in the middle, but I was sure that what he thought was more likely to be right than what I thought and, on my return to the States, I used his gift rod in the Skish fly event at the National. I found out, too late, that if I made a fraction of an inch of error when I directed the rod toward the target, the soft butt section would magnify the error to be measured in feet. Instead of casting in the high eighties or low nineties, as I had always done, my score this time was *thirteen*. I retired the parabolic rod to the attic. I find myself wondering, now, how Charlie could have been comfortable with parabolic rods and his "high speed/high line" casting instruction, but Charlie moved from one rod action to another as long as he lived, each one being the best that ever was and the one action that would change the fly-fishing world. I loved him, as others did, for his enthusiasm and for his love of both fly fishing and fly fishermen, but I could not be comfortable with many of the rod actions he originated.

Trust your own judgment.

Fly Reels

Line capacity, weight, and whether or not a drag system is included, are the determining factors in choosing your fly reel.

The capacity includes room for your fly line and "backing," if you need it, for fish that make runs longer than your 100 feet of flyline will allow. Backing is usually braided dacron and is attached to the reel behind the fly line. Fifty yards would be the minimum for trout fishing; 150 yards the minimum for tarpon. Backing also cushions the fly line, giving the core a wider diameter around which the line will be wound to eliminate kinking in its backend yardage.

Reels with perforated spools are lightweight compared to those which have solid spools, and drag systems too add weight. Don't use a complex drag system if you don't really need it. Most single-action reels have a click to keep the line from overrunning when a fish makes a quick dash for freedom, and that is usually enough for trout and bass fishing.

Automatic reels are heavy and "dangerous." Dangerous because it is so easy to lose fish with them. Drags should be lightened as fish increase the distance they move from the angler. An automatic reel tightens the tension as the distance increases, often allowing the fish to pop the leader.

Early in the book I mentioned left-hand reeling for right-handed people. Left-hand reeling lets you play a fish more effectively, partly because your primary hand on the rod is stronger than your secondary hand and partly because of eye/hand coordination. It is sometimes difficult to learn to wind left-handed, but you can do as I did. I held the reel handle still and wound the rod, for the first step. Then I progressed to winding both the reel and the rod at the same time, and finally was able to hold the rod still and use only the left hand. (The reel must be adjusted, internally, before it can be wound opposite the way the manufacturer intended.)

nine

SPECIES

Fly Casting for Bass

A long rod that has "the guts" to move an air-resistant fly against the wind, is a good choice for this fine sport. If you are in a boat with a companion, keeping the fly above his head, as well as yours, is a first priority.

Your choice of fly lines will probably be a bass-bug taper or a triangle-taper bass line, each designed to handle the relatively bulky or air-resistant flies and shoot the necessary length of line with a minimum number of casts. Bass are not known for long runs, so you don't really need backing unless you want to cushion your line.

To keep a large bass bug from coming off the water with a flat trajectory, be sure to make your pickup precisely. On the loading move, start with the rod tip low and all slack removed, then pick up not just the line, but the leader too, so that your power snap needs only to take the bug, itself, off the water. You'll get a nice quiet pickup this way on a good angle above your head. A single or double haul may help, depending on wind conditions. Experiment to find out.

The timing on the backcast will be a little different than with a light fly. Wait until the heavy bug is fully extended before the forward cast is begun, to make the turnaround a smooth one. On the forward cast, use the slower acceleration of the loading move to get the bug moving at the same speed as the rod and line, before you pick up speed for the power snap.

Even if you are in a sitting position, body motion is likely to rock the boat. To help with this, use your casting arm relatively high on the backcast (having started with the rod tip low) to extend the casting arc as much as

A huge fly-rod-caught bass, West Palm Beach, Florida.

possible under these restricted conditions. If you can sit sideward, it will simulate an open-body position and give you room to lengthen your stroke comfortably.

The presentation cast with heavy flies works best with a wide loop and the line put on the water at about its middle to unroll from there. (Lower the rod's path to finish the stroke *below* the hand/target line.)

Your leader length can be as short as four to six feet, for good control of the heavier or air-resistant flies. Line weight range is from #7 to #10.

Fly Casting for Atlantic Salmon

The challenge of fishing for Atlantic salmon is an unparalleled one. These anadromous fish are on a spawning run, when you have access to them—super-charged with energy to see them through the long months they will spend in the river before returning to the sea. Because they are not feeding, your fly must trigger a response that reaches back to their early years in the stream when, as parr, they pounced on anything that moved.

It can be very demanding fishing: wind, deep wading, rocky shores, hours of casting, and black flies (on *this* continent) are among the conditions you may have to contend with. Use the technique of quartering downstream (see "Casting Patterns for Stream Coverage") for wet fly coverage, or, if the water is relatively low and you know the location of a salmon's lie, dry-fly fishing can be incredibly exciting!

In the biggest rivers, canoes and guides are necessary, and, if you fish on only one side of the boat, the pattern will be the same as when you are wading. If you must cover water on both sides of the canoe, you can cover one side at a time, retrieving all of the line between sides; or you can do it in the pattern shown in the illustration.

1. Make a short cast (let's say to the right side first) and fish it.

2. Cast to the left side, with the same length of line.

3. Extend the line by your measured amount and make a second cast to the left.

4. Keep that length and cast to the right.

5. Extend the line and make a second cast on the right.

After the first cast, you'll be making two casts to each side of the canoe, lengthening the line on the second cast. If you think a particular length swing is more likely to produce a rise than another, you can always repeat it.

If a salmon rises to your fly but misses it, length marks on your line (see "Marking Lines for Weight and Distance") will enable you to duplicate the cast exactly.

Choose your tackle carefully to make what may turn out to be hundreds of casts in a fishing day. The range of line weights from which to choose is #7 to #10 and the lines can be of weight-forward, triangle-taper, or shooting-head design.

ATLANTIC SALMON: COVERAGE FROM A BOAT

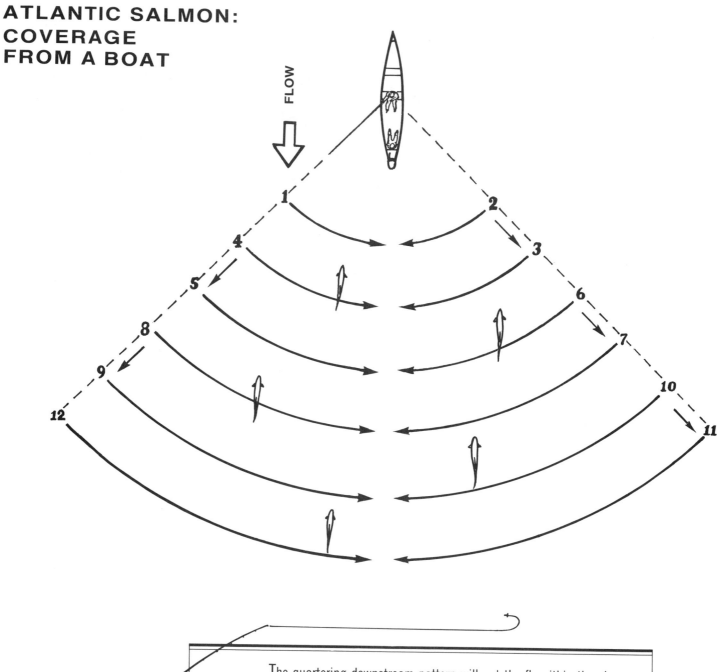

The quartering downstream pattern will put the fly within the view of every fish in the pool (within your casting range) with your repetitive maximum length cast, but a shorter line, as used at the beginning of the coverage, will bring the fly to the fish at a different angle. It is, therefore, good technique to retrieve the long line and start the pattern over again with short casts, as you come to the best holding sections in any given pool. The fish will then have seen the fly from two different angles.

Casting on the Spey River in Scotland. *Photo by Arthur Oglesby.*

On the Forks Pool on the Grand Cascapedia. *Photo by Lee Wulff.*

Typical Atlantic Salmon Tackle
> 9-foot to 9½ foot rod with extension butt
> #9 or #10 weight, intermediate sinking line, or a floating line with a sinking tip
> 200 yards of 20 lb. test dacron backing
> large-capacity reel with drag system

Light Atlantic Salmon Tackle
> 8-foot to 9-foot rod
> #7 weight-forward floating line
> 200 yards of 20 lb. test dacron backing
> Single-action reel with only a click to keep the line from overrunning

Leader lengths can range from nine to fifteen feet, with the tippet strength chosen according to water conditions, fly size, and your skill in playing fish.

Two-Handed Rods

A few years ago, Lee and I had the pleasure of fishing on the River Spey, in Scotland, with Arthur and Grace Oglesby, both of whom use two-handed rods with skill and artistry. Arthur has taken over the reins from the late, great instructor, Tommy Edwards, as one of Great Britain's premier salmon fishermen.

Because my own experience with two-handed rods had been limited to a brief fling, as a tournament caster, with tackle that was too heavy for me, I asked the Oglesbys to bring me up to date on technique. Gracie responded by demonstrating Edwards' instruction to hold the rod lightly, with just the thumb and forefinger, at the two pressure points, the top and bottom of the long-rod grip. She made it look relaxed and easy.

Two-handed rods are somewhat in fashion for American salmon fishermen, at least as a back-up when they visit the hallowed streams of Europe. A two-handed rod, used from a boat, can keep the heavy (up to 7/0), traditional salmon flies well above the heads of companions. In wading, the beat you may be given to fish could include only one bank (and a high one at that) of a very wide river, and the two-handed rod with *Spey* casting techniques, is the best and sometimes, the only method that will make your fishing effective.

The Mechanics

Hold the rod at the top and bottom of the grip, with the thumb and forefinger dominant in the holding. Use your primary hand on top to begin, but, at some point in your practice, exchange the hand positions to use the other on top. Depending on which bank of the stream you may be given for a wading beat, or the direction of the wind, you may well have to cast with your secondary hand at the top of the grip.

TWO-HANDED ROD: BASIC HOLDING POSITION

Because using two hands centers the rod on your body, use a closed-body stance, with a foot dropped back for straight-line casting. The casting mechanics are the ones you are familiar with. On the backcast, as your rod hand (on top) lifts and pulls the rod back, the lower hand will push the rod grip forward. On the forward stroke, the rod hand will push forward as the lower hand pulls the grip back. Keep the path straight, using the top of the grip as your indicator. Because of the length of the rod, you need not angle the path of the rod as sharply as you did with a single-handed rod. Your upper hand should travel just above shoulder level. On false casts, make the strokes parallel to the water.

Hold the fly line with the middle finger of each hand and keep it tight, between hands, along the rod butt, to avoid catching it on the reel. Hang loops for shooting from the fingers of the lower hand.

Spey Casting

Spey casts were originally roll casts. The Spey moves, which precede the presentation cast, are made to position the fly, up or downstream of the angler, so there will be no crossing of line and leader as the cast is made. The pattern of coverage is quartering downstream.

If the fly line used is a full-length single or double taper, the presentation cast will be a standard roll cast, with the line unrolling on the water. With lines of weight-forward design, or shooting heads, the presentation cast is made *above* the water, to allow for the shooting of line.

Single Spey

Position yourself against the left bank of an imaginary river (left or right, banks are determined by a view downstream). Start with an extended line, downstream of you, and find your target area at a 45° angle toward the other bank. The move of the backcast will be to reposition the fly from downstream to just upstream of the angler, before the forward cast.

1. Lift the line (on the loading move), ending with the rod in front of your left shoulder.

2. Your power snap will be a *curved* one, moving across your body from left front to right rear, lifting from the water the leader and fly. Let the forward end of the curved loop of line touch down on the water long enough to create surface friction, as

3. you *drift* your arms upward, repositioning

4. to make the forward stroke above the water, shooting line to the target area.

In this **single-Spey** technique, you are, in effect, placing the portion of the line that lands on the water, *opposite* where you want your forward cast to go. This is the same principle you used with a single-handed rod to bridge the angle of change of direction. The difference is that this time part of the line touches the water.

SINGLE SPEY CAST

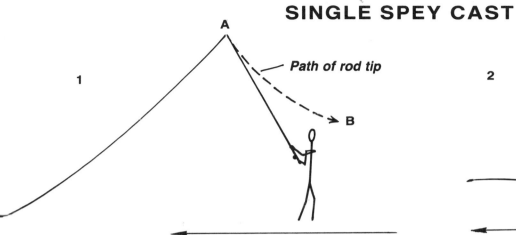

Path of rod tip

1. A is end of loading move

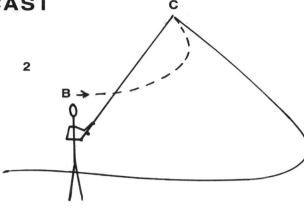

2. A to B to C is curving power snap.

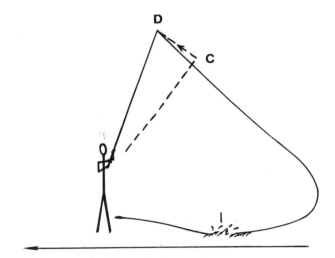

3. Section of line touches water briefly
   as rod is drifted upward C to D. (Splashdown)

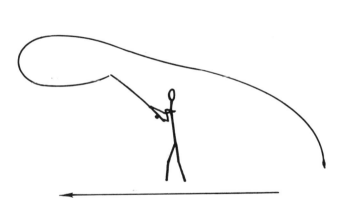

4. Forward cast is made above the water.

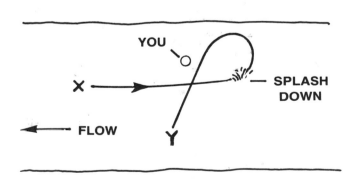

Path of fly line for Single Spey.

Double Spey

This has a Figure-eight form for your rod tip to follow. Once it starts, the moves are continuous.

Position yourself on the right bank of your river. The line is extended downstream of you. Your target is at a 45° angle across the river. On the **double Spey**, you'll reposition the fly upstream but to a point still below the angle of the coming presentation cast.

1. Lift the line (loading move) to bring the fly to the surface.

2. Start the figure eight. To move the line upstream, swing the rod upstream in an underhand curving move that passes by your left shoulder.

3. Swing the rod forward with a *soft* power snap, to form a loop that remains connected to the water (for a short length).

4. Take the rod back to your right shoulder to swing the loop of line behind it and

5. make the presentation cast above the surface to shoot line.

The direction of the wind is very important in your choice of techniques: single or double Spey. You already know that if the wind is blowing from your casting side when you do a simple roll cast, you must make the cast off your other shoulder, backhanded. So too, with the Spey. The final move before presentation must be made on the downwind side of your body so that the line will not blow into you. Therefore, if the wind is blowing upstream, choose the single Spey, and if it is blowing downstream, use the double Spey. Whichever bank you are on will determine whether the right hand or the left hand will be at the top of the grip.

Tackle

If you plan to just roll cast with the Spey techniques, use a double-tapered line, unless you can find a full-length single taper. For an aerial presentation, on which you will shoot line, the shooting head design is best.

General Range

Rods:	13 to 17 feet long
Lines:	#10 to #14, from 35 to 45 feet in length. The general formula is to make a shooting head from half of a double-tapered line and splice shooting line to it
Shooting line:	Oval monofilament or floating fly line in light sizes (#4)

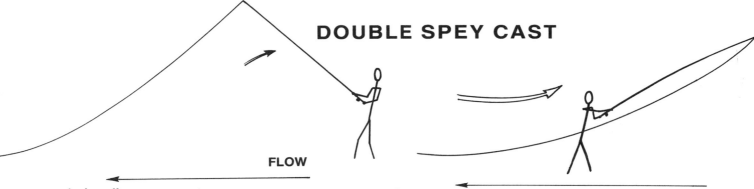

DOUBLE SPEY CAST

FLOW

1. Loading move.

2. Swing rod upstream to angler's left for beginning of figure 8. Fly moves upstream but remains in water.

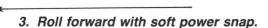

3. Roll forward with soft power snap.

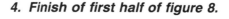

4. Finish of first half of figure 8.

5. Swing rod to right side for final roll-cast position. (Raise rod at this point.)

6. Line unrolls above the water for the shooting presentation.

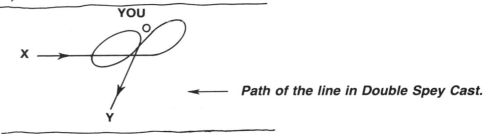

YOU

X

Y

Path of the line in Double Spey Cast.

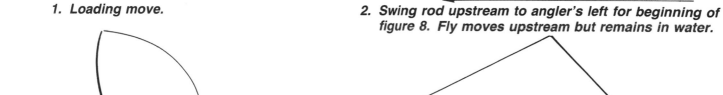

Arthur Oglesby uses 36 feet of a double-tapered #11 line, backed by oval monofilament of 25 to 30 lb. test, on rods of 15 to 16½ feet in length.

Fly Casting on the Salt-Water Flats

In July of 1950 a national Skish casting tournament was held on the campus of the University of Miami at Coral Gables. It was my first look at Florida and I was invited to fish afterward, at Tavernier, with guide Holly Hollenbeck. The Florida keys were pretty empty in those days and I found Holly and his brother, Rollie, sitting on the steps of their tackle shop on the Overseas Highway when I arrived. The bonefish skiff was tied to the dock right behind the building, on the Gulf side, and we took off under the early morning sun. We never saw a bonefish that day, but I did cast behind a ray, as instructed, and hooked what Holly screamed *was* a bonefish ("Just like I tole ya"), keeping the gag going until I could see that it was a jack crevalle. My first jack . . . the tough, sunfish-shaped fighter that anglers "break their teeth on," in that country. They are always good exercise.

I fell in love with the flats and our fishing for bonefish, permit, and tarpon and have never had enough of it. Flats fishing is a different kind of game from trout, salmon, or bass fishing. It is hunt, spot, and intercept. You stand ready to make the cast, your eyes—as are those of your guide—sweeping the bottom over which he poles the boat, for a shadowy form or some movement that will indicate the presence of your quarry. The guide will suddenly say something like, "Fish fifty feet . . . ten o'clock!"—then the presentation must be made with as few false casts as possible, to intercept the moving fish and/or keep from spooking it if it is not moving.

It is demanding fishing, requiring good eyes, sharp reflexes, well-trained casting muscles, and stamina. Tension can be a factor if your guide has poled for long periods of time and you've seen few fish. Every move becomes terribly important; you don't want to blow any opportunity, and sometimes there is undue pressure put on the angler. Have a few words with your guide, beforehand, about what he can reasonably expect of you, and be prepared with mastery of the **quick cast**, a technique that will let you reach sixty feet or more, in two to three seconds.

Success with quick casts lies in the design of the line and the angler's being properly set up ahead of time. The line must be of weight-forward design; choose a saltwater taper, triangle taper (sizes ten and up were designed for this cast), or shooting head. In setting up, the line's effective weight should be just out of the rod tip before you begin the cast.

An 84-pound tarpoon, taken on a #9 line during the Islamoradora Gold Cup Tarpon Tournament in 1966.

Setting Up

Long before the guide spots your first fish, make your longest cast and retrieve the line so that it lies on the casting platform in large coils. As the head, or back end of the line's belly, reaches the rod tip, secure some line under your rod hand and swing the remaining line in to you, so that you may arrange it, from that point forward, as shown in the illustration. It is a roll-cast position, but you will hold loops of the front end of the line, plus the leader and the fly, in your line hand. How much you must hold depends on your height, the rod's length, and the platform height above the water.

Start the arrangement of the line by holding the fly between thumb and forefinger, then form the necessary loops of the leader and front end of the line on other fingers. Two loops are usually sufficient, even if you are short in height. You can trail the bellied line in the water if there are no weeds to obstruct it; that connection with the surface tension will anchor the line to make your first forward move a more efficient one than if the line were hanging freely above the water, or lying on the deck.

1. The forward roll. Make a forward stroke, aimed well above the water. Don't release the loops all at once but let the momentum of the fly line "pull" the loops from your line hand, *ending* with the release of the fly.

As soon as the fly leaves the fingers of your line hand, reach forward to take the line from where it has been secured, against the rod grip, under your rod-hand's middle finger, in preparation for the double haul to come.

2. The backcast. Begin a double haul on the backcast stroke, shooting line during drift time, to reach your optimum overhang.

3. The forward cast. Use the second haul and shoot the line needed to reach the target.

Three moves in two-to-three seconds to distances of sixty feet or more. It's magical, once you can do it. The first move, with the sequence of the roll forward, the release of the fly, and the taking of the line from the rod hand —all accomplished before the line falls too low or loses its tension—is the part of the cast that really requires practice.

If, because of the fishing circumstances, you are not able to stand with your rod in the roll-cast position, with the line bellied behind your shoulder, you will have to make an additional move. You'll have to move the rod

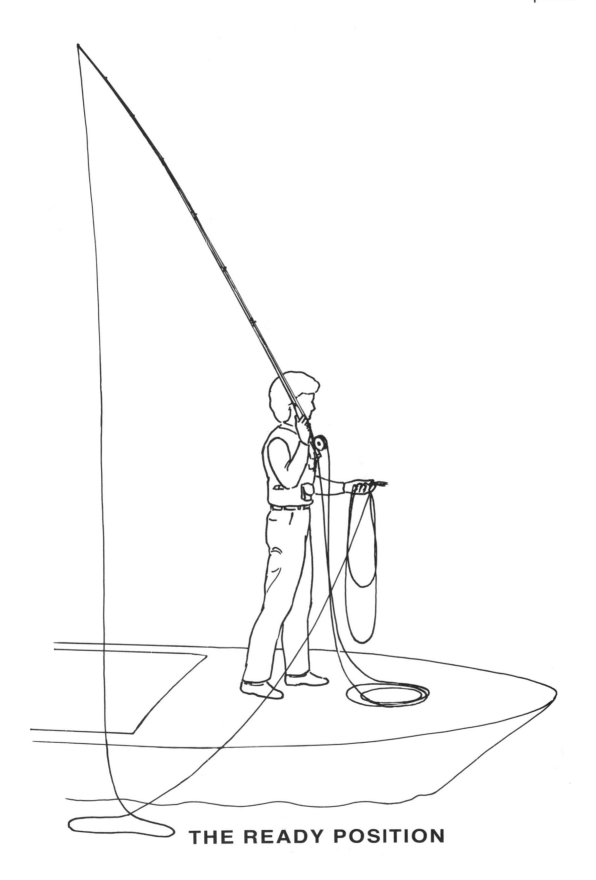

THE READY POSITION

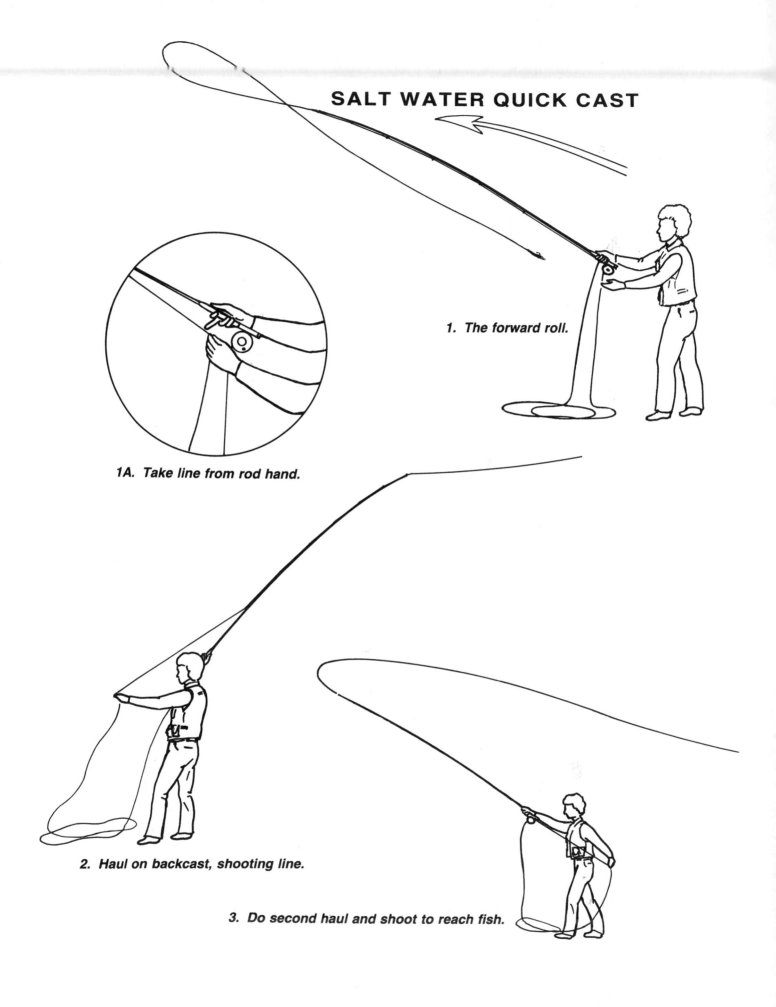

SALT WATER QUICK CAST

1. The forward roll.

1A. Take line from rod hand.

2. Haul on backcast, shooting line.

3. Do second haul and shoot to reach fish.

backward, without releasing the line, before the roll forward, *or* you might do it all in *two* moves. Make the first move the backcast, shooting line, and shoot the rest on the forward stroke.

The weight of the tackle is very important to the success of the quick cast. Size #9 and up will work most easily because of the dramatic difference between the effective line weight and the running line.

Suggested Tackle

Light: for bonefish, permit, barracuda, sea trout, redfish
   9 foot rod, or shorter, weighing 3½ ounces or less
   #6 to #8 weight, floating or intermediate sinking line of weight-forward or triangle-taper design
   150 to 200 yards of 20-pound-test dacron backing
   A single-action reel, with only a click to keep the line from overrunning.

Heavy: for tarpon
   9 to 9½-foot rod, weighing 4 to 6 ounces
   #9 to #12 weight, floating or intermediate saltwater taper, triangle taper or shooting head
   200 yards of 20-pound-test dacron backing; 30-pound-test for #11 to #12 weight lines
   A large capacity reel with a drag system.

Saltwater leaders must be constructed to protect against abrasion or the sharp teeth of some species. Wire, or heavy monofilament shock leaders of 80-to-100-pound test next to the fly, serve this purpose. It is best to check with the outfitter, or guide, about special leader components before a trip.

Off Shore

In deep water, exciting surface action can be yours with other species on tackle similar to that used for fresh-water bass.

Intermediate weight: For such fish as bluefish, mackerel, and stripers
   9-foot rod
   #8 to #10 floating or intermediate line

150 yards of 20-pound-test dacron backing
Single action reel with just a click to keep it from overrunning.

Many anglers enjoy the challenge of fishing with a fly for amberjack and other species that are found near what bass fishermen call "structure" in deep water. The challenge in this kind of fly fishing is not in the casting but is in the difficulty of pumping the fish up to the surface once it is hooked.

ten

PRACTICE

Outdoor Practice

Casting practice is "dullsville" unless you have set some goals and challenges for yourself to make it interesting. Practicing often is more important than practicing for long sessions. Practice while you are sharp and fresh; if you get tired, stop!

I wish I could tell you exactly how long it will take for you to become a good caster, but you and I both know that it depends on too many things. You must train your muscles to do their job *without thought* from you, just *direction*. Whatever time you put in will be productive if you understand what you are doing. The tough part is that you could be doing something wrong and not know it, but you'll find clues in the way the cast looks to you and whether or not you feel anything hurt. You can expect that your hand and arm muscles will tire, but if you have pain in your upper arm or shoulder area, something is probably out of line as you make the cast. Use the drawings for reference and be very aware of the "area of focus," mentioned in the beginning of the book. It might be helpful for you to tape your own reading of the instruction to play back outdoors as you practice.

Even if you can get to a pond or stream on which to practice, you'll do better if you divide your practice time to include sessions around the house, without water, where you can use parts of buildings, vehicles, bushes or trees, alleys—all of the natural set-ups in which you can cast your fly to simulate fishing conditions. Here are some suggestions:

1. The **picking leaves** exercise is one of the most important. It will perfect your accuracy, your turnover arc for narrow loops, your change-of-direction backcasts, and give you practice in the whole 180° spectrum.

2. **Getting the whole picture** will always remind you of within what parameters the cast must be executed, and help you to see what happens as a result of your actions. Stroke length, line speed, and backcast timing will be improved with this exercise.

3. Practice **hovering** a fly over a trash can, or in small openings in anything available.

4. Practice **curve casts** around bushes, trees, the dog that is lying patiently watching you, or the back wheel of your car.

5. Practice **reverse casting** using your garage, shed, van, truck, or some medium-high obstacle if you don't have a large, spreading tree with a slot of space between its branches.

6. Practice making **long casts** to place the fly in "slots" of space. Use an alley, the narrow space between two vehicles, or an open doorway. Use a partially open overhead garage door or the window of your car. These last are good targets because you can vary the opening.

7. Practice **air rolls**, with limited backcast room, by decreasing the distance between yourself and an obstacle. Use any vehicle, building, or bush.

8. Practice casting in the **wind**, changing your position relative to it, through 360°, to experience the condition in all possible ways. This will heighten your awareness of how and when you must vary timing and power, sometimes instantly, as the need arises. It will also give you practice in combining forehand and backhand casts to keep the fly line from colliding with the rod.

You can benefit from a headwind when you are perfecting your double haul or the technique of shooting line on the final backcast. Cast into the headwind to feel more strongly the backward extension of your fly line.

When you get very good at all of these exercises (and others you may originate), try them with your secondary hand. Every once in a while, you may need that skill, when the stream's direction or the wind or your position in a boat, dictates it. Be the best that you can be!

And when you are moving from one target area to another, don't just walk, *false cast* as you go!

Arrange for someone to video-tape parts of your practice sessions. Using the illustrations in the book for reference, you can then analyze your efforts.

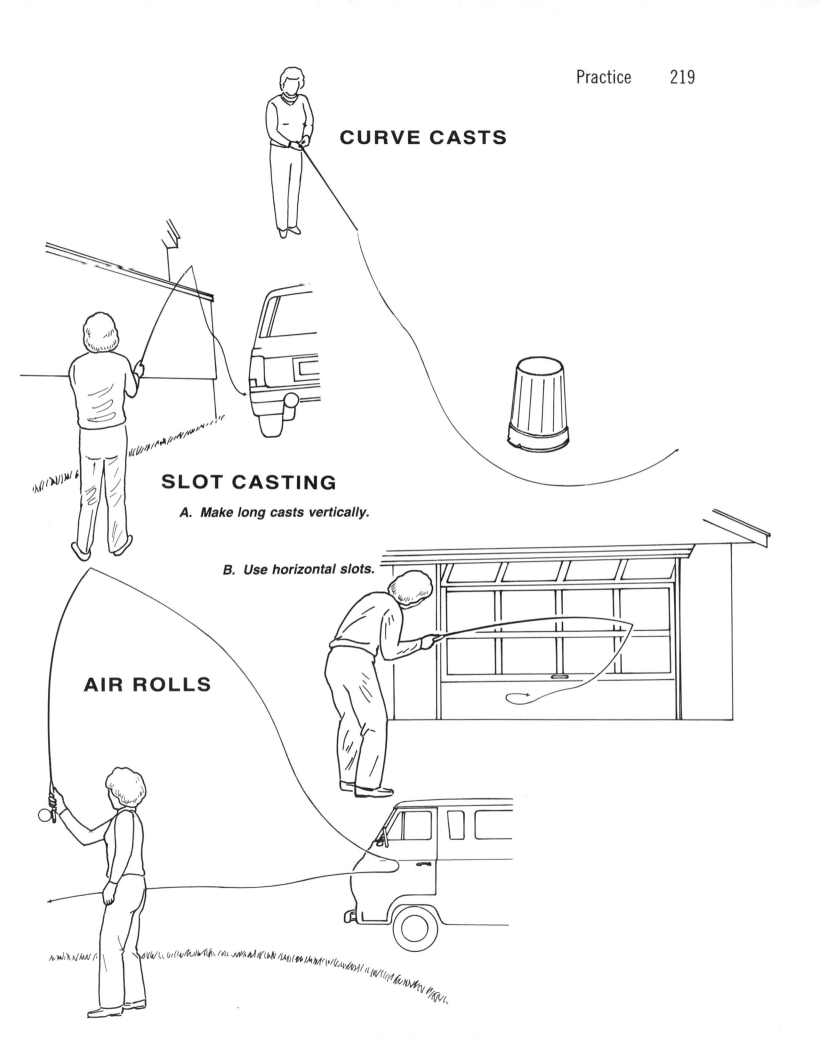

CURVE CASTS

SLOT CASTING

A. Make long casts vertically.

B. Use horizontal slots.

AIR ROLLS

Casting Practice Axioms

I will:

1. *Mark* my fly line at thirty, forty, and fifty feet.

2. Start the backcast and end the forward cast with the end of the rod against the underside of my forearm.

3. When taking line off the water, start the pickup with the rod tip low to the water and with no slack in the line. OR, use a *roll pickup* technique to solve the problem of slack.

4. On the pickup, end the backcast stroke as the fly comes out of the water.

5. End all backcast strokes with my rod hand in front of, above, or in line with, my shoulder, but not behind it.

6. Use a *squeeze stop* on the backcast, with a straight, but not stiff, wrist.

7. Make sure that my grip on the rod handle does not change during the cast.

8. Use a stroke length that will unroll the fly line along a 180° line.

9. Use the *drift move*, between the back and forward casts, to reposition my arm and rod backward, sideward, upward, or downward, but *never* forward.

10. *Aim* at a particular inch of water on every cast.

11. Determine a *hand/target line* before beginning the forward cast and make a straight-line path along it with the rod hand.

12. Use enough *acceleration* to unroll the line completely above the water before any of it touches the water.

13. Use *hand/wrist action* on the forward cast power snap by pushing with my thumb as far forward as it can go.

14. As the line lengthens, use *body motion* as it is needed to lengthen the casting stroke.

15. Watch and analyze the way in which the line unrolls on every forward cast.

16. Cast with the *hand/target line* overlapping the *eye/target line*, to be accurate with short casts.

17. On longer casts, be sure to do a *loading move* at the beginning of every forward cast so as not to create a tailing loop with a power-snap start.

18. Keep slack from forming between the line hand and the first guide on the rod, during the cast.

19. Exercise precise control with the line hand, shooting line only after the *power snap*.

20. Look for the feeling of *constant pressure*, of the fly line on the rod tip, throughout the cast.

Indoor Practice with Fly-O

Outdoor practice is ideal, but the amount of time it takes to get outdoors and set up tackle is not always as available to you as the small increments of time you might find indoors, whether at home or at work. Think of the many five-minute time periods you have in a day when you could pick up a tiny, indoor fly rod and work on your accuracy by sending the unrolling line to targets like the wastebasket, the finial on a lamp shade, or, in a horizontal cast, under an overhanging chair or table. If you have twenty-five feet of hallway to use, you can practice long casts.

There *is* such an indoor fly rod, and the idea was Lee's. In the early fifties, he decided that if golfers could practice their swing indoors with nets and soft balls, there should be the equivalent for fly fishermen to use. He put bulky yarn on a small rod, wrote about it, and went on to other things. In 1969 we developed the idea together.

Fly rods short enough to use indoors are hard to come by, so we made one from the upper section of a spinning rod; the three-foot tip had some stiffness in its lower section and wasn't too soft at the top. It was converted by adding three or four inches of cork rings for the hand grip. We found a bulky acrylic yarn, about three-eighths of an inch in diameter, that worked perfectly as a line. It is carded by Hallmark as gift-wrapping yarn, in 18-foot lengths and in myriad colors. We chose blaze orange.

A family Fly-O session—Joan, Douglas Cummings, Lee, and Stuart Cummings.

Photo by Jack Hegarty.

Although the yarn, unlike a fly line, has no effective weight, its bulk creates air resistance, which requires real power in the cast to push it through the air. We estimate that for the same effort, the proportion of this yarn to real fly line is about one to four; i.e., one foot of yarn equals four or five feet of fly line. You can mark the yarn with one-inch black marks at 6, 8, 10 and 12 feet, working first with the 6-foot mark positioned at the tip of the rod (comparable to 24 to 30 feet of fly line), and adding a foot or two at a time as you master each length. Lengthening the yarn will require longer strokes, more power, and slower timing, just as it does with real tackle.

The indoor training tool, Fly-O, used in front of a mirror, is faster than a video instant replay!

When my elder son, Douglas Cummings, was twelve years old, he learned to cast with "Fly-O," as we named it. After a couple of months' practice, in the winter, he could perfectly straighten out exactly ten feet of yarn, on the floor. As soon as the ice went off our pond in the spring, we made an occasion of his first try with real tackle and set up an 8½-foot rod with a #8 weight line. At the end of a twenty-minute session, he had made a cast of *60 feet*! He held 35 to 40 feet of line and leader in the air, false casting, and shot the rest. It was a natural extension of what he had learned indoors.

Because the yarn line cannot slide or shoot through the guides, the rod hand gets all of your concentration, and well it should. I have suggested that, as you read the instruction, you use a pencil to simulate a rod, or use the butt of your rod with a reel on it. If you have Fly-O to follow up with, you'll save endless amounts of time in learning the techniques in this book. You can work on the *basic discipline* up to and including *line hand tension*, and then you can practice the circular casts, pickups and presentations, and even aerial mending. The "picking leaves" exercise is a natural for indoor practice. You can find oodles of targets among your home or office furnishings. Sitting on a chair, or kneeling on the floor, may help you use the space in small rooms, and can also put the outfit in better perspective. You are pretty safe with Fly-O, with regard to movable treasures it may touch that are in the path of the backcast. But you might get into trouble if you snap your backcast forward before it has unrolled. Look for clear backcast space.

INDOOR PRACTICE—FLY-O

To keep the practice interesting, set goals for yourself in accuracy and distance. The marks on the yarn will help. Your objectives in long-line casting can be reached if you learn to unroll the yarn line completely (no curls) on the floor, at various lengths. The form of the cast should be like a real fly line, with narrow loops and wide loops at your command. If you can straighten twelve feet of yarn, it will be the equivalent of forty-eight to sixty feet of fly line. The basic mechanics will be important; as well as the stroke length, the overall acceleration, and the positioning of the power snap on your hand/target line. Practice in both open- and closed-body stances, although the length of the rod will make the open-body stance a better choice for long casts. You may be surprised at the amount of power you will have to generate in the casting stroke with twelve feet or more of yarn.

Whatever time you invest will give you a great return. The visual images, the eye/hand/rod coordination, and even the toning of your casting muscles, can be carried from indoors to outdoors, from the yarn line to a real line.

You can tell that I believe in this tool. Without Fly-O I might never have analyzed fly casting to the degree that I have—nor written this book. I hope you will make one, as we did originally, or buy one.

eleven

SPECIAL SITUATIONS

Hand Casting

Hand casting has been developed to an art by very few people. Lee Wulff, in his campaign to prove that rod *length* didn't really matter in the catching of Atlantic salmon, first hand-cast a fly line and salmon fly thirty-five to forty feet, in the Southwest River of Newfoundland, in 1941. He hooked, played, and landed a ten-pound salmon without any fly rod at all and won credence for his six-foot rods.

The late Ellis Newman was probably the most famous handcaster of recent times. He taught fly casting in the Catskills in the fifties and made hand casting an exhibition specialty. It is reported by A. J. McClane that Ellis could cast a whole 90-foot HCH (#7) fly line. Quite a feat. He was a powerfully built man and was dedicated to the development of this particular skill.

Hand casting will help your basic understanding of the weight and character of the fly line. It is fun to do and you may amaze yourself and your friends with the distances you can cast.

Use a #7 weight line if you have it, going heavier rather than lighter for another size. Stand as you did in "Getting the Whole Picture," casting from left to right rather than backward and forward.

Stretch ten feet of line on the lawn to your left, placed a little ahead of you. Start with a bent arm.

Start the whole length of line moving a few inches to the right, and then, keeping your hand's path on a straight line, accelerate in a power snap. When the fly comes off the grass, end the stroke—just as you do with a rod. The line should curl over your hand and unroll above the grass, to land to your right. You can drift after the power snap to reposition for a good forward cast.

Make a forward stroke within the same parameters and let it land to your left. You *are* using imaginary targets, aren't you?

When making the strokes one at a time is comfortable, try false casting. The critical elements are: keeping the path of the hand straight and good acceleration. This false casting with one hand is tough. Let's make it easier and add a haul.

To the right:

For a starting position, hold the hands a few inches apart, right hand forward of the left. Cup the line with the right and hold it with the left.

1. The rod hand will not keep a firm grip on the line, but will, instead, *slide* as the line hand *pulls the line* in the opposite direction. The line can move across the rod hand's cupped fingers or you can reverse the rod hand and run the line in the crotch between thumb and forefinger.

2. Accelerate to a stop.

3. While the line unrolls, "disconnect" your rod hand and reposition both hands for the cast to the left. The left hand will cup and the right hand will hold.

HAND CASTING

1. Start.

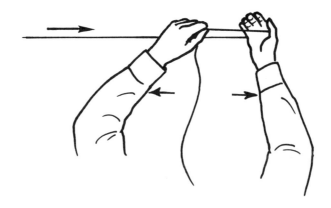

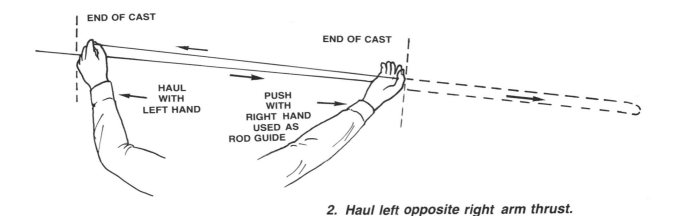

END OF CAST

END OF CAST

HAUL
WITH
LEFT HAND

PUSH
WITH
RIGHT HAND
USED AS
ROD GUIDE

2. Haul left opposite right arm thrust.

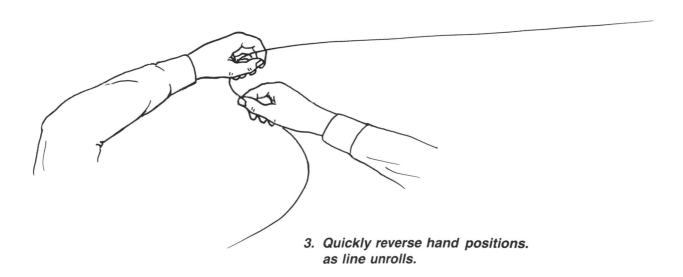

3. Quickly reverse hand positions.
as line unrolls.

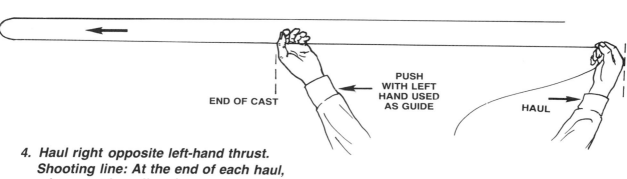

PUSH
WITH LEFT
HAND USED
AS GUIDE

END OF CAST

HAUL

4. Haul right opposite left-hand thrust.
Shooting line: At the end of each haul,
when cast is well under way,
release line with haul hand to lengthen cast.

To the left:

Follow the same mechanics, letting the left hand slide along the line and the rod hand pull opposite it. You can shoot line in both directions.

As you false cast, changing the hand positions between strokes requires quick reflexes—but you've got them.

Your stroke length can be only the length of your arm, stretching as far as it can go without straightening. People with long arms may outcast those with shorter arms.

There is only one thing about this you might not like, and that is that the line can burn your hand on the acceleration as you develop your skill. You might wear a thin glove, or coat your hand with something, as Ellis Newman did, if you get serious about it.

Teaching Your Youngster

A phone call from the local inn asked me to set aside lesson time for two pupils, a man and his six-and-a-half-year-old son. I agreed, anticipating difficulty with the younger student, either through lack of concentration to correct what would be his "natural," but all-wrong cast, or in the restricted length of his periods of concentration. I was wrong on both counts.

My two sessions with six-and-a-half-year-old Daniel turned out to be the highlight of my teaching season. Not only did Daniel listen, but he could direct the use of parts of his arm (hand, forearm, and whole arm) once he was shown their effect on his cast. He was uncanny; I found myself wondering if he wasn't a man in a child's body.

In two one-hour sessions, shared with his father, Daniel learned the roll cast, the basic cast, false casting, and shooting line—no mean feat even for an adult. Toward the end of each session, when he showed weariness, I taught him how to retrieve line, pretend to strike a fish on a dead-drifted dry fly, and how to play and land a fish (I was the fish). It was fun for both of us.

Daniel was not a man in a kid's body. He was a *motivated* child. He wanted to learn to fly cast so that he could catch fish on a fly. I don't know the root of his motivation but it is the essential element in the successful teaching of youngsters. If your youngster isn't interested, don't waste your time or his; and when he or she is ready, age won't make much difference. Here are some guidelines.

1. Limit the length of the session to the time the child will concentrate, and end on a high note.

2. Set limited and specific goals for identification of the casting motions, such as movement of parts of the arm, stopping the rod as it reaches a particular spot, learning the difference between clutching the rod with full strength, and holding it firmly. These are difficult things for a child to grasp all at once; take them one at a time.

3. Use targets of any kind, so there is instant reward for a good cast.

4. Be honest. Offer praise when a cast is perfect and non-committal comment when it is not. Use "not so good" "good" and "Perfect!"

I had Daniel use a 7½-foot rod for a #5 line. It had a small grip to fit his small hand, but he lacked the strength to accelerate it to a dead stop and so I had him use his second hand at the very bottom of the rod grip.

First I taught him the **roll cast**, stressing the slowness with which the rod and line are drawn back to a position that bellies the line just behind the shoulder (determined by looking). I had him push his rod hand toward a target in the water, for the roll itself, and introduced the idea of pushing with his thumb.

When he could do the roll cast without help, I alternated, then, between **horizontal false casting**—as I've described in "Getting the Whole Picture" (on grass)—and taking the fly line off the water for a **basic cast**. The pitfall for all beginners, is the change from no backcast stroke on the roll cast, to a forceful backcast stroke on the basic cast. The horizontal casting is so different there is usually no confusion, so I chose to use it first.

I took off my shoes and put them on the grass for targets, 90° off the rod tip, and kept Daniel to a short line. He started by "waving" the rod back and forth without letting the line unroll completely. It seemed difficult for his eyes to follow the form of the unrolling line. So I picked out obstacles *behind* the spot at which I wanted him to stop the rod in each direction, and stood behind him to guide his rod to those spots. He caught on quickly then. His timing was no problem and I think this is true of most youngsters. Because it takes just as much time for a cast to unroll behind the rod as in front of the rod, there is a cadence easily recognized by children.

For the basic cast I had him lift his hands to a position between his eyes ("Accuracy: Lining Up"), to center the rod action and to keep him from breaking his wrist, which was less likely with two hands on the rod. On the forward cast, I made him look at the target and push his top hand and the rod shaft toward it. Instead of using loading and power snap for the parts of the stroke, I used "lift-SNAP" interchangeably with "slow-FAST" and "easy-HARD" when his efforts at acceleration or hand pressure wavered. When he did a perfect backcast I told him so and asked him to recognize the feeling of the line behind the rod tip as "tight."

Following up on false casting the "Picking Leaves" exercise was introduced so that he could practice at home on a nearby bush. He would surely remember it.

The final technique was **shooting line**. I had him hold the fly line under the middle finger of his rod hand and "stick that finger out straight" at the end of the forward cast, to release the line. Shooting line delighted him.

Daniel may well have been an exception, but he *was* a six-year-old child with limited concepts and understanding of what he was trying to learn. He relied on the feeling of what he was doing rather than understanding the mechanics. This was true of my own experience as a ten-year-old beginner.

The ideal way to teach children to fly cast is to have them begin indoors with Fly-O. Use the instant replay of a mirror or a home video camera where it can be helpful.

Outdoors, a real outfit should be no less than 7½ feet with a #5 line, for younger students (8 years and under). A #6 line on an 8- to 8½-foot rod is best for older, stronger youngsters. Keep the rod weight under 3 ounces, and the rod grip thickness in proportion to the student's hand size.

When there is real progress made in the casting skills, add fishing to the program, choosing places to go, and times to be there, when the potential for success is very high.

Fly Casting for the Handicapped

Salmon fisherman Tom Lamont, of Connecticut and New Brunswick, lost his left arm in World War II. He started to fish for Atlantic salmon, five years later, with an automatic fly reel, thinking it was his only choice. After losing as many as four salmon in one day because of the reel's drag system (the drag tightens as the fish increases its distance from the angler), Tom changed to a conventional Hardy St. John and has been happy ever since, using practically no drag. He fishes with either of two rods: a 9-foot Orvis graphite for a #9 line or a 10½-foot Fenwick Boron X, for a #9 line. He chose a line of weight-forward design.

Tom uses an artificial arm which has a hook to hold a fly or to strip in line. He can lock it, at an angle, which he does when he hooks a fish, bracing the end of the rod against his body at waist level so that he can reel with his right hand. He can put playing pressure on the fish by leaning his body backward.

Tom Lamont, stripping line in . . .

. . . and at the beginning of a forward power snap.

Tom covers the water as other salmon fishermen do, and when he reaches his maximum length cast (which I measured to be eighty feet on the day we fished together) moves downriver a few feet between casts. He makes three or four strips with the hook, to retrieve twelve to fifteen feet of line. He forms one large loop and one smaller one, holding them in his rod hand fingers. Then, starting with his rod tip just above the water, he makes his pickup and perhaps shoots the first loop on the backcast (if the wind is right), shooting the rest on the forward cast. No false casts; no double haul.

Tom can change direction with that one cast by angling his pickup to help facilitate the change, and then he turns his body to the presentation angle. He's remarkable. He has figured out the factors that are critical to his performance and disciplined himself to perfect them.

In the 1950s I knew a tournament caster with one arm who had no prosthesis. He used his mouth to hold loops of line, one of the techniques anglers use with shooting head lines.

If you have arthritic casting arms, or muscles that have been damaged, I would suggest that you use two hands on the rod, the second one at the very end of the grip, to take advantage of the strength of a good arm. You may have to use long rods with an extension below the grip, but it will be worth it to make good casts.

If your problem is with your legs, longer rods and the double haul will be helpful, because of your possibly limited body motion potential. Using two hands on the rod might work better in particular conditions, without the double haul. Within this book you can surely find a technique that you can work with.

The fly fishing community is giving some attention to the problem of access for the handicapped fly fisherman. In New York City, the Theodore Gordon Flyfishers Club has, in motion, a "Project Access" to have areas set aside and improved for handicapped anglers on eastern streams. Write to: Theodore Gordon Flyfisher, 24 East 39th Street, New York, NY 10016.

Perfect Casts

As a teacher I want my knowledge to become your knowledge, to be a part of your confidence when you fish. I wish I could be with you to see your eyes light up as you bring a fish to your fly by performing a casting technique you once thought beyond your reach. Throughout the learning experience you will have your share of good casts and bad, some that are better than expected, others that will make you wonder if you'll ever get it right. And there will be some casts that are absolutely perfect!

A perfect cast is a thing of beauty. It is like a note of music extended and held. In all other sports the moment of impact separates you from the very thing you are projecting in beautiful flight, but the execution of a perfect cast can be seen and felt, from its inception until the fly touches down on the water.

May your percentage of perfect casts—and fish you entice to the fly— grow and grow and grow.

Glossary

Accelerate   To start slow and end fast.

Aerial Mending   An alteration, on the presentation, of all or a portion of the extending fly line, through movement of the rod *after* the power snap and *before* the line touches the water.

Backhand Casting   Any cast to the left of a vertical line centered on the body from head to toe (for a right-handed caster). It includes any angle from vertical to horizontal.

Basic Cast   A cast taken off the water and returned to the water, without false casting.

Casting Loop   The open-ended form of the unrolling fly line, off the tip of the rod, on both backcast and forward cast.

Closed-body Stance   The stance in which the body faces the target area, with feet side by side or with one foot dropped back.

Diameter   A measurement, in thousandths of an inch, of the thickness of the fly line or of leader material.

Drift   1. Follow-through on the backcast stroke.   2. A repositioning of the rod hand (and rod) between backcast and forward cast, in either the same plane or to a different plane.

Drift Time   The time during which the line unrolls, on the backcast.

Extending Line   To lengthen the line that is out of the rod tip.

Eye/Target Line   An imaginary line between your eyes and the center of the target area.

False Cast   A forward cast made to extend fully above the water but not allowed to land on the water.

Fly Line Design   The placement and length of tapered and/or level diameter sections within the whole fly line.

Follow-Through   The movement of the casting arm and rod, after the power snap on the forward cast, in a natural continuation of the casting stroke.

Hand/Target Line   An imaginary line between your hand and the target, at the beginning of the forward cast.

Leader   Made of monofilament, it is the relatively invisible, tapered, connection between fly line and fly.

Line-Hand Tension   Movement by the line hand parallel to that of the rod hand, to keep undesirable slack from forming between the line hand and the first guide. There is no movement of the line through the guides.

Loading Move   The first move of the casting stroke, which gets rod, line, leader, and fly moving as a unit. It begins the *loading* of the rod. The loading move acts as a positioning move for the coming power snap.

Loading the Rod   Making the rod bend, from the tip downward, with the weight of the fly line on it. The rod must be in motion.

Mending the Line   The caster's movement of the whole line, or a portion of it, to alter its form on the water in order to control the speed of the fly or to prevent drag on the fly.

Off-Vertical Casting   Casting in the area between a vertical rod position and one that is 45° to the right or left of vertical. The rod will be tilted outward.

Open-Body Stance   The stance in which the body is turned 90° sideward from the target area, with the feet spread apart.

Overhang   The distance that the back end of the weighted portion of the fly line hangs from the rod tip.

Pickup   Taking the line off the water.

Power Snap   The heart of the cast, in which the forearm, hand, and rod *snap* from one position to the other, to move the line from one side of the rod tip to the other and form a new directional loop.

Presentation   The cast that presents the fly to the fish.

Recoil   To spring back in a reversal of direction.

Rod Arc   The movement of the rod as a segment of a curve.

Shooting   The releasing of additional line to be pulled out through the guides by the momentum of the unrolling casting loop.

Slack Line   1. Line that is not under tension either as the cast begins or during the cast.   2. Line that hangs between the fly reel and the line hand ready for shooting.

Slipping Line   Slack line is released from the line hand to slide through the guides in coordination with dramatic directional movement of the rod, before or after the casting stroke. There must be tension on the line (1) as it lies on the water before or after the cast, or (2) as it hangs in the air, after the power snap.

Stroke   The path of the hand as it executes the backward or forward cast. It encompasses a power snap and, when needed, a loading move ahead of the power snap.

Stroke Length   The measurable distance the rod hand moves, in the execution of a backcast or forward cast.

Stroking Line   Movement of the rod, side to side, or up and down, with the rod tip close to the water, to lengthen fly line already on the water. Movement at the hand is two or three inches; at the rod tip, two or three feet.

Tailing Loop   The closing of the loop on the cast.

Tapered   The changing of diameters within the length of fly line or leader.

Ticking the Water   The fly, or part of the leader or line, touches the water on the backcast or forward cast—unintentional on the part of the caster.

Turnover   The power snap portion of the cast, when the line turns over the rod tip, from one side to the other, to form a new loop.

Unloading of the Rod   The reverse or opposite bend of the rod from its first, deepest, bend in the power snap. The rod tip flips over, oscillates, and then becomes quiet again, "unloaded" until the fly line's weight once again begins to bend it.

Vertical Plane Casting   The rod moves back and forth in an upright plane in a range between the center of the head and the outside edge of the casting shoulder.

Wind knot   An overhand or figure-eight knot formed in the leader through imperfect casting in fair wind, or foul, or no wind at all.

Index